Glory, Grace, and Culture

Glory, Grace, and Culture

The Work of Hans Urs von Balthasar

Edited by Ed Block, Jr.

Paulist Press
New York/Mahwah, N.J.

Cover design by Sharyn Banks
Book design by Lynn Else

Library of Congress Cataloging-in-Publication Data

Glory, grace, and culture : the work of Hans Urs von Balthasar / edited by Ed Block, Jr.
p. cm.
Includes bibliographical references and index.
ISBN 0-8091-4305-4 (alk. paper)
1. Balthasar, Hans Urs von, 1905–1988. I. Block, Ed.
BX4705.B163G59 2005
230'.2'092—dc22

2004022085

Published by Paulist Press
997 Macarthur Boulevard
Mahwah, New Jersey 07430

www.paulistpress.com

Printed and bound in the
United States of America

Contents

Contents

Acknowledgments

This collection owes its existence to a number of people. Besides the contributors, to whom I am grateful for sharing their insights into the work of Hans Urs von Balthasar, I must thank the Marquette University College of Arts and Sciences, and Dean Michael McKinney, who supported the project from the beginning. The original impetus came from an Andrew Mellon grant for a semester-long Balthasar Colloquium, at which a number of the essays were originally read. The four other essays first appeared as a special Balthasar issue of *Renascence: Essays on Values in Literature*. A grant from Mellon funds also aided in publication.

I also want to thank my two research assistants, Jill Roskos and Moon-Ju Shin, for their painstaking editorial work, without whose help the collection could not have appeared. As always, I thank my wife and family for the continued support and encouragement that make my work possible.

Abbreviations

A	*Apokalypse der deutschen Seele*
ASI	*Against the Self-Images of the Age*
CT	"Current Trends in Catholic Theology and the Responsibility of the Christian"
Ep.	*Epilog*
ET I or III	*Explorations in Theology: Volume I: The Word Made Flesh* *Volume III: Creator Spirit*
Ex	"Exegese und Dogmatik"
G	*The Grain of Wheat*
GF	*Das Ganze im Fragment*
GL 1-7	*The Glory of the Lord: A Theological Aesthetic* (Citations from the German version, *Herrlichkeit* are given in the text.)
KB	*The Theology of Karl Barth: Exposition and Interpretation*
KL	*Komische Liturgie: Das Weltbild Maximus' der Bekenners*
LA	*Love Alone*
MW	*My Work in Retrospect*; also cited as *Mein Werk. Durchblicke*
PSO	"Patristic, Scholastics, and Ourselves"
Résumé	"A Résumé of My Thought"
SG	"Die Sprache Gottes"
SPA	*Short Primer for Unsettled Laymen*

SRC	*Science, Religion, and Christianity*
2*SS*	*Two Sisters in the Spirit*
TCP	"On the Tasks of Catholic Philosophy in Our Time"
TD 1-5	*Theo-Drama*
TH	*Theology of History*
TL I-II	*Theologik I-II*
UBC	*Unless You Become Like This Child*
WC	"Why I Am Still a Christian"
WIS	*Die Wahrheit 1st Symphonisch: Aspekte des Christlichen Pluralismus*
WST	"The Word, Scripture, and Tradition"

1

Introduction

Ed Block, Jr.

The life and work of Hans Urs von Balthasar mark an unusual and highly significant juncture in twentieth-century Catholic thought and culture. A quick overview of Balthasar's early life and education suggests why. Born in Basel, Switzerland, in 1905, Balthasar was educated, after high school with the Benedictines and the Jesuits, in Vienna, Berlin, and Zurich. There he experienced firsthand the rich German-European culture of the early twentieth century. His later work often reflects something of the aristocratic values of Stefan George and R. M. Rilke, the love for dramatic pageantry found in Hugo von Hofmannsthal's plays and opera libretti, and the fascination with actors and acting that characterized the ambience of German and Viennese culture at the turn of the century.

Balthasar brought his intelligence and aesthetic taste—he was an accomplished musician—to the study of such German poets as Goethe, Hofmannsthal, and Rilke. He then carried this love for the German classics over to his study of German idealist philosophy. This combination of interests yielded a monumental doctoral work, *Apokalypse der deutschen Seele*, which critiqued the rise of German idealism from the Romantic to the modern period. The first volume of *Apokalypse* was published in 1937. It demonstrates Balthasar's erudition and contains chapters on Kant, Schiller, Fichte, and Schelling—to name but a few of the most significant. Among its highlights are the detailed contrast of

Kierkegaard and Nietzsche as idealist thinkers. The second and third volumes appeared in 1939. The former contains chapters on Bergson, Hofmannsthal, and others. The latter includes studies of Scheler, Rilke, and—perhaps most notably—Heidegger as a seminal modernist thinker. In *Apokalypse* the outline of Balthasar's career-long concern with the relation of nature and grace, the immanent and the transcendent, receives its first articulation.

Before he had finished that doctoral work, however, another formative event had occurred. In summer, 1927, Balthasar made a thirty-day retreat in the Black Forest, under the guidance of Fr. Friedrich Kronseder, SJ. During this retreat he experienced a call to the priesthood.[1] When Balthasar joined the Jesuit order in 1929, he began another stage in his education, but one which he remembered in later life as being less than stimulating. However, there were numerous highlights. From the Jesuit philosopher Erich Pryzwara—never his teacher, but a close intellectual friend—Balthasar borrowed a dynamic interpretation of the *analogia entis* that became a mainstay of his philosophical method. While studying at Fouviere in southern France, he found time to drink deeply of the wisdom of the Greek Fathers of the Church. There, too, he became friends with Henri de Lubac, another theologian who further shaped his philosophical and theological outlook.[2] While studying in France, Balthasar also developed a love for French literature, particularly the work of Charles Péguy, Georges Bernanos, and Paul Claudel. In time Balthasar became the German translator of Claudel and produced a monumental study of Bernanos. Péguy's work—citations to it occur in Balthasar's earliest publications—is a pervasive influence and forms a key part in *The Glory of the Lord,* the first section of Balthasar's monumental trilogy, which also comprises *Theo-Drama,* and *Theologik.*

Balthasar was ordained in 1936, and soon after that he was sent to Munich where he served as associate editor of the journal *Stimmen der Zeit* from 1937 to 1939. During this time he completed three books on the Fathers. The first two, *Kosmische Liturgie: Höhe und Krise des griechischen*

Weltbilds bei Maximus Confessor and *Die Gnostischen Centurien des Maximus Confessor,* were published in 1941. The third volume, *Présence et Pensée: Essai sur la Philosophie Religieuse de Grégoire de Nysee,* was published in 1942.

During his years at *Stimmen der Zeit,* Balthasar also produced a number of translations as well as forewords and afterwords to collections of both translations and a variety of selected works. One of the most prominent of these was his "Nachwort zur deutschen Übersetzung," the "Afterword to the German translation" of Claudel's panoramic drama, *The Satin Slipper.* Those who care to read the "Afterword" will find that it contains not only an insightful interpretation of Claudel's play, but also the seeds of many of Balthasar's later works. Particularly prominent are themes that find their way into *Theo-Drama.* These include the dialectical role of male and female, and the self-transcending potential of human erotic love. Adopting Claudel's epigraph from a Portuguese proverb ("God writes straight with crooked lines"), Balthasar shows how the play's chief characters represent a struggle of the finite for the infinite. In Balthasar's view, the principal female character of the play experiences her love for the protagonist as total self-emptying, an analogy of Jesus' kenotic love, a theme which becomes a central part of Balthasar's Christology. Also apparent in the "Afterword" are three further themes: role-playing, a concern with the metaphor of *theatrum mundi* ("theater of the world"), and an awareness of the microcosmic/macrocosmic dimension. The first two become central in the *Prolegomena,* volume one of *Theo-Drama.* The third expresses a thoroughly Catholic perspective found throughout Balthasar's work, but perhaps most notably in his *Theology of History.* As Balthasar succinctly states near the end of the "Afterword": "[T]here is, finally, no individual fate [in the play] which is not at the same time social and historical."[3] This idea also animates the theological anthropology evident in Balthasar's major works.

Another, too-little known work of this early period is Balthasar's book of aphorisms, *Das Weizenkorn,* which was first published in 1944.[4] A blend of commonplace and original aphorisms, *The Grain of Wheat*—

like the earlier *Apokalypse* and the "Afterword" to *The Satin Slipper*—represents both a summary of some of Balthasar's central ideas and, because of its brevity, a much more accessible introduction to his thought than the longer, and also more difficult to find, *Apokalypse der deutschen Seele.* In the very first of the six sections into which the collection is divided, we find a passage that not only echoes the Jesuit spirituality of the "Suscipe,"[5] but also recalls the theme of self-emptying love found in the "Afterword" to *The Satin Slipper:*

> God's Face like a countenance beaming forth from the darkness: in order to see it we throw everything we possess into the fire—the world, our joys, our hopes. The flame leaps forth, consumes it all, and in its glow the beloved Face lights up. But the flame dies down, and we feed it with what little remains to us: honor, success, our will, the intellect, our temperament, finally our very self: *absume et suscipe*—"take and receive." This is not simple self-giving but, increasingly, the knowledge that I am being taken, that I must surrender. (G, p. 1)

A host of other themes and images link *The Grain of Wheat* with Balthasar's earlier and later writings. One of the more enigmatic reflections manifests Balthasar's early and continuing interest in the analogy between the experience of beauty and the experience of the divine. It also thematizes the title of the work, *The Grain of Wheat.* "At times," Balthasar says,

> when we stand before works of art or also before people, we often feel the need to exert ourselves in bringing to life the dead, cold, alien existence before us and, as it were, making it talk. At such moments we can experience, as by a stroke of lightning, the great extent to which we actualize ourselves in all our love of creatures: we lend ourselves

> to things in order to receive ourselves back from them. It is as if a small, hard, cold object were thrown into our soul, and our soul warmed it and softened it and made it grow bigger, until what came out of it again consisted of our own substance as chief ingredient. Thus it is when we read a poem. And even when the seed planted in us is alive and has an activity of its own (as is the case of people or of the Word of God), the result remains thoroughly synergistic. (G, p. 30)

Following a tertianship in 1939, and another thirty-day retreat, Balthasar was ready for his next assignment. As Henrici notes:

> At the beginning of the war his superiors gave von Balthasar the choice of going either to Rome as a professor at the Gregorian University or to Basel as a student chaplain....Von Balthasar chose Basel—certainly not out of patriotism, but because pastoral work was closer to his heart than lecturing.[6]

In Basel, von Balthasar became acquainted with one of the most influential figures in his life, the Protestant theologian Karl Barth. According to Henrici, Barth was the third great influence on Balthasar's thinking—along with Pryzwara and de Lubac.[7] That influence is manifest in both Balthasar's notion of "call," and in the emphasis on the cross in his Christology. Besides carrying on a dialogue with Barth—which some thought was bent on the theologian's conversion[8]—during the early days in Basel, Balthasar also edited and translated a number of classic works of German and other literatures for the "European Series" being published by Sammlung Klosterberg (the Klosterberg Collection). One of these, according to the bibliography of his works compiled at the Johannes Verlag, included *Friedrich Nietzsche: Vom vornehmen Menschen*, published under a pseudonym, Hans

Werner. It was also in Basel at this time that Balthasar's engagement with cultural life reemerged. As Henrici notes: "In 1943 the Zurich Playhouse...staged the premiere of his [Balthasar's] translation of *The Satin Slipper.* Von Balthasar himself collaborated in the production in an advisory capacity."[9] It was also in Basel that Balthasar began the long series of works that would eventually make his name as a theologian and single him out to such influential clerics as Joseph Ratzinger and Karol Wojtyla.

For the purposes of brevity, neither this introduction nor this collection concerns itself directly with Balthasar's later life, before or after 1950, when he reluctantly left the Jesuit order to found a lay institute, the Society of St. John, with convert, friend, and mystic Adrienne von Speyr. Nor does it concern itself with a number of controversies that have sometimes cast Balthasar in the role of "conservative theologian." If anything, the essays in this collection should help dispel the notion that Balthasar's work is in any way one-dimensional, polemical, or easily set aside. As a deepening familiarity with his work will show, he is, if anything, one of the most comprehensive, capacious, and generous thinkers and theologians of the twentieth century.

Balthasar, it has been said, was so fascinated by the doctrine of the Trinity that his work often reflects it in unaccountable ways. It is little wonder, then, that one might summarize some of Balthasar's key ideas in triads. One such triad is form, action, and truth, which corresponds to the different focus taken by each of the three parts of the trilogy, *The Glory of the Lord, Theo-Drama,* and *Theologik* (the first two, in German, are titled *Herrlichkeit* and *Theo-Dramatik*). Also central to Balthasar's thinking from early on are a trilogy of "analogies" that, he argues, provide windows on the divine. They are the experience of love, of art, and of one's own mortality. In *Love Alone* Balthasar states:

> When one experiences startling beauty (in nature or in art) then phenomena normally veiled are perceived in their uniqueness. What confronts us is overpowering, like a miracle, and only as a miracle can it be understood. The appearance of its inner unfathomable necessity is both binding and freeing, for it is seen clearly to be the appearance of freedom itself. (*LA*, p. 44)

In *Why I Am Still A Christian*, Balthasar relates these two analogies to the experience of death (in a manner which, by the way, echoes Rilke):

> In order objectively to apprehend and then judge the unique work of art, one must create for oneself the appropriate mode of receptivity. In order to love personally, one must let there be opened in the beloved a value already present in one, which may perhaps be reserved for that person alone to see and to come forward to encounter. In order to approach one's death responsibly, one must accept this frontier and project one's actions toward it. At each of these three points we find the provocation of uniqueness, in that each eludes the tribunal of the comprehensive. (WC, p. 23–24).

Together, all three of these experiences point to what Balthasar calls the uniqueness, the singularity, that he argues the encounter with Christ is.

A further reflection on Balthasar's abiding themes surfaces the following, which also forms the context for this collection's individual essays. From his study of classical philosophy and the early Church Fathers, Balthasar derives a sense of Being that is grounded in both ontology and philosophy of religion. As he had stated so succinctly in *The Grain of Wheat*:

> All great thought springs from the conflict between two dominant insights: that the rift in Being is incurable and that it must nonetheless be healed. Since the solution of this contradiction lies in the hand of Christ alone, all philosophy is oriented toward his existence. (p. 53)

Balthasar understands Being as fundamentally open to and then related to the divine. According to Balthasar, such openness, in human beings, is constitutive of their humanity. The individual person's genuine identity, in turn, is constituted by that person's realization of his/her unique mission. Hence, part of Balthasar's theological project is a reinterpretation of Being, via the three transcendentals and the analogy of being. At the heart of this reinterpretation is the centrality of intersubjective experience. Intersubjective experience, for its part, is based on Balthasar's dialogic conception of how the person's awareness of self, other, and all of being is made manifest, first of all, through the mother's love for her child.

> Now man exists only in dialogue with his neighbor. The infant is brought to consciousness of himself only by love, by the smile of his mother. In that encounter the horizon of all unlimited being opens itself for him, revealing four things to him: 1) that he is one in love with the mother, even in being other than his mother, therefore all being is one; 2) that that love is good, therefore all being is good; 3) that that love is true, therefore all being is true; 4) that that love evokes joy, therefore all being is beautiful. (Résumé, p. 471)

From this insight also derives Balthasar's notion of personal identity discovered or fulfilled through the simultaneous discovery of one's mission. Though the term "mission" may evoke negative connotations, in Balthasar's work the idea of mission is—on the contrary—

most often related to the traditional Catholic idea of vocation. For Balthasar an individual experiences—in good Biblical fashion—a call which not only defines a mission but also confers a sense of Christian personhood. It will be apparent to anyone familiar with Jesuit spirituality that such thinking derives at least in part from the order which had formed the young Balthasar, and whose influence continued to manifest itself throughout his career.

As the essays which follow will demonstrate, Balthasar's work is enriched by its implicit and explicit dialogue with numerous thinkers. Professors Schindler and Oakes remind us of Balthasar's knowledge of Nietzsche. Fr. Oakes also notices Balthasar's resistance to reductive Hegelian dialectic—and its temptation to a deterministic reading of history. Other essays allude to the significance of such varied figures as Chateaubriand, Kierkegaard, Ricoeur, and Heidegger. This collection, then, reflects the richness and complexity, the breadth and depth that Balthasar's thought comprises. It should also suggest a number of directions which subsequent research in Balthasar's work might take. Also central to these essays are a number of key themes (in addition to those mentioned above) that, together, relate the various contributors' essays.

Articulated in different ways by almost all the contributors to this collection is the centrality of openness: divine openness to human beings and human beings' openness to God. The latter openness is what David Schindler calls "contemplative receptivity." All contributors agree, at least implicitly, with Balthasar's fundamental insight that the experience of gratuitous beauty is the beginning of philosophy and theology, and that (as contributor David Yeago says in his later chapter), "it is an elementary criterion of good theology that it communicate a kind of aesthetic wonder at the surprisingness and extravagance of the divine love." The experience of beauty, what contributor Christophe Potworowski refers to as the "epiphany of being," is the desire, or drive, toward what the desire, or drive, is toward what is transcendent. For all the contributors, then, finite nature is redefined in "narrative-dramatic terms." This means that in response to the "radiance shining through form" (and analyzed in *The Glory of the Lord*), human beings experience a unique call to which they respond in freedom (an issue discussed at length in *Theo-Drama*). Of course, in Balthasar's formulation, this finite freedom is seen in the context of God's infinite freedom. But lest the human being feel left alone in making his or her free decision for God, Balthasar offers the example of Jesus. Fr. Oakes highlights Jesus' "theodramatic" embeddedness in time, saying that, like us, "he must face the future with the same sense of darkness as all the rest of us do." As a corollary, Fr. Oakes reminds us that living within our own mortality[10] makes us better able to understand Balthasar's Christology, which is the heart of his theology.

All the authors would agree, at least implicitly, with David Schindler, who sees Balthasar's work emphasizing the crucial nature of our relation to God as incarnated in Jesus Christ. It is the loss of this relation which makes for the superficiality of modern culture and—another key Balthasarian insight—the modern fragmentation of being. The infinity of God means that God affects everything all the time. In response to Balthasar's emphasis on "openness," Schindler calls for that "contemplative receptivity" which becomes a way to reintegrate the aesthetic, the religious, the moral, and the philosophical strains of our culture and our very beings.

Receptivity and the openness of the person are similar emphases in Peter Casarella's essay. Approaching Balthasar's work on language as expression and form, and human language as an analogue to God's mode of expression, Professor Casarella explores the implications of Balthasar's idea of language, discovering that "dialogue derives from the dynamic relation of form and expression within being." Openness of the person to modes of expression mirrors our openness to God. But expression is not merely a subjective experience. It is, in fact, always an expression of the truth of being, a truth fundamentally mysterious.

Focusing on *The Glory of the Lord,* Fr. Aidan Nichols underscores Balthasar's assertion that receptivity to beauty is related to receptivity to the divine. Nichols highlights the way in which Balthasar traces "the primordial phenomenon of the beautiful" from its roots in classical antiquity, through the early Church Fathers, to Thomas Aquinas. Seconding a number of the other contributors, Nichols shows how Balthasar traces to Aquinas the idea that "being [is] always in the process of pouring itself out into the things that are." This dynamic quality of the "divine Essence" is also related to "being's simultaneous poverty." From this source comes another of Balthasar's characteristic ideas, and one reflected thematically in almost all the essays: namely, the kenotic self-emptying, or self-dispossessing, of Christ in his obedience to the Father. Or, as Nichols summarizes it, "in its self-dispossessing glory being finds its fulfillment in the self-emptying Son of God." Like Schindler, Nichols finds that the subsequent devaluation of this understanding of Being results, finally, in Hegelian and Nietzschean critiques.

Professor Nemoianu's essay places Balthasar in a rich context of secular and Christian humanism from the time of the Fathers to the present day. Surveying late classical and early Common Era pagan antiquity, he—like other contributors—locates the intersection of Balthasar's interests in the Eastern Fathers of the Church. Nemoianu also sees Balthasar's appropriation of ideas from the Middle Ages, through the Renaissance, and both Enlightenment and Romantic periods as "a good parallel" to the "appropriation" of Neoplatonism by the Cappadocian and other early Christian Fathers. He sees Balthasar's work as a *summa* of the tradition which developed from the engagement of the Eastern Fathers with Neoplatonic ideas. Among the specific Neoplatonic ideas that Nemoianu sees Balthasar appropriating, by far the most important is the intimate relation of Beauty to Truth and Goodness. In the medieval and Renaissance periods, Nemoianu also identifies a tension between skepticism and belief that is reflected in Balthasar's willingness to take into account not only medieval and Renaissance thought but also Romantic and idealist traditions from Chateaubriand to Nietzsche and Heidegger.

Nemoianu also argues that there has occurred a "globalization of Christianity" whose implications help us appreciate Balthasar's sometimes-overlooked cosmopolitan vision. Just as Balthasar's early work had seen in the vision of a writer like Paul Claudel the most catholic—that is, the most comprehensive and, as it were, worldwide—of "horizons," so in *Truth Is Symphonic* and *New Elucidations*, Balthasar sympathetically critiques both the fundamental premises and some key religious practices of the East. Nemoianu also highlights the commonalities of humanism and Christianity, focusing on the processes and dialectics of the Trinitarian doctrine. He sees in the doctrine an allowance for the freedom, the openness, and the gratuitousness of creativity analogous to that found in literature. He also notes the resemblance of the Gospel accounts to the operation of literature. This highlights Balthasar's own efforts—in the trilogy—to see Revelation in terms of form, drama, and idea. In the operation of tradition, the openness to transcendence, and the relation of the mundane to the divine as constitutive of the human, Nemoianu sees three other key features linking Christian humanism to its secular counterpart.

While Nemoianu focuses on the early Romantic period (particularly Chateaubriand's *Genius of Christianity*) as a time when "the beautiful emerges as an indispensable key to any grasp of the true and of the beautiful," he credits Balthasar with seeing both the philosophical potential and the theme of striving which characterize the Romantic age. Its resurgent desire for the transcendent, as well as its collapse, are perhaps most notably apparent in the philosophy of Nietzsche. Echoing Balthasar, Nemoianu observes: "Aesthetic culture is that which seeks to articulate the opening toward transcendence that appears as a constant in all human societies."

Like Professor Nemoianu, Professor Oakes also sees Balthasar's insights as in harmony with both premodern and postmodern hermeneutics. And like Professor Schindler, he makes much of

Balthasar's deep understanding of Nietzsche's place in the development of the postmodern philosophical climate. Citing Balthasar's definition of inspiration—which "involves a permanent quality, in virtue of which the Holy Spirit as *acutor primarius* is always behind the word, always ready to lead to deeper levels of divine truth those who seek to understand his word"—he says:

> This view actually dovetails very nicely with the best of recent theory of literary criticism, which insists that the meaning of a text is not some hard nugget called the "intent of the original author" waiting to be retrieved by the panning-for-gold skills of our exegetical Gold-rushers. On the contrary, meaning always involves a listener as well as a speaker, a reader as well as a writer.

In his *Vorlesungen über die Ãsthetik,* G. W. F. Hegel argued that drama represented the highest form of literature. In *Theo-Drama,* which takes Hegel as both an explicit and an implicit partner in dialogue, Balthasar makes a strong argument for drama's significance, not only in its own right, but also as a source of terms and concepts for developing a "theology for the twentieth [and twenty-first] century." Premised on the unique revelation of beauty outlined in *Glory of the Lord* and supported by Balthasar's dialogical—or intersubjective—conception of human existence, *Theo-Drama* foregrounds the human response to God's call. In drama, Balthasar says, human beings invite revelation about themselves, who they are, their roles in life, and the ultimate significance of their actions.

A central force or power which Balthasar sees in the relation of the dramatist, the director, the actor, and the audience is the self-giving, self-emptying that is Balthasar's central insight into the reality of Christ and the Trinity. Balthasar suggests by analogy that all of the chief participants in drama—dramatist, director, actors, and audience—assume roles whose defining features are self-giving if not self-emptying. The structure of the dramatic ensemble, Balthasar argues, reflects the "procession" within the Trinity. Balthasar seeks to find in drama the terms and concepts for a "dramatic theology" for the twentieth century, but in the process, his wide-ranging investigations of Western drama make *Theo-Drama* a rich resource for discovering mutual revelations between theology and literary criticism. It is the burden of the collection's final essay to sketch out some of those mutual relations.

Among the works which these essays reference, none is so central as the first part of Balthasar's trilogy, *Herrlickeit,* translated as *The Glory of the Lord.* Almost equally important are the second and third parts, *Theo-Dramatik (Theo-Drama)* and *Theologik.* Other works of importance include *Love Alone,* which Balthasar himself referred to as a kind summary of *Glory,* a book written about the same time he was completing the larger work. Also referenced are a number of the essays in the series *Explorations in Theology.* Not to be overlooked, of course, are such other works as *Heart of the World* and *Truth Is Symphonic.*

This collection, then, may serve as an advanced primer to a study of Balthasar's life and work. Taken as a companion to Dr. Schindler's groundbreaking *Hans Urs von Balthasar: His Life and Work,* and Fr. Oakes' scholarly *Pattern of Redemption,* my own *Glory, Grace, and Culture* means to further the study of the person Henri de Lubac referred to as "perhaps the most cultivated man in Europe," and one of Catholicism's three or four greatest thinkers of the twentieth century.

Notes

1. Peter Henrici, "A Sketch of von Balthasar's Life," in *Hans Urs von Balthasar: His Life and Work,* ed. David Schindler (San Francisco: Ignatius, 1991), p. 11.
2. Two of the earliest authors contributing biographical sketches of Balthasar's life, Henrici and Medard Kehl, are in some disagreement about facts and interpretations having to do with Balthasar's early philosophical

and theological influences. For Kehl's essay, see *The von Balthasar Reader,* eds. Medard Kehl, SJ, and Werner Löser, SJ (New York: Crossroads, 1985).

3. "Nachwort zur deutschen Übersetzung," *Der Seidne Schuh* (Salzburg: Otto Müller, 1939), p. 460. Translation my own.
4. Reissued in German in 1953, *Das Weizenkorn* was translated into English (as *The Grain of Wheat*) only in 1993.
5. "Suscipe" is the title given a prayer found in the *Principle and Foundation* of the Society of Jesus, a document with which the young Jesuit Balthasar would have been intimately familiar.
6. Henrici, p. 14.
7. Ibid., 17, 18.
8. Ibid., 18.
9. Ibid., 15.
10. Oakes' observation makes understandable why Balthasar, in *Love Alone,* should analogize the experiences of love, art, *and* one's own mortality with the experience of God's love and divine call.

2

The Significance of Hans Urs von Balthasar in the Contemporary Cultural Situation*

David L. Schindler

The tremendous event [of the death of God] is still on its way, still wandering; it has not yet reached the ears of men. Lightning and thunder require time;...deeds, though done, still require time to be seen and heard.[1] (Friedrich Nietzsche)

[Following the death of God, we stray] as through an infinite nothing.[2] (Friedrich Nietzsche)

[T]he world has become 'infinite' for us all over again, inasmuch as we cannot reject the possibility that it may include infinite interpretations. Once more we are seized with a great shudder; but who would feel inclined to deify again after the old manner the monster of an unknown world.[3] (Friedrich Nietzsche)

Only a god can save us.[4] (Martin Heidegger)

The sign and divinity have the same place and time of birth. The age of the sign is essentially theological.[5] (Jacques Derrida)

The very ground of being smiles upon us in the face of Jesus Christ, as a father or mother might smile at us. We are his creatures and so a seed of love, God's image, lies dormant within us. But just as no child can awaken to love until it is loved, no human heart can come to knowledge of God without the free gift of his grace, in the image of his Son....[Man can respond adequately to the love of God only] under the "protective mantle" of the *fiat* spoken archetypically for him and all men by the bride and mother, *Maria-ecclesia*.[6] (Hans Urs von Balthasar)

But whenever the relationship between nature and grace [between the world and the God of Jesus Christ] is severed..., then the whole of worldly being falls under the dominion of "knowledge," and the springs and forces of love immanent in the world are overpowered and finally suffocated by science, technology and cybernetics. The result is a world without women, without children, without reverence for love in poverty and humiliation—a world in which power and the profit margin are the sole criteria, where the disinterested, the useless, the purposeless is despised, persecuted and in the end exterminated—a world in which art itself is forced to wear the mask and features of technique.[7] (Hans Urs von Balthasar)

The Spirit meets the burning questions of the age with an utterance that is the keyword, the answer to the riddle. Never in the form of an abstract statement...; but almost always in the form of a new, concrete supernatural mission:

> the creation of a new saint whose life is a presentation to his own age of the message that heaven is sending to it, a person who is, here and now, the right and relevant interpretation of the Gospel, who is given to this particular age as its way of approach to the perennial truth of Christ. How else can life be expounded except by living? The saints are Tradition at its most living, Tradition as the word is meant whenever Scripture speaks of the unfolding of the riches of Christ, and the application to history of the norm which is Christ....St. Bernard and St. Francis, St. Ignatius and St. Theresa were all of them...like volcanoes pouring forth molten fire from the inmost depths of revelation; they were irrefutable proof, all horizontal tradition notwithstanding, of the vertical presence of the living *Kyrios* here, now, and today.[8] (Hans Urs von Balthasar)

The crisis we face in the current situation is primarily theological in nature. "Crisis" is understood etymologically, as a moment requiring judgment, hence a decisive moment, a turning point. The purpose of the present article is to attempt a reading of this thesis in light of the writings of Friedrich Nietzsche and Hans Urs von Balthasar.

Literally, theology means "a study or account or interpretation of God." As indicated in the texts cited from Nietzsche, an interpretation of God can take a "negative" form. The crucial point, as we will see, is that, even in his absence, or "death," God retains his fundamental, precisely ultimate, significance in and for human culture.

For Balthasar, theology has a positive if equally radical meaning. In accord with Aquinas's notion of *"sacra doctrina,"* theology for Balthasar includes an interpretation not only of God, but also of the entire cosmos in the light of God, both interpretations based first on God's own self-revelation. The foundations for this comprehensive notion of theology lie in the great christological text of Colossians

1:15–18, which says that Christ is the firstborn of creatures, that all things were made in him and through him and for him, that the Church is his body. The anthropological meaning of this text is highlighted in the Second Vatican Council's *Gaudium et Spes,* which states that it is in the mystery of Jesus Christ that the mystery of man becomes clear: "Jesus Christ, in the very revelation of the Father and his love, reveals man to himself" (n. 22). The cosmological meaning is highlighted in Pope John Paul II's *Dominum et Vivificantem:* in uniting himself with the individual humanity of Christ, the second person of the Trinity in some way unites himself with the entire reality of man, and in this reality, with the whole of creation (n. 50).

The claim, then, is that our cultural crisis turns on the reality of God in our lives. Nietzsche—and Derrida, or, in general, what we will call the "postmoderns"—makes this clear, albeit in "negative" terms: the reality of God is such that his presence or absence changes everything. Balthasar agrees with this judgment, but in positive terms. The infinite God of Christianity, as trinitarian, is a God of love. This God of love is revealed in the person of Jesus Christ, and thus has a form or "*logos*" that is best termed beautiful. This God of love is revealed likewise in the entire cosmos that is created in Christ: all of creation, made in the image of God in Jesus Christ, thus bears, through an intrinsic relation interpreted analogously, the image of love and beauty.

For Balthasar, therefore, the crisis of the present time likewise concerns the absence of God in the dominant patterns of our cultural life and thought. For Balthasar, the death of God in the cosmos leads, logically and over time, to the death of love and beauty in the cosmos. There is a mutually causal relation between the two events—the absence of God and the absence of love and beauty—even though, within this mutual causal relation, the absence of God has an absolute (ontological) priority.

I

Now, several possible objections to this thesis surface almost immediately: that it is false, that it is banal, that it is breathtaking in the scope of its generalization. A common thread runs through these objections: namely, that the thesis indicates a theological reduction, or at any rate a reduction of problems to a precipitous unity. In a word, the thesis is at once too simple and too theologically—or indeed Christianly—imperialistic. The problems facing us hardly seem to be problems that concern ultimacy primarily, or at any rate exclusively. Why?

First of all, public opinion polls give abundant evidence of Americans' continuing belief in God. And, even if this were not so, the problems would still hardly reduce to the question of God: there are political-social-economic problems; problems of poverty and wealth distribution; moral problems regarding abortion, drugs, the integrity of the family; personal problems concerning relationships and career choices, of boredom and anxiety about the future. There are also institutional, scientific, and technical dimensions of these problems; and on and on.

Furthermore, when we turn to love and beauty, the generalization of the thesis seems even more extreme. Surely American society, as evidenced, for example, in its great history of "volunteerism" and of aid to foreign peoples in need, reveals a vast reservoir of moral generosity. Who in any case is to judge that there is somehow less love and less beauty in contemporary culture, such that we are warranted in speaking of a crisis regarding these? And even if we concede that there is a crisis of love and beauty, on what grounds do we rightfully insist that this crisis has, most basically, a *theological* origin? Surely, the integrity of anthropological and cosmic realities is such that we need to account for any absence of love and beauty in these realities first in terms of their own intrinsic ("natural") properties.

Recognizing that all of these issues cannot be dealt with adequately in the present forum, my response is that the objections—

insofar as they imply that the thesis offered at the outset is false, banal, or overly generalized—fail to grasp the radicality and comprehensiveness of the reality of God: that God is infinite. At the same time, they fail to see the concrete meaning of this infinite God: that this God, revealed in the singular person Jesus Christ, is the *logos* of love and beauty.

Now, in saying this, I do not mean to reduce all of the problems listed above to God, or indeed to love and beauty. The point, simply, is that the infinity of the God of Jesus Christ entails that he cannot but—in some significant sense—affect everything, all the time. This is why Balthasar says that Jesus Christ is the *"universale concretum et personale"*;[9] he is the divine *person* who, precisely in his *singular* and *concrete*—hence unique—historical existence, bears a *universal* meaning.

This is what is implied by St. Augustine, for example, when he says that God is "more interior to me than I am to myself." The foundation of Augustine's claim is given in Colossians 1:15–18, and is confirmed and deepened in the texts from *Gaudium et Spes* and *Dominum et Vivificantem* cited earlier. These texts do not deny but on the contrary presuppose both the infinite transcendence of God and the integrity of the creature. Indeed, it is the creature's constitutive relation to God that precisely makes the creature itself be.

Thus the creature's relation to God is such that the creature is never, in the "logic" of its being, or in any of its thoughts or actions, neutral toward God. No abstraction from God, be it only for methodological or strategic reasons, is without implications with respect to the existence and meaning of God. Simple neutrality toward God, in any moment of the creature's being, action, or thought—even a moment of methodological abstraction—implies that the relation between God and the creature is just so far a relation between two entities, each of whose reality or meaning *ends* at the *boundary* or *limit* of the other. It implies the external relation that is properly termed a relation of addition. (I use the term "addition" here precisely: after the manner of two entities that are first [simply] outside of each other and whose positive relation thereby equals their *sum*.) But if the relation between God and the creature is properly the external one of addition, then God just so far becomes finite.

Note that the non-neutrality of the creature toward God indicated here does not mean that the creature's relation to God is—or need be made—thematic or explicit at every moment. It means only that relation to God is *implied* at every moment and that this *implication* is always-already significant for the being and meaning of the creature.[10]

The point, then, is that simple neutrality toward God, in any moment of the creature's being, action, or thought, implies just so far a finite God: and a finite God is not really a God at all. In other words, any such moment of simple neutrality already and in principle implies the absence of God—implies, at least in that (logical–"onto-logical") moment, the death of God.

It is the great merit of the postmoderns cited at the outset to have drawn this to our attention: that is, with respect to the empirical, consumerist culture of modern Western liberalism. Characteristic of liberal culture, especially in its Anglo-American form, is not a theoretical or explicit denial of God's existence, but a methodological or practical abstraction from God as we go about the whole range of our culture-building activities. What the postmoderns see, and what most contemporary liberals do not see, is that this practical abstraction from God already indicates the dying of God, and that the consequences of this death are fundamental. The postmoderns unmask what is now rightly seen to be the ultimate implication of emptiness or nothingness within the beings and meanings of liberal culture (hence nihilism).

The first inference to draw from this insight of the postmoderns, then, is a paradoxical one: It discloses the objections noted above—that is, insofar as these objections contend that our thesis is false, banal, or overly generalized—to be themselves already signs of cultural atheism. The notion that a plurality of cultural problems precludes a primitive unity within this plurality itself already expresses the dispersal of being and meaning into fragments whose ultimate source lies in the absence of God.

Now, as I said, the great merit of Nietzsche is that he unmasks this (methodological) fragmentation of modern culture and reveals it for what it most truly is: atheism. And, as should already be clear, this atheism is such that it can exist even in the souls of those who sincerely profess theism. For the question is not whether one professes God's existence, but whether one sees that God is infinite and whether one grasps the "integrative" implications of God's infinity for all aspects of human and cosmic existence.[11] The question is whether relation to this infinite God gives form to everything the creature does.

What Nietzsche's "analysis" makes clear is that we moderns cannot have it both ways: we cannot both kill God through our practical or methodological self- or human-centeredness, and pretend there is still a real God out there who can be called in from time to time to save the (normative) moral or indeed aesthetic day. For the God who then arrives has already been rendered altogether too feeble now to help: the lateness of his arrival is just the point.

The inference Nietzsche draws from this analysis of our situation is that we should make the implied atheism (or feeble nihilism) of liberal modernity into the explicit atheism (or energetic nihilism) of postmodernity. We should embrace the consequences of God's death, realizing that we ourselves must now become God.

Balthasar shares much of the negative side of Nietzsche's judgment regarding the fragmentation of being and meaning in modern culture. He agrees that the fragmented being and meaning of this culture have their source in the death of God: in atheism.

However, it will hardly come as a surprise that it is at just this point that Balthasar takes Nietzsche's critique in an opposite direction. For Balthasar, the answer to the death of God lies, not in becoming gods ourselves, but in renewing the authentic presence of God in ourselves and the cosmos. Or better—if we can initially risk a more radical formulation of Balthasar's response, which recalls the opening passages cited from him—the answer to our crisis *does* lie, in some significant sense, in becoming "gods" ourselves: that is, precisely through our graced (or "adopted") participation in the life of God himself effected by Jesus Christ, in and through the Church, by the power of the Holy Spirit. This participation is called sanctification. Balthasar's response to the absence of God in modern culture, in other words, is to urge a renewal of God's presence precisely through the generation of saints.[12]

Two points must be kept in mind if we are to understand the distinctiveness of Balthasar's position. First, the creature's participation in divine life always remains a gift from God. The participation in divine life to which we are all called at conception and which is effected in the sacrament of baptism always remains a graced or adopted and hence creaturely participation. Secondly, as this already implies, such participation comes about only through the absolutely singular person Jesus Christ, via the singular woman Mary, and the singular sacramental-eucharistic Church.

It is by means of this participation that the reality of God truly takes effect *in the world*. Through the encounter with man that God initiates through the gift of himself in Jesus Christ, an encounter that is enabled by the Holy Spirit and finally occurs only within the receptive *fiat* of Mary-Church, God intends to draw—and indeed always-already has begun to draw—all of creation into a relation of communion with himself.

This is what Balthasar means when he says that the very ground of being smiles upon us in the face of Jesus Christ; that the seed of love that consequently lies dormant within us can nonetheless awaken only under the protective mantle of the *fiat* spoken by *Maria-ecclesia*. The saints represent the place where the seed of love planted in all of us by God has taken root and grown. Through the saints, this relation is meant now to be extended outward, to the ends of the earth.

It is crucial that the gratuitousness and singularity of God's way of sharing his life not be understood such that either the (physical) realism or the universal scope of this intended sharing be attenuated.

In other words: in Jesus Christ, heaven has come to earth—has sunk into earth—in order that, beginning already now, earth might be lifted to heaven. Those whom the Church calls saints, beginning with Mary, represent the place where this mutual immanence of heaven and earth is most deeply actualized. This mutual immanence, lived fully only by the saints, is now to be extended throughout the cosmos, in and through their presence.

II

Thus, in a crucial sense, Nietzsche is right: to face our cultural problems at the requisite depth, we must now bring "God," or heaven, to earth. But recall what this means for him: we ourselves must assume the role formerly held by God. Hence the meaning of what Nietzsche calls the *Übermensch* or "Overman": we must assume the absolute or infinite creativity of "God" into ourselves. Thus the bringing of heaven to earth for Nietzsche represents, as it were, the *fusion* of heaven and earth, through man's *seizure* of heaven.

For Balthasar it is also the case that our crisis consists in the separation of earth from heaven. But here again the parting of ways between the two thinkers is fundamental. For Nietzsche, we bring heaven to earth by seizing it; for Balthasar, this bringing of heaven to earth occurs—and indeed, by the very nature of what is involved, namely, the coming of heaven, can *only* occur—through the utterly free gift of heaven itself. In the movement of heaven to earth, earth itself in the first instance *does* precisely nothing: it can only wait, and then *receive*. And the resulting union of heaven and earth, because it remains ever a *gift from* heaven, is consequently never a *possession*, properly speaking, of earth.

Thus the needed response to the present situation is, first of all, one that earth itself cannot produce. It begins, on the contrary, in the incarnation: in God's free decision to incarnate himself in the singular person Jesus Christ, and thus to unite himself with all of us, with all of creation. There is only one hypostatic union between God and man. But the spousal union indicated in God's hypostatic union with Jesus Christ is meant somehow to be passed on, in the order of grace, by means of Christ's sacrament, the Church, hence by the communion of saints, through the power of the Holy Spirit.

The further point to be emphasized is that God's invitation to union with himself in Jesus Christ is extended first through Mary. God becomes man through the free *fiat* of Mary (*fiat*: "let it be done unto me according to your Word") that is empowered by the grace of the Holy Spirit. Through her *fiat*, Mary *magnifies* the Lord and his greatness. Indeed, the point is that through the *fiat* she becomes the *Theotokos*—literally, the *bearer of God*.[13]

Thus, for Nietzsche, the world becomes divine again through ("masculine") seizure: through the absolutizing of creativity, and thereby through taking possession of what is proper to deity. For Balthasar, on the contrary, the world becomes divine—charged with divinity—only through the ("feminine") "disponibility" of the Virgin Mary, the first saint within the sacramental *communio sanctorum* that is the Church: through the deepening of contemplative receptivity, and thereby through an ever-deeper sharing in what remains properly a gift from God.

The crucial point is that the Nietzschean Overman, in "infinitizing" human creativity, becomes thoroughly Promethean or "titanizing" in nature. Fundamentally, the bringing of god to earth signifies the elimination of any and all sense of *gift from* an *other*. The dynamic is exhaustively in the direction of construction, domination, and possession, and away from any moment of anterior contemplativeness. The dynamic is away from communion—either with an infinite "Other" or with any others.

To be sure, Nietzsche is a profoundly complex thinker, and there is much in his work that rejects *hubris*[14] and indeed affirms obedience as a necessary inner condition of any authentic act of freedom.[15] And he does assert a kind of community between "great souls" that transcends the ages.[16] But in the end his basic "project" is to overcome the pettiness of the modern soul through recovery of the capacity for willing something grand. And this can take place, on his presuppositions, only through the radical subsumption of the heavenly infinite creativity of the gods into man himself, *by* man.

For Balthasar, on the contrary, the bringing of God to earth occurs through Mary, the *Theotokos*. God comes to earth and takes on its very flesh through the contemplative obedience of the woman-mother Mary, and indeed, the God who comes as a child of this mother. The bringing of God to earth, in other words, is first a *receiving* of God *from* heaven: a receiving of the *gift* of God *from* God. The bringing of God to earth is thus an act that effects communion and whose purpose is communion—first between human beings and God, and consequently among all human beings. And the God who comes is a God not of power, but of humility, vulnerability, innocence, and "littleness."[17]

In a word, Nietzsche sees the "restoration" of God at the heart of our culture as occurring first by means of the masculine *Übermensch*. (Not surprisingly, Nietzsche always preferred the masculine warrior-gods.)[18] Balthasar on the contrary sees this "restoration" as occurring first by means of the Marian-feminine *Theotokos*, and hence by means of a relation that is first motherly feminine and indeed childlike in nature.[19] The one who, from the side of earth, enables the entry of heaven into earth, and thus "completes" the disclosure of the cosmos as gift, is a woman and a mother; and the God who enters earth enters first as a child.

Note how all of this comes together in terms of what we noted earlier as Balthasar's understanding of the current cultural crisis also as one of love and beauty. The key lies in the notion of *gift*, whose "foundational" meaning, we can now see, is theological in nature. The meaning of gift is revealed most fundamentally in the incarnation, which is God's gift of himself to creation (Col. 1:15–18); at the same time, the meaning is revealed in creation, which is God's gift of the creature to itself. But the meaning of this gift, in both senses, is completed only through its being received. And the reception itself is completed—in the one real order of history—only through the free fiat of the obedient woman Mary.

Here, then, in this theological notion of gift, the meaning of love and beauty is revealed. Love in its basic meaning is just this giving and receiving initiated by God in heaven and completed on earth in Mary through the Holy Spirit.[20] And beauty is but the *form* or *logos* of this giving and receiving of God's love in and through Jesus, whose meaning is amplified further in Mary's *fiat* and the sacramental communion of the Church.

The upshot is stunning in its comprehensiveness: the crisis of our culture, as a crisis consisting in the absence of God in the dominant patterns of thought and behavior, is disclosed by Balthasar as a crisis at once also of the absence of love and beauty in these dominant patterns. Finally, God, love, and beauty in any human culture can only live and die together.

III

We return now to the problem specifically of the liberal culture of Anglo-America. As we have seen, for both Nietzsche and Balthasar, the fundamental problem of our time is the death of God. Both men recognize that the peculiar nature of the modern liberal killing of God lies in its timidity. The modern death of God is a death which occurs only implicitly, by means of methodological or practical abstraction. In the words of Alasdair MacIntyre: "The difficulty lies in the combination of atheism in the practice of the life of the vast majority, with the profession of either superstition or theism by that same majority. The creed of the English is that there is no God and that it is wise to pray to him from time to time."[21]

Thus for Nietzsche the point is not that the moderns characteristically deny the existence of God. The point, rather, is that they live *as though* God did not exist, even as they are for the most part sincere and explicit in their profession of God's existence. Modern liberals are content to construct the world on their own—precisely finite—terms. God may and often does still exist for most of these liberals, but he is kept at a distance (for positive reasons for some: to protect his transcendence; for negative reasons for others: to keep him out of worldly affairs). But the relevant point in either case is that the transcendent God is never an immanent shaper of worldly being, thought, and action.

Nietzsche's response is that we now need to give a robust shove in the direction toward which liberalism has already begun to move of its own inner dynamic. That is, we need now to acknowledge the noneffectiveness, or effective nonexistence, of God in our lives and embrace the consequences of this fact. The feeble creativity characteristic of liberalism now needs to be transformed into the absolute creativity of an authentic postliberalism.

It is important to see the vast implications of Nietzsche's reading of modern liberal culture. Here is the source of what would be his criticism, even disdain, for so many of the dominant features of this culture: its consumerism; its tendency to confuse genuine thinking with the taking of empirical public-opinion polls, and to replace substantive judgment with the following of formal-legal procedures (proceduralism); its tendency, in the academy, to replace philosophical reflection with "analysis," history, and archaeology—the gathering of bits of data; its reduction of the meaning of freedom to mere freedom of choice.

What all of these tendencies have in common, for Nietzsche, is precisely their surface character. The methodological-practical abstraction from God characteristic of liberalism entails a surface, or superficial (*"super-facies"*), existence. That is, for all practical purposes, liberals are absorbed in and with the finite, which typically means the empirically or sensibly accessible finite. To be sure, and once again, this absorption does not preclude the (eventual or part-time) addition of God. The point is that this addition now, *eo ipso,* finitizes God. The god who is only a god of or in "the gaps" is no god at all. More accurately stated, what liberalism does, from the perspective of Nietzsche, is replace true infinity with unending finiteness—what may be called a "bad infinity." All of the tendencies of a liberal culture noted above—consumerism, academic "analysis," freedom of choice, and the like—in the end represent but different varieties of this "bad infinity."

The superficiality of liberalism is thus revealed in the fact that it permits no breaking open of the infinite *within the finite.* Transcendence has no *immanent,* or *human-earthly,* home. But it is only the breaking open of the infinite within the finite, and the consequent immanence of the transcendent in the finite, that enables the human-earthly to achieve any genuine depth or profundity: that is, truly to go beyond the surface boundaries that constitute its reality *as finite.*

Of course, as we have seen, Nietzsche's response is forcibly himself to bring the infinite within the finite, thus rendering the transcendent itself, as it were, immanent. Nietzsche "trans-finitizes" all that is finite (all that has boundaries), even as he thereby "immanentizes" all that is transcendent. This, in a word, is what he means when he insists that the timid nihilism of liberalism needs to promote itself into the energetic nihilism of postliberalism.

It is nonetheless important to see the "unity" that Nietzsche has uncovered at the heart of our culture. To put it in a word, the problems that face us today are not in the first instance political or moral or procedural or institutional; our problems do not disperse into a pluralism of such categories. On the contrary, as indicated throughout, our problems are most fundamentally theological: they stem from the slow dying of God. The relevant point, again, is that God is such that his death affects precisely everything. Hence, for Nietzsche, the renewal of politics and morality and institutions requires, as its anterior condition, the re-forming of these realities in terms of their "divine" source and shape.

The problem, of course, is that divinity, for Nietzsche, has in the meantime become precisely nothing ("no-thing") in itself, and hence is to be wholly (re-)generated by humanity.

When we return one final time to Balthasar, we note again that he agrees with the radicality of Nietzsche's judgment: our cultural problem is above all the problem of the nature and presence of God. But again, it is also at just this point that Balthasar diverges profoundly from Nietzsche. Indeed, from the perspective of Balthasar, Nietzsche, in his response to liberal culture, in the end extends liberalism. For the problem with liberalism, according to Nietzsche, is not that it has (effectively) replaced God with human creativity and constructiveness, but that it has done so unconsciously. The problem with liberalism is not the primacy it accords human creativity, but the timidity with which it accords such primacy. The death of God that is the basic problem of modern liberal culture lies precisely in this timidity. The death of God is thus to be overturned by a renewal of the presence of God: by becoming God ourselves.

Thus Nietzsche, in construing the problem of liberalism as one of timidity rather than of the primacy accorded human creativity, now makes matters worse—infinitely worse—by absolutizing human creativity.

Balthasar insists, on the contrary, that we need to recover the primacy of the true creator God, the infinitely creative Father of Jesus Christ, and thus to "relativize" human or earthly creativity. Balthasar intends thereby not to deny human creativity, but to restore its rightful nature, which consists in being truly creaturely, always and everywhere first a *responsive* creativity: a creativity that begins in grateful and wonder-full receiving.

The point, in other words, is that an authentic recovery of heaven, of relation to the true God, to the truly infinite and truly transcendent, requires that the first act (onto-logically) on the part of earth be contemplative.

Only such a primacy of the contemplative enables the real depth that Nietzsche rightly seeks: for only when the true infinite has himself entered the finite and been *received* by the finite is the finite then enabled to reach infinitely beyond itself. Any effort by the finite to seize the infinite can, from the perspective of Balthasar, result only in a further extension of the "bad infinity" of liberalism that Nietzsche himself decried. That is, while the unending successive finiteness of liberalism may be overcome in favor of infinity, this infinity remains empty, albeit now explicitly and resolutely so.

Further, this recovery of the true depth of things, through recovering the truly infinite and transcendent God, entails the recovery simultaneously of a sense of the deepest reality of all things as a gift of the creator and thus of love and beauty as the deepest meaning of all things. A true sense of reality as gift comes about only through one's being first receptive to God's generosity.

In short, for Balthasar, the depth that is lacking in liberalism can be overcome only by opening up in receptive wonder and obedience to the God who is infinitely generous—and thus by letting God be God.

Note, then, the paradox that results regarding the respective dispositions of Nietzsche and Balthasar toward liberal modernity. Nietzsche is first of all violent in his rejection of all that is characteristically modern: he disdains its feeble freedom and creativity. Nevertheless, in locating the problem in the timidity of, and not in the primacy accorded to, creativity, Nietzsche, at least from the point of view of Balthasar, ends by extending modernity, by absolutizing its (mostly implicit) primacy of human creativity. Nietzsche's emphatic postmodernism in the end is still too modern.[22] He leaves us with a culture that is still too human- or self-centered, in that it lacks the true sense of other-centeredness that can come only from a notion of reality as gift, which in turn presupposes, finally, that there is a transcendent and generous Giver (a genuine Other).

Balthasar, however paradoxically, is thus able, in contrast to Nietzsche, to *integrate* the achievements of modernity, while at the same time moving us truly beyond modernity, because of the generosity of his God and his consequent sense of all of reality as gift, hence something to be wondered at. Balthasar is able to integrate the achievements of modernity while moving decisively beyond modernity because he has, paradoxically, returned us to *the constitutive relation to the Other lying at the heart of the self*.

It is Balthasar's sense of the "*pre*modern," in a word, that precisely enables his genuine *post*modernity.[23]

Thus for Balthasar all of the features of modernity indicated above can find a true home by being related in form and content to the deeper context of giving and receiving that signifies their character as *imago Christi*. For example, power is not rejected but transformed into what is now understood first as generosity; the external "analytic" kind of knowledge that prevails in the academy is not simply rejected but placed within the prior and deeper kind of knowledge that is interior and integrative; freedom of choice is not rejected but situated from the beginning within its primitive ordering from and toward God.

In all of this, it is important that we draw attention once again to what is for Balthasar the essential link between the cosmic universal on the one hand, and the theological-ecclesial singular on the other. The retrieval of love and beauty in the cosmos, always and everywhere, occurs through the utterly singular relation that God has established in Jesus Christ. The whole world, in each of its beings and activities, is destined to be an encounter with God in Jesus Christ, an encounter given form in the Church through the power of the Holy Spirit. It is through Mary and the Church that the world is properly a contemplative, wonder-filled, thankful response to God's gift of himself to and for the world. It is therefore through the extended presence of the Church—the sacramental communion of saints—throughout the world, that the true encounter with God can finally take place.[24]

Thus, in the words of Pope John Paul II, the Church is the *forma mundi*: she is destined to form from within everything in the cosmos: every act, every relationship, every cultural or social or economic order. It is in this singular Church that the definitive encounter between God and man has truly—infallibly—taken place, which is nonetheless the destiny of all of creation. This, it seems to me, is the authentic meaning, not only of Balthasar, but of the Second Vatican Council's *Lumen Gentium*, when it states that the Church is the sacrament—the sign and instrument—of humanity's communion with God and of the final unity of humankind itself (no. 1); and as well of *Gaudium et Spes*, when it states that Jesus Christ reveals the human person to itself (no. 22). The encounter with God, in short, always has cosmic-universal implications and always occurs within a movement from and toward the concrete realities of Christ and the Church, through the power of the Holy Spirit. It is just here, in this paradoxical coincidence of the universal and the singular, that we see how, in Balthasar, the most radical and the most traditional responses to our present crisis come together. The renewal of God, gift, love, and beauty in the cosmos occurs finally only in the context of the mother's smile, and this smile, which is first that of the woman Mary, has now become the inner form of the sacramental communion of saints making up the Church.[25]

In a word, the radical problems of our age can be met only via a renewed encounter with the scandalously singular realities of the magisterial-creedal Christian faith. This is what it means for Balthasar, finally, to say that the crisis of our time is theological in nature. This, finally, is his rendering of Heidegger's pronouncement that "only a god can save us."

Notes

* First published as "Modernity, Postmodernity, and the Problem of Atheism" in *Communio* 24, no. 3 (1997): 563–79.

1. *The Gay Science: With a Prelude in Rhymes and an Appendix of Songs*, trans. with commentary by Walter Kaufman (New York: Vintage Books, 1994), #125.
2. Ibid., #125.
3. Ibid., #374.
4. Interview, *Der Spiegel*, 1976.
5. *Of Grammatology* (Baltimore: John Hopkins University Press, 1976), 13–14.
6. *Love Alone* (London: Sheed & Ward, 1968; fifth impression, 1992), 62, 65.
7. Ibid., 114–15.
8. *A Theology of History* (San Francisco: Ignatius Press, 1994), 109–10.
9. Ibid., 92.
10. Cf. Aquinas: "Every knower knows God implicitly in all that he or she knows" (*De Veritate*, 22 ad 2). For a helpful discussion pertinent to the argument here, see Henri de Lubac, *The Discovery of God* (Grand Rapids, MI: Eerdmans, 1996). Again, it is important to understand that our argument does not imply a rejection of all methodological abstractions from God—of course not. It implies only that even methodological or strategic abstractions are always-already fraught with implications relative to the existence of God, and hence that these can be made rightly or wrongly but in any case not neutrally.
11. Cf. Derrida's statement cited at the outset: "The age of the sign is essentially theological." This implies that theology, or God, plays an essential role ultimately in the "oneness" or "wholeness" necessary for the meaningfulness of any given sign (necessary, that is, for the sign to be a sign). Of course, Derrida says this in the context of the need to move beyond or "deconstruct" meaning or sign—and God. Cf. Balthasar, *Love Alone* (New York: Herder and Herder, 1969), 103: man's constitutive relation to God in Jesus Christ "opens him to the infinite and leads him towards a fulfilling unity."
12. That is, the sanctification of human persons and, in turn—by means of the bodily-cultural activity of persons—the sanctification as well of the entire cosmos: cf. "Sanctity and the Intellectual Life," Chapter 7 of my *Heart of the World, Center of the Church* (Grand Rapids, MI: Eerdmans, 1996).

13. Note the realism and the real immanence: God takes flesh *in* and *from* Mary's body, while of course remaining a distinct person within that body.
14. See, for example, *Genealogy of Morals,* third essay, no. 9.
15. See, for example, *Beyond Good and Evil,* no. 188.
16. See *Philosophy in the Tragic Age of the Greeks* (Washington, D.C.: Regnery Gateway, 1962), 32.
17. See Balthasar, *Unless You Become Like This Child* (San Francisco: Ignatius Press, 1991); and Christoph Potworowski, "The Attitude of the Child in the Theology of Hans Urs von Balthasar," *Communio* 22 (Spring 1995): 44–55. The theme of "littleness" and "childlikeness" is one which Balthasar shares with, and indeed draws from, authors such as St. Thérèse of Lisieux, Charles Péguy, and Georges Bernanos. It is interesting here again to note that Nietzsche himself emphasizes that the spirit—the great soul—needs to undergo three metamorphoses: into a camel, then into a lion, and finally into a child. But of course, the child represents for Nietzsche a "new beginning," a new willing of one's own will, in a sense quite different from that of Balthasar: cf. *Thus Spoke Zarathustra,* Pt. I, no. 1.
18. See *The Antichrist,* Sections 59–60; *The Will to Power,* no. 145.
19. This implies not at all a denial of the importance of the masculine and of human fatherhood, but merely highlights the necessary inner condition for a proper sense of these realities in the order of creation. In this connection, see Karol Wojtyla's "The Radiation of Fatherhood," in his *Collected Plays and Writings on Theater* (Berkeley: University of California Press, 1987), 323–68.
20. In the distinctness within union of the orders of creation and incarnation (redemption).
21. *Against the Self-Images of the Age* (New York: Schocken Books, 1971), 26.
22. In this connection, see Kenneth Schmitz, "Postmodern or Modern-Plus?" in *Communio* 17 (Summer, 1990): 152–66.
23. See the pertinent discussion in Balthasar's remarkable early (1939) essay "Patristic, Scholastics, and Ourselves," *Communio* 24 (Summer 1997): 347–96.
24. This, of course, does not mean that there are not authentic elements of sanctification and truth outside the confines of the visible Church, but only that the true encounter with God "subsists" in the visible Church: cf. *Lumen Gentium,* no. 8.
25. That the first form of the Church is given in Mary is implied by the *Catechism of the Catholic Church,* when it notes that the Marian dimension of the Church precedes the Petrine dimension in the order of holiness (no. 773).

3

The Expression and Form of the Word: Trinitarian Hermeneutics and the Sacramentality of Language in Hans Urs von Balthasar's Theology

Peter J. Casarella

> God's utterance of himself in himself is God the Word, outside himself is this world. This world then is word, expression, news of God. Therefore its end, its purpose, its purport, its meaning, is God and its life or work to name and praise him.[1]
>
> G. M. Hopkins

Central to Hans Urs von Balthasar's trinitarian theology is the notion that the person of God the Word is the "exegesis" of God the Father: "No one has ever seen God. It is God the only Son, in the bosom of the Father, who has revealed him" (John 1:18; *TL* II, 13–23; *ET* I, 92).[2] For von Balthasar, as for his predecessor Bonaventure, the Son is the perfect image whose *distinctissima expressio* proclaims both all that can be experienced of the Father and the fullness of God's creative expression in the world (*GL* 2, 260–362). By reading and interpreting God the Word, those possessing the eyes of faith see the dynamism and fecundity of the Father expressed in a concrete, human form. As Bonaventure states, the Son is the very language of the Father.[3]

One can deduce from this doctrine that human expression is an adequate analogue to the perfectly unique mode of expression by which the Word "exegetes" the Father. In other words, language imitates the outpouring within the divine Trinity in that it manifests a unique gift for self-expression. Human speech also mirrors the generation of God the Word by revealing that its silent ground is inseparable but not indistinguishable from its expression. Von Balthasar sometimes states that "the Father is ground, the Son is appearance." This trinitarian relation points to a dynamic polarity of form and expression in the Word that obtains analogously for all appearances of the Word, divine and human, linguistic and otherwise (*GL* 1, 610; 2, 282–308).

Stated in terms of a philosophy of language, a spoken word does not signify a static mental word but makes what is meaningful in the world really present through the expressiveness of speech itself. Although von Balthasar does not avail himself of this term, it is consonant with his theory that words can express meaning through performative utterances.[4]

In letting his theory of language be influenced by Christian doctrine and vice versa, von Balthasar has created a hybrid that has few, if any, parallels in the contemporary intellectual milieu. An explicitly theological theory of language would seem foreign to philosophers of language, who doubtlessly object to the intrusion of trinitarian dogma. By the same token, contemporary theologians, assuming they still lend credence to distinctly divine intratrinitarian processions, might fear that a foundational inquiry into the linguistic presuppositions of the expression of the divine Word leads ineluctably to an anthropomorphic reduction of the triune God.[5] What warrants this bold intermingling of trinitarian dogma with speculation about language? Is it possible to elicit the principles of interpretation presupposed by von Balthasar's apparent hybrid?

One clue may derive from the hermeneutical theory of Paul Ricoeur. Ricoeur writes:

> The object of theology is the word become flesh, but as flesh it is man and the fact that man is language. Becoming flesh is for the word *(parole)* becoming language in the human and worldly sense of the word *(mot)*. That the Logos became flesh is raised to the level of our words *(mots)*. Here indeed is the *Geschehen* which created the encounter between the theology of the word *(parole)* and studies of language.[6]

Ricoeur argues for the mutual encounter between the Christian task of elaborating a theology of God's Word and the study of language itself. He contends that a theology of the Word which truly comprehends the "event" in the incarnation of the Word cannot ignore its consequences for a hermeneutical theory of language. Conversely, and equally important to Ricoeur, Christian theologians must face the critical task of opening up their understanding of the divine Word to an ontology of language, one preferably based upon Heidegger's claim in *Being and Time* that language itself is a fundamental determination of *Dasein*.[7]

Two of von Balthasar's most astute Protestant interpreters, Rowan Williams and Aldo Moda, have noted an affinity between Ricoeur's call for an ontology of language and von Balthasar's theology of language.[8] While Williams is correct to note "the implicit community of interest between Balthasar and the whole post-Heideggerian approach to philosophical hermeneutics," he also acknowledges that "Balthasar makes little attempt at stating a sustained and coherent account of the 'ontology of language' he regularly presupposes."[9] Although von

Balthasar occasionally mentions Heidegger, he does not speak about an ontology of language in exclusively Heideggerian terms.

In *Das Ganze im Fragment,* the text in which Williams claims that von Balthasar worked out an explicit ontology of language, von Balthasar's starting point is not even philosophical hermeneutics but a theology of history derived primarily from "the vision of Augustine."[10] In this volume von Balthasar explores the natural kinship between human history and human language. Just as history attests equally to human glory and foibles, so too is *das Wunder der Sprache* a blessing and a curse. For example, according to the creation myth of the Yahwist, the power to name gives Adam a special place in creation. More so even than human deeds, words in their finitude and arbitrariness of expression reveal human mortality.[11] In the same volume he refers to his own thoughts on language as a first attempt at a science that has still hardly begun, what he terms a *Geschichts-Theologie des Wortes.* As forebears in this effort he cites several German philosophers on language: Heidegger's *On the Way to Language,* J. G. Hamann, Wilhelm von Humboldt, Franz von Baader, Max Picard, and Gustav Siewerth.[12]

A comprehensive investigation of von Balthasar's theological theory of language has never been undertaken. This essay will give more precise definition to the theory by investigating its relation to his theology of the Word. Like Ricoeur, von Balthasar correlates the Christian understanding of God's *parole* with the ontological or semiological status of human *mots.* Unlike Ricoeur, however, what is revealed through a study of human language is not just the post-Heideggerian awareness that consciousness is not self-originated.[13] In the end, von Balthasar's interweaving of a theology of the divine Word made flesh with an investigation of the nature and function of human words belies conventional labels such as "post-Heideggerian" or "ontology of language."

What is the basic structure of von Balthasar's theological theory of language? First, human dialogue—while unique among other forms of expressivity in creation—nonetheless evinces an ordered and dynamic relation deriving from the polarity between expression and form within being itself. Second, the openness of the human person to diverse modes of expression (including the spoken word) mirrors the openness by which we become molded into a word responsive to God's call.

Most of what follows will dwell upon the first point as the foundation for the second; however, as will become clearer below, the relationship of philosophy to theology is by no means one of absolute priority. For von Balthasar, philosophy of language and theology of the Word determine one another. The order of exposition must therefore remain somewhat circular. The first and longest section examines the basis for the theory of language in his metaphysics of the polarity of expression and form. The second section lays out the convergence of hermeneutics with Christian doctrine in his theological theory of language. The third section returns to the notion of language by showing how its unique mode of expressiveness discloses the sacramental form of creation.

So far we have argued that von Balthasar's theory of language is heavily indebted to a trinitarian view of the Word made flesh. Von Balthasar nonetheless also demands that human language be investigated independently of strictly theological claims (*TL* I, xxii). The *Geschichts-Theologie des Wortes* presupposes a *general phenomenology of expression and form,* which is applied in turn to the phenomenon of the word.

His most complete exposition of the expression and form of the word lies in "The World of Images," a highly condensed section of the early philosophical work *Wahrheit der Welt* (145–200).[14] The key to "The World of Images" is the claim that the truth of the world, being insuperably mysterious and incapable of total self-disclosure, is always suspended between the polarity of expression and form. Von Balthasar is also reported to have identified the polarity of expression and form as "the very center of his construction" in *Wahrheit der Welt.*[15] Even though he does not apply his own terminology with complete consistency, "expression and form" generally refer to the dynamic of manifestness and hiddenness of the world's truth as it appears in three different modes of expression: images *(das Wesenlose)*, signification *(das Bedeutende)*, and the word *(das Wort)*.[16]

Von Balthasar follows the basic pattern of post-Romantic hermeneutics in rejecting the idea that "expression" refers primarily to a subjective manifestation of human consciousness, particularly human emotive consciousness.[17] He contends that a comprehensive definition of expression must encompass all modes of manifestation in the world, not just those emanating from the psychology of emotions.

Expression is always in some fashion an expression of the truth of being, a truth which reveals itself as fundamentally mysterious. Every revelation of being carries with it a moment of concealment. Images conceal the most, for by themselves they only reflect the surface of appearances. Words reveal the most because their signification gives expression to truth in the appearance of an image, that is, through a sign or name.

The etymology of the word itself *(ex-primere, Aus-druck)* indicates a pressing outward of inward content in all forms of "ex-pression" (*TL* I, 153). Yet the outward form is not a detached product or mere medium of the expression. The form poured into appearances constitutes as well as conveys meaning. M. Waldstein summarizes:

> A medium of expression is not merely an external sign, but a sign that is filled with manifest content. The paradox of this mediate immediacy is precisely the fundamental structure of expression. Balthasar formulates this paradox most clearly by saying that truth (as disclosedness) in expression lies in a suspended middle between the appearance and the being that appears. He does not mean that the manifestness of expressed content lies neither in itself nor in the external appearance. He rather asserts that it lies in the organic whole constituted by the poles of exterior and

> interior. The mind cannot simply rest in either one or the other of these poles, but must hold both in their unity.[18]

The "appearing of inner content in expression is an essentially and permanently mediate appearing."[19] In other words, form is not merely cloaked by a particular expression, but the emergence of a concrete expression codetermines the expressed content.

Although mediation is a necessary condition for expression, von Balthasar sometimes speaks of expressed content appearing *immediately* in a sensible form. Form can be said to appear immediately in expression because the content does not lie behind the form but in it. Content is only intelligible if one learns to interpret expression within the form: "Whoever cannot see and read the form also misses the content. Whoever does not see the form will not be enlightened by the content" (*GL* 1, 151). Grasping expressed content involves seeing and "reading" forms.

Von Balthasar often refers to expression as the mediated appearing of an interior in an exterior. The spatial metaphors "inner" and "outer" need clarification. Exteriorization does not denote an additional vestment for the expressed content.[20] Exteriorization and interiorization are two different modes of knowing and being an expression. The distinction between expressed content as such and its exteriorization lies as much in the mode of knowing and being of the viewer of form as it does in the appearance of form. Similarly, the interiorization of an expressed content points inward to what is expressible rather than to a detached, suprasensible *eidos*.

Another characteristic of expression is that the medium of expression is not an instrument of the content. As von Balthasar states, "the image is an original expression, a creation, not a poor imitation (*TL* I, 153). Expression is never a mechanical reproduction of an exemplar *(Urbild)* in an image *(Bild)*. The process of coming to expression, what Ricoeur refers to as the *Geschehen* ("event") of the word, allows for expression in a form that remains distinct from the content. Expression itself is called "creative" because it brings to perfection a relatively independent act of the intellect without destroying or removing what von Balthasar calls the depth or freedom of the mind (*Geist*). We return to the idea that expression has its own type of freedom below.

A key to von Balthasar's notion of expression is found in the theology of St. Bonaventure.[21] According to Bonaventure, the *expressio* and *impressio* of God's Word are inseparable. In Bonaventure's rendering of the stigmatization of St. Francis, for example, the intratrinitarian outpouring of love appears simultaneously with its concrete imprint on the life of the saint (*GL* 2, 270ff). The crucified seraph expresses by impressing himself upon St. Francis. Accordingly, Bonaventure writes in his *Legenda minor sancti Francisci* that "the servant of the Lord bore on his breast expressively an impressed likeness of the crucified one."[22]

In the first instance, form refers to the concrete manifestation of the world as representation, what Nicholas of Cusa in his speculative theology refers to as a "contraction" of the absolutely infinite. To see the representation of the infinite in the finite is to view the form of the finite world as open to ever-greater interpretation. The interpretation of the world's form is only grasped by first attending to the expressiveness of form itself (*GL* 4, 28–39).[23]

Form is both in and not in its expression. Moved by the power of an organizing principle, content is expressed in the manner of a form (*gestalthaft*) without losing itself to the outward appearance (*GL* 1, 441–42). Form is not a separate entity from its expression. Form has the same being and is grasped by the same act of knowing as its expression. Form differs from expression, however, in that it is viewed from the standpoint of its articulated exterior.

Forms appear differentiated in the world. The differentiation of forms reveals not only an infinite diversity of appearances but also an implicit hierarchy. To see the hierarchy of form requires some grasp of the height or exaltedness (*die Höhe*) of each form in the world. Von

Balthasar's notion of the height of form was developed in dialogue with Christian von Ehrenfels, an Austrian philosopher best known for his contribution to the study of morphology.[24] In von Ehrenfel's theory of form, the height of form is discernible by a form's capacity to unify diverse parts. A melody, according to von Ehrenfels, is a particularly exalted form because it can be transposed from one key to another with its expressed content intact and undiminished. The form of a plant likewise manifests greater internal unity than the form of a stone, for the outward appearance of the plant reveals the system of growth of the form. Unlike von Ehrenfels, von Balthasar does not contend that there is a finitely knowable, transcendental *Urform* that unifies every expressed form. The melody is only known in and through its different expressions.

Unity in diversity is therefore not the central characteristic of the height of form according to von Balthasar. He characterizes form's height primarily by its free, transcending center of being. Rather than denoting a static supramundane synthesis of diverse parts, form is born of the freedom of the intellect to operate in and above matter, a freedom derived from form's own inner transcendentality.

Theologians have frequently noted that von Balthasar rejects the deduction of the spontaneous, *a priori* structures of subjective experience in the Kantian sense and favors instead the path prepared by Goethe's theory of nature, that is, starting with the visible evidence for spiritual interiority irradiating from within form itself.[25] Von Balthasar contends that the manifest appearance of form is prior to strictly transcendental categories of subjectivity. Instead of a formal deduction of the conditions for the possibility of transcendental experience, he lays bare the movement of spirit from sensible appearance to what the scholastics called the *splendor formae.* His account of transcendental experience does not ignore the more basic relationship between appearance and nature (*TL* II, 168–69).

This understanding of the transcendental conditions of experience could be called "expressive transcendentality," for it proceeds from an inner light that breaks through sensible appearance to let form appear:

> The light which breaks out of form and opens it to understanding is therefore inseparably the light of form itself (thus the scholastics speak of the *splendor formae*) and the light of being as a whole in which form bathes in order to be able to have really unified form *(überhaupt einshafte Gestalt)*.[26]

Light shines forth from within form without being projected onto it. The subjective disposition for the appearance of form is a disposition to let form be expressed. The "height" of form is not determined by unity in the appearance of diversity even though such a pattern can also be discerned. The height of form is determined by the light whose origin, though not tied to appearance, nonetheless radiates form through it.

Von Balthasar compares his theory of form to Gerard Manley Hopkins's notion of "inscape" (*GL* 3, 336).[27] Inscape gives language to what the poetic eye sees in nature and thereby names the expressed form implicit in the poet's vision of creation. In journal entries, for example, Hopkins describes a winter landscape in which nature's concrete detail reveals the expressed form of the world:

> In the snow flat-topped hillocks and shoulders outlined with wavy edges, ridge below ridge, very like the grain of wood in line and in projection like relief maps *[sic]*. These the wind makes I think and of course drifts, which are in fact snow waves. The sharp nape of a drift is sometimes broken by slant flutes or channels. I think this must be when the wind after shaping the drift first has changed and cast waves in the body of the wave itself. *All the world is full of inscape and chance left free to act falls into an order as well as purpose:* looking out of my window I caught

> it in the random clods and broken heaps of snow made
> by the cast of a broom.[28]

By proclaiming the world full of inscape, the poet sees and names the illumination of form expressed in snowdrifts.

Another entry alludes to the ancient metaphor of language as the speech of nature. On April 20, 1874, Hopkins described springtime fields of "white daisies, yellower fresh green of leaves above which bathes the skirts of the elms, and their tops are touched and worded with leaf too."[29] Commenting on the description, von Balthasar writes: "The form thus grasped is the key to the word, is itself already an objective word. *Formed* can also mean *worded*" (*GL* 3, 366). Language imitates Hopkins's inscape because of the implicit analogy between the expression of the word in language and nature. In the spoken word and in nature's speech, expression is illuminated by an interior splendor providing concrete form and meaning.[30]

Von Balthasar contends that the interpretation of finite beings draws upon the phenomenon of polarity. Since expression and form is seen in every image, in every signification, and in every word, grasping the metaphysics of their polarity becomes a prerequisite for understanding von Balthasar's theory of language. To understand the essence of a being truly is to accept that a finite nature cannot be reduced to a metaphysical composition constructed out of different parts and elements, for the irreducibility of form to expression is intrinsic to each being and manifest in being itself.

For von Balthasar, the metaphysical teaching about the polarity of being is most fully articulated by the Thomist real distinction between existence and essence in finite beings (*GL* 4, 395).[31] In any given finite being, that whereby a being exists is distinct from that which essentially defines it. The polarity of being and essence in finite beings does not imply the separation of being and essence. Whoever attempts to grasp the barest "that" cannot do so without expressing "what" it is. Being and essence are composed and divided in creatures because each finite essence can participate and subsist in the fullness of being itself. Through its participatory being, creaturely being is "caught" between an expressed form (its definable essence) and its expressivity of being itself (*esse ab alio*). The act of being a creature is irreducible to either its form (essence) or its source of expression because essence coincides with the pure act of being in God alone.

Only if expression and form are understood together in a polar relation can one grasp the basic configuration of being. Von Balthasar refutes the idealist supposition that the category of expression can by itself do justice to the analogy of being (*GL* 5, 620). He maintains that by itself the term "expression" can suggest a self-exhaustion of the fullness of being (*esse*) in a finite form. In other words, the difference between the participating essence of the creature and being itself is destroyed when self-expression alone becomes the governing category for a metaphysics of being. The polarity of expression and form reveals that each being in the world has an immanent ground that manifests itself in a definite form. Von Balthasar chose the word "polarity" because it denotes a unity based upon free activity, namely, a relation which can never be formalized into a systematic formula or analogy of direct proportion. This unity itself implies that expression and form are not identical modes of being.

The polarity of expression and form implies both a unity and a difference. Unity is defended against those who claim that expression is an epiphenomenon or mere representation of form.[32] The polarity of form and expression implies that expression is not a photographic copy of what is being expressed. When we say "I see you, the "you" does not refer to a pictorial representation of the person seen. A blind man could grasp the expressed form of that person and could therefore "see" her or him. Moreover, the appearance of the expressed form of a person is "seen" as neither mere expression of the nature nor as pure form. The unity of expression and form signifies that someone appears as expressed form when the words "I see you" are spoken in truth.[33] The person appears without a mental picture but not without the expression of that person's form.

On the other hand, polarity also signifies a clear distinction between expression and form. The phenomenon of pretense shows that any given expression does not necessarily correspond to a fixed content. A smile, for instance, may express the pleasure of malice or lasciviousness. A smile may also express the depth of love which a mother holds for the child in her lap.[34] The distinguishability of expression from form must therefore be underscored against those who deny the distinction between interior and exterior and against those who ignore the true depth of interiority possible in an expressed form.[35]

We can now return to "The World of Images," in which von Balthasar interprets the expression of the world in terms of the polar relationship within the being of all manifestations and appearances. This section makes the metaphysical teaching about the polarity of form and expression concrete by applying it to real modes of expression in the world. Three forms of manifestation—the image *(das Wesenlose)*, signification *(das Bedeutende)*, and word *(das Wort)*—constitute the most basic modes of disclosure of being and its representations (*TL* I, 233).

Images are deceptive because they appear to mediate meaning even though they are in and of themselves without meaning.[36] Von Balthasar refers to them as *das Wesenlose* because they have no nature of their own: "Pure mutability is their perduring nature; pure irreality is their form of existence."[37] They are not more than appearances and can only barely be differentiated from nonbeing: "Their pure superficiality lets nothing penetrate from another dimension. They are not nothing since they are actually readily apparent as images."[38] Something is disclosed through an image, but the being of an image as such can be readily called into question. Images waver. Without the expressed content that they transport, images are pure, insubstantial reflection.

Images are still essential for signification. Finite existence has no other language than images to reveal itself.[39] Images are therefore sensible signs of reality, and there is no act of knowledge without a sensible sign.[40] The mediating role of the image lends credence to the adage that nothing can be in the intellect that was not first in the senses.[41] As in all expression, images evince the polarity of being. They do not offer a static picture or mere "representation" of a pregiven meaning.

We come to understand through what images signify in a sensible form, but the act of understanding is not limited to the assimilation of sensible signs. "One has to close the gates of the senses in order to hear the voice of reason within oneself and to see the light of the mind. Only they can liberate from the kingdom of deception and open up the world of truth."[42] Knowledge requires the assimilation of what is acquired through the "gates of the senses." However, once one has acquired what is communicated through a sensible sign, then one must turn inward to "see" beyond the surface appearance of the sign.

Von Balthasar's point in this metaphor is that the insubstantiality of the image indicates its capacity not only to deceive but also to reveal. Rationalists and certain mystics describe the image as a realm without any truth or as a mere copy of the truth. Von Balthasar by contrast contends that in an image "the essentiality of the existing world triumphs over the insubstantiality of mere appearance."[43] Images reveal that the relationship between objective appearances and the experience of the subject is veiled in mystery which is not empty and meaningless.

> The subject is in the truth as long as it sticks to the assimilation of images and devotes itself completely to their acceptance. If previously the insubstantiality of images led to anchoring truth outside of them, now it leads to handing the features of insubstantiality over to the truth itself.[44]

Without the dim light of the truth of being, the way of images would support a methodical skepticism regarding the reality of the objective world. For von Balthasar, an insubstantial appearance in an image can still reflect a true, albeit diminished, expression of being.

Signification refers to the meaningful expression of form in an appearance. If expression is the mediated appearing of an interior in an exterior, then signification is a mode of expression in which the interiority of being is reflected in an exterior form. In signification, however, the interiority of being does not become known in itself. The truth of being lies neither in the appearances nor behind them. "Truth is the undisclosed. It can only be found hovering between the appearance and that which appears."[45] The complete and univocal translucency of being is therefore permanently veiled by the mystery of truth's appearance.

The phenomenon of signification confirms that the world in the most fundamental sense is unsurpassably open to greater interpretation. For Hopkins, "being formed" was synonymous with "being worded." Von Balthasar likewise contends that the appearance of *das Bedeutende* ("signification") means that the world needs to be read as the book of nature in which each form represents a letter or word (*GL* 3, 241ff).[46] In the alphabet of nature the entire field of revelatory images is open to a meaningful interpretation.

> The whole world of images which surrounds us is a unique field of significations. Every flower which we see is an expression, every landscape has its meaning, every animal and human face speaks a wordless speech. It would be completely in vain to want to translate this speech into concepts. We could attempt to circumscribe or describe the expression, but our attempts at an adequate rendering would never succeed. The speech of expression does not apply primarily to conceptual thinking. It addresses itself

> to thinking which understands and interprets forms *(das verstehende, das gestaltlesende Denken).*[47]

Meaning and image coincide in the world of forms. Everything that has been expressed has found its form. The result is a vision of the world in which the perfection of expression remains a perfect mystery. At the same time mystery conceals and reveals. In grasping the presence of signification in an image, the mystery of being appears as a "quality of the most lucid revelation."[48]

Signification derives from the dynamic polarity between form and expression and discloses a twofold movement within being itself. Most apparent is the movement from inner to outer in which expressed content is revealed through a concrete form. But von Balthasar also speaks of a movement in the other direction, a movement from outer to inner.[49] The first movement is predicated upon the power of the image to give expression to being itself. The reverse movement is predicated on the insubstantiality of the image. In every expression the image fades away and drops out of appearance to make a place for the "essential fruit of being." The fading of the image allows the mind to distinguish between being and mere appearances. The fading of the image does not mean that its function has changed or that truth can be surgically removed from the images that express it. Nor does the fading of the image remove the veil from the mystery of being. Even when appearances qua appearances disappear, there is still no direct, unmediated intuition of raw being.

The reverse movement of the image into its ground is the condition for the possibility of reflection upon being.[50] Von Balthasar's metaphysics of expressive transcendentality also becomes more concrete in the realm of signification. The twofold movement of expression on the part of the subject mirrors the objective structure of the polarity. The subject experiences the turning back of appearance into a nature that does not appear. Von Balthasar refers to this motion as *das Erscheinen des Wesens im Nicht-mehr-erscheinen der Erscheinung.*[51] The appearance of form in the nonappearance of appearance is the point at which reflection must transcend the empirical conditions for the possibility of sense perception. Von Balthasar is not a transcendental idealist because he rejects the spontaneity of the subject established solely by its *a priori* system of categories. Transcendental reflection is established by the apparent emergence of expressed being as an interior movement of the subject. He writes:

> Knowledge of truth is only possible when the subject is able to mirror the reflection of being immediately in the appearance through its [the subject's] own interior connection between sensory perception and spirit. Such mirroring—the standing still of all that can be assimilated in a realm that is immediately more than sensory, in fact a spiritual realm—permits a second step. In the second step, appearance returns to being through its own movement in order to let it appear as being. Thereby intuition is also resolved into a concept in order to make insight into the essence of beings possible.[52]

Von Balthasar assumes that there is a twofold movement between being and appearance on the level of sense experience. His supposition of an experience of being that is in some sense prior to the *a posteriori* expression of being is not meant as a strict proof for the conditions for the possibility of being's appearance as being. Nor is he assuming that transcendental reflection emerges spontaneously through an *Aufhebung* of the polarity of form and expression. Polarity remains even as *Geist* moves beyond the assimilation of the sensory data toward an insight into the essence of beings. The subject experiences being as being through, not beyond, the polarity of expression and form.

The highest function of an image appears in a word, for the insubstantiality of the image is fully overcome in a word. A word is a sensible sign filled with meaning in which signification emanates not from the sensible sign but from an interior and hidden act. Speech is therefore the outward expression of this dynamic inner word.

In a world of mere images, the verbal sign appears to be just a copy of the inner word. In the world of meaningful discourse, however, the form of a word is distinguishable from its verbal sign. The distinguishability of inner and outer words betrays the unique gift of human speech, "the marvelous and multifarious interplay of nature and spirit in our speech, the gradual transition from natural images to half-emancipated symbols and then to freely chosen signs" (*ET* I, 82).

Up to this point, we have been using the terms "word," "speech," and "language" rather broadly. This is not the case in von Balthasar's own writings. He not only distinguishes inner and outer words but also verbal and nonverbal speech, and language as a form of human communication from language as the form of creation. Mental or inner words receive their paradigmatic form in the spoken word while nonverbal forms of expression such as laughing, crying, turning one's back, and modulating one's tone of voice change the expressed content of a verbal sign in a dramatic way (*ET* I, 82; SG 34).

The presence of inner and outer in the spoken word shows the polarity of expression and form in its linguistic articulation. Freedom for self-exteriorization in speech displays the unity and difference of the subjective and objective poles of expression. Von Balthasar analyses the polarity of speech in terms of: 1) the word as an expression of a free person, and 2) the word as a function of standing in the world and community.

The freedom of the word is the freedom to use a natural expression as a self-offering. Even though sensible images are temporally prior to natural words, a mental word still has an essential priority to the verbal sign (*TL* I, 185). The distinction between the inner and outer form of the word is the source of speech's freedom. A contrast with ordinary language will clarify. Our everyday notion of "self-expression" usually assumes an opposition between the arbitrariness of a culturally determined sign and the liberating representation of an individual's subjective, emotive self. The glory of free speech is quite different for von Balthasar. Speech is free because of its rootedness in a basically objective source. The free expression of an inner word in an outward form becomes the objective measure of the polarity of form and expression: "[The mental word] hands a relation of truth over to the I and at the same time—through perduring identity—a standard with which to measure this relation" (*TL* I, 183) Free self-expression is therefore an offering of self over to the expression of truth rather than a liberation of the passions. This free self-offering makes an authentic dialogue between an *I* and a *You* possible.

Speech utilizes sensible signs, and sensible signs are drawn from the social world. Since the metaphysics of expression and form does not discount outward expression as a diminution of reality, the social world of the expressed sign is *a fortiori* an enrichment of an inner word. The interpersonal environment in which a word is uttered is not an addendum to the act of expression but its culmination and unifying center.

The social expression of meaning in words is fraught with ambiguity. The viciousness of not meaning what we say goes deeper than outright deception, for we can also instrumentalize words for personal gain, for example, when aggressive locutions serve only to distance or silence the other. In these cases, the words themselves are no longer meaningful centers of interiority but fragmented images signifying nothing.

On the other hand, the social environment of speech can make dialogue possible in the form of love, the final goal of the polar movement of form and expression:

> As soon as the direction of the disclosure of being surpasses the I to perfect itself in a You and as soon as the Logos of being enters into dialogue in the sense of an inconclusive communication, at that moment love emerges as the final explanation of the whole movement. (*TL* I, 195)

In the end love is the true justification for authentic self-expression. Love justifies speech because the expression of love is the most comprehensive norm by which the word can be judged. The self-emptying expression of oneself to another becomes circumscribed by the external situation and eventually meaningless if expression is not somehow an expression of love. "Without [love] every nearness and communion would necessarily seem uncomfortable, embarrassing, and indiscrete. Everyone would have enough of his own truth and would probably use the truth of the other to gather up his own treasure and need for knowledge" (*TL* I, 195). Love justifies speech not as a verbal entity hanging in the air in front of someone's lips but through the entire expression of that person's moral acts (*TL* I, 197–200; SG 44–45).[53] Each word spoken is measured by the testimony of a life just as the Christian expression of the truth is measured by its correspondence to the Word and Deed of the Incarnate One. This christological insight leads us to the third part of our investigation.

The polarity of expression and form is the foundation for von Balthasar's theory of language and the basis for his trinitarian hermeneutics. In this section we will explore more fully the theological dimension of language by examining the horizontal and vertical dimensions of human speech (SG 32–36).[54]

The two dimensions of human language follow von Balthasar's verbal anthropology: we are, in a word, God's own speech (*GF* 264–68; *ET* I, 69–94). Because the Word has truly become flesh, God's Word speaks in the human language. The language of being human is situated along a twofold axis. As human language it is subject to human modes of interpretation. As God's speech in human form, it remains continually open to God's address.

The horizontal dimension of language refers to the insoluble connection between the corporeality of human speech on the one hand and the freedom of the human imagination on the other. The expression of the word is not just emptied into a material environment but actually enriched by its verbal signs. Human speech mirrors the hylomorphic unity out of which we are composed. The freedom of the act of speech is bound but not imprisoned by the conventionality of verbal expression. The senses *actively* assimilate the material world around them so that speech is not a mechanical exteriorization of an inner word but an ethical expression of the uniquely human capacity to stand in and above nature. Among creatures only the human displays such a seemingly infinite variety of hylomorphic expressions—smiles, shouts, hand gestures, salutations, sign language, groans, mime, stop signs, and, of course, books. In sum, the horizontal dimension of language follows the polarity of all human expression.

The vertical dimension, however, is not reducible to a human source or finite mode of interpretation. Even as we occupy a unique place among creatures, our speech is still more fundamentally determined by a higher law. Von Balthasar compares the peculiar human form of existence in the world to that of a ruler *without* absolute power:

> He has in the world which surrounds him a superior, "royal" position, which enables him to form both himself and the world. But a king is neither a god nor a tyrant capable of sheer autocracy. He carries a twofold responsibility for formation: to himself corresponding to his mission in the world and to the world in accordance with his own law, inseparable from that mission. (SG 33)

Even though the human gift of speech gives us a relative superiority over creatures, the verbal expressiveness of human existence makes life contingent upon the utterance of the divine speaker. This seemingly metaphorical relation of human and divine speech is more than figurative, for it follows the metaphysics of being sketched above. The real distinction between being and essence in creatures assumes such a polarity. Since finite being is caught between an expressed form and its expressivity of being itself, dependent being (*esse ab alio*) is always-already expressed in the speech of a creature (SG 35).

Human speech has a capacity to respond to and even imitate divine speech. What does that mean concretely? The answer depends in part upon what is meant by divine speech, for God's speech takes on different forms. According to von Balthasar, the forms of divine speech can be derived from St. Maximus Confessor's notion of the threefold "thickening" of the Word: he speaks in creation, in the covenant with his chosen people, and in the incarnate Word (SG 36–47; *ET* I, 23). An ever more vocal response to God's Word gradually emerges within this triad (SG 51; *GF* 260ff).

Creation speaks, for example, when we perceive the expression of the world's inscape. Von Balthasar, following Ignatius of Antioch, interprets the wordless speech of creation as the trinitarian background to the emanation of the divine Word. The silent emanation of the Son from the Father is actually expressed in the mystery of creation itself. God's Word in creation is not other than the Word who takes on human flesh (Prov 8). The human response to God's first speech is to praise the seeds of the Logos in creation as silent manifestations. The taking on flesh of the Word in creation has already been expressed in a real but incomplete fashion. Our response can embrace both St. Paul's speech at the Areopagus and Moses' exhortation upon returning to the base of Mt. Sinai. At a particular moment we may be called either to witness to the creative presence of the Logos at the altars of unnamed gods or to enjoin our kin to smash their idols.

Our response to God's second speech is more than silent worship and praise for the unknown God. It is a disposition to respond in active obedience. At this stage the precise words with which we respond are not crucial so long as we are capable of recognizing with Moses that the Lord is the one "who gives one man speech and makes another deaf and dumb" (Exod 4:11). The words of his prophets and the verbal readiness of the Israelites (e.g., Abraham's "Here I am LORD!") are not just a slave's response to a Lord's command. Israel's loyalty to Yahweh does not stand opposed to God's decision to place himself near his people. God literally "incorporates" the faithful obedience of his people into the activity of his own Word (SG 40). The unity that binds Yahweh's call with Israel's word already begins to exhibit a christological shape in the old covenant.

God's verbal presence is not only heard but seen in the Old Testament. The prohibition against idols highlights and preserves the fearful beauty of God's theophany. The appearance of glory *(kabod)* of the Lord at Mt. Sinai and in the Ark of the Covenant discloses the sovereignty and freedom of God's Word to Israel. Israel's faithful response to the offer of a covenant *(hesed)* shows that God's speech becomes concrete in the life and history of his people. For Christians, von Balthasar notes, the covenant with Israel can nonetheless express a contradictory and paradoxical form since it hovers between the election of a particular nation and God's universal proclamation to offer himself to all.

God's third speech is expressed in the concrete *Gestalt Christi.* After the Father has spoken through his Son, no more can be said (SG 42). Christ is the self-interpretation or exegesis of the Father because he alone is the perfect image of the invisible God (Col 1:15). It is easy to misconstrue von Balthasar's teaching about Christ as the image of God as a kind of static exemplarism separate from the activity of human history. By contrast, the true logic of Christ's form is self-involving.[55]

There is a truth analogous to the polarity of expression and form in the logic of the incarnate Word. The expressed content of what is revealed in the Word is the Father's free decision to make himself visible to all. "No one knows the Son but the Father, and no one knows the Father but the Son—and anyone to whom the Son wishes to reveal him" (Matt 11:27). The form of this disclosure is the life and words of Jesus. In taking on human flesh, God's Word is expressed in human form (*ET* I, 69–94). The mysterious truth revealed in the incarnate man Jesus Christ is not *(pace Arius)* a second god. Nor is it a Nestorian truth whereby the inner content does not enter into full union with the incarnate form of human expression. The Chalcedonian confession of faith gives us a language to express the dogmatic truth of the incarnate Word's unique mode of verbal presence.

God's perfect word is also his perfect deed. Everything that is expressed in this fully human deed—including, paradoxically, God's own kenotic self-expression on the cross, "My God, my God, why have you abandoned me?"—reveals something about the triune life of God. The Son undergoes the experience of having been abandoned by the Father on the cross. God's highest and last statement is finally disclosed through the self-abandonment of the cross (John 3:16; Rom 8:32).

In the passion of the Word, the unity of expression and form appears ripped apart (*GF* 298–308). The image of the invisible God no longer seems capable of expressing form. He becomes, in von Balthasar's words, a "non-image *(Unbild)* of the Father," for "the icon of God has been deformed on the cross *(die Ikone Gottes, die...in Ungestalt zerbricht)*" (SG 45, 46).[56]

How do we respond to the paradoxical breaking of God's own image on the cross? Our response comes through the breath of the Spirit.[57] "The role of the Holy Spirit in this mutual abandonment (for the sake of the unifying of the world) consists of nothing other than effecting this division to the end, whereby the unity of the Father's as well as the Son's will is shown" (SG 47). The Spirit of the Word is the inseparable bond of love between Father and Son. The love which restores the image broken on the cross is the Spirit of the resurrected Word. The Son becomes his own exegesis in the forty days after the resurrection, namely, the spiritual exegesis of the Word which St. Paul speaks about in Romans 8.[58] "The Holy Spirit given to faith at Easter is the first one to make God's language in Christ really intelligible. It is a language which expresses the triune love not by stammering but in an adequate speech" (SG 47). Because the risen Christ hands his spirit over to the Church through an act of trinitarian self-interpretation, we are able to participate in God's Word through the firstfruits of the Spirit. Through the Spirit's gift of love, we form ourselves into a human speech adequate to the self-emptying love of the triune God.

Von Balthasar's trinitarian hermeneutics encompasses both a theological and a pre-theological theory of linguistic expression. The metaphysics of expression and form make the silent speech of the Father in his Word more intelligible to the believer. This intelligibility is relatively independent from the strictly theological claims revealed in Scripture and tradition. The conditional independence of philosophy needs to be emphasized, for the revelation of the triune life can never be rendered into an alien tongue. As von Balthasar states, "God is his own exegete."[59] He proposes a theory of expression and form as no more and no less than a *preparatio evangelica* for a clearer and more concrete vision of the trinitarian form of God's self-expression.

The horizontal and vertical dimensions of language show that von Balthasar's trinitarian hermeneutics extends to the act of human speech. The peculiar human capacity to rise above nature as a servant of the Lord makes human speech simultaneously self-expressive and disposed to self-emptying, obediential love. The believer stands before God's speech as a quasi-independent utterance, actively awaiting the performance of the Word.

Having uncovered the verbal aspects of von Balthasar's trinitarian and anthropological doctrines, we will now examine von Balthasar's view of language in light of his theology of the Word. Von Balthasar sees an interior sacramentality within language itself. Rowan Williams writes, "Language, for Balthasar, is the means of opening the human subject to 'being', it is the sacrament, we might say, of the totality to which we belong...."[60] Language is sacramental because speech is paradigmatic of the human capacity to give expression in a finite form to the totality of the world.[61] The inner sacramentality of language points to a human capacity to make an expressed content really present in and through the performance of an incarnate word. This does not mean that spoken language is always necessarily consecrated, for human words sometimes compete with God's Word and are thereby disclosed as broken and prideful (*GF* 258–63).

The exteriorization of a word does not transfer a mental word to a verbal form nor does it vest an inner word with the garment of speech. As Claudel states, "The word is not merely the formula of an object. It is the image of myself as informed by this object."[62] If truth can be spoken in a performative utterance, then what is represented in a word is a kind of self-offering. Since no words convey what we want to say with absolute precision, the sacrificial act of speech is always performed on the altar of concepts and ideas.[63] Genuine communication or dialogue between two persons can express a substantial handing over of self in the form of words.

In the essay "God Speaks as Man," von Balthasar develops two analogies between human speech and sacred liturgy.[64] First, speech is fully corporeal and organic, but at the same time it reveals that man is the summit of the whole material and organic creation. In an analogous manner, Christian liturgy takes over natural signs and human practices common to many different religions and cultures and endows them with a meaning that is not reducible to a natural religion. The expression of language and the expression of liturgy both presuppose and perfect natural forms without destroying them.

The second way in which speech transcends itself is in its ends. Speech is generally the beginning of action, but spoken words are seldom self-sufficient acts. Speech is not its own fulfillment, according to von Balthasar, for it goes beyond itself in its involvement with life's activities. Without the witness of the whole person, "as in married love, in politics, in the apostolate, in martyrdom," all speech, especially speech addressed to God, begins to disintegrate.[65] In speech as in liturgy, the spiritual presence of the word continues even when its outward expression has faded away. The word of Christ becomes act in the sacraments. According to von Balthasar, there is no Christian liturgy without the sacrifice of the cross: "The two are one and the same."[66] The activity of the word in the eucharistic sacrifice is analogous to the kenotic expression of inner form in the true speech act. In both cases the self-surrender of the true word remains in, but also transcends, outward expression. Both forms of expression occur within and beyond natural, organic forms, and both are truly meaningful only if freely transformed into an act of self-giving. Hopkins likewise recognizes an analogy between the poetic act and sacrament in the fourth stanza of "The Wreck of the Deutschland":

> I am soft sift
> In an hourglass—at the wall
> Fast, but mined with a motion, a drift,
> And it crowds and it combs to the fall;
> I steady as a water in a well, to a poise, to a pane,
> But roped with, always, all the way down from the tall
> Fells or flanks of the voel, a vein
> Of the gospel proffer, a pressure, a principle, Christ's gift.[67]

These lines reenact the procession from self to altar, culminating in the eucharistic offer in "Christ's gift."[68] The dramatic images of desperation in the first three lines are said to express Hopkins's own poetic experience: "I have prescribed for myself twenty-four hourglasses a day...even this does not stop the ravages of time."[69] The poet's fall in line four is stilled suddenly by the liturgical image of a life-giving well. The offering of self to Christ in the last line builds upon the equally kenotic "fling of the heart to the heart of the Host" mentioned in the previous stanza. Poetic form is the expression of the inner sacramentality of the word—"That is Christ being me and me being Christ."[70]

Some will contend that employing concepts derived from the Christian view of eucharistic presence to illuminate a theory of language constitutes a category error, for it results in an unnecessary and unwarranted mixture of philosophy and theology. To be sure, a sacramental theory of language can stand on its own only after being justified in the realm of philosophical hermeneutics and philosophy of language. Such justification goes beyond the bounds of this essay but would begin with a theory of what language makes present that neither instrumentalizes the function of the linguistic sign nor hypostatizes the active polarity between the expression and form of the word.

Finally, the potential contribution of this view of language to a renewal of Christian theology and the Christian state of life in the world should not go unnoticed. For Christians the Word is the site of the Father's kenotic love revealed in the form of a slave (Phil 2:7). The world created in and through his Son expresses itself in the form of cosmic liturgy *(KL)*. God's revealed speech in his Son presupposes and perfects the natural speech of creation. Liturgy, understood as both a sacrament in and the form of creation, binds these two modes of divine self-expression. The presence of the Word in the liturgy is the source, summit, and fulfillment of all that creation can express. To the degree that the flesh and blood of the Word is truly represented in the liturgy, language is necessarily fulfilled in sacrament.

Notes

1. Gerard Manley Hopkins, *The Sermons and Devotional Writings of Gerard Manley Hopkins,* ed. Christopher Devlin (London: Oxford University Press, 1959). 129.
2. Thomas Rodolf Krenski, *Passio Caritatis: Trinitarische Passiologie im Werk Hans Urs von Balthasar* (Einsiedeln, Freiburg: Johannes, 1990), 97–103.
3. Ewert H. Cousins, "Bonaventure's Mysticism of Language," in *Mysticism and Language,* ed. Steven T. Katz (New York: Oxford University Press, 1992), 240–43.
4. Von Balthasar would agree with J. L. Austin that human speech is a mode of expression in which the utterer can perform, as well as describe, what is being said. Unlike Austin, von Balthasar does not distinguish between performative and constative utterances. His theory of polarity may be more applicable to the former than the latter. On the other hand, I do not think that von Balthasar would agree with John Searle's "theory of expressibility" whereby whatever can be meant can be said. For von Balthasar, the disclosure of meaning in speech is always simultaneously a form of concealment. In his view language reenacts the fundamental mystery of human interiority in a concrete form. If whatever can be meant can be said, then what von Balthasar refers to as the

spiritual depth of human interiority could never be expressed as a polarity of concealment and disclosure. Unlike some ordinary language philosophers, von Balthasar does not accept a classification of the rules and forms of life that govern "speech acts" as an exhaustive determination of what language discloses. It is most likely for this reason that he refers to post-Wittgensteinian analytic philosophy as "a dead-end" and "a game of ratio" in "*Die Sprache Gottes*," 31.

5. One exception is Gerhard Ebeling, *Introduction to a Theological Theory of Language* (Philadelphia: Fortress, 1973). Ebeling's approach is well-suited to the Protestant dialectic of law and gospel, whereas von Balthasar's theory of language is rooted in the trinitarian confession of faith and its expression in sacrament.
6. Paul Ricoeur, "Contribution d'une réflexion sur le langage à une théologie de la parole," in *Exegese et Hermeneutique*, eds. Roland Barthes et al. (Paris, 1971), 303; my translation.
7. Ibid., 315.
8. Aldo Moda, *Hans Urs von Balthasar, Un' esposizione critica del suo pensiero* (Bari: Ecumenica Editrice, 1976), 510ff; Rowan Williams, "Balthasar and Rahner, " in *The Analogy of Beauty: The Theology of Hans Urs von Balthasar*, ed. John Riches (Edinburgh: T. and T. Clark, 1986), 28–29.
9. Rowan Williams, 31.
10. The English translation of this volume, *A Theological Anthropology* (New York: Sheed and Ward, 1967), leaves much to be desired as is evident from the rather arbitrary rendering of the title.
11. Hans Urs von Balthasar, *Das Ganze im Fragment: Aspekte der Geschichtstheologie* (Einsiedeln: Benziger, 1963). Cf. its English translation, *A Theological Anthropology*, 246ff.
12. *Balthasar, A Theological Anthropology*, 228.
13. Rowan Williams, "Balthasar and Rahner," 29.
14. *Wahrheit der Welt* was originally published in 1947. I am citing from the virtually unchanged edition included as the first volume of *Theologik*. In *The Glory of the Lord* I, he notes how his theological aesthetics builds upon the theory of expression first developed in *Wahrheit* (610).
15. Michael M. Waldstein, "Expression and Form: Principles of a Philosophical Aesthetics According to Hans Urs von Balthasar" (PhD diss., University of Dallas, 1981), 33.
16. Von Balthasar sometimes uses other terms to identify this polarity. In *The Glory of the Lord* I, for example, he refers to "form and radiance" (*Gestalt und Glanz, species et splendor*) as inseparable from one another and constituting together the basic configuration of being (111).

17. Hans-George Gadamer, *Truth and Method* (New York: Continuum, 1991), 458–59; Martin Heidegger, *Being and Time* (New York: Harper and Row, 1962), 205; Joel Weinsheimer, *Philosophical Hermeneutics and Literary Theory* (New Haven: Yale University Press, 1991), 87–123.
18. Waldstein, "Expression and Form," 44.
19. Ibid.
20. Ibid., 41, 62.
21. John O'Donnell, SJ, "Alles Sein ist Leibe," in *Hans Urs von Balthasar, Gestalt und Werk,* eds. K. Lehmann and W. Kasper (Cologne: Communio, 1989), 269.
22. Bonaventure, *Opera Omnia,* Vol. 8 (Quarrachi edition, 1898), 576a.
23. Cf. Louis Dupré, "Hans Urs von Balthasar's Theology of Aesthetic Form," *Theological Studies* 49 (1988): 299–318.
24. Christian von Ehrenfels, *Gestalthaftes Sehen: Ergebnisse und Aufgaben der Morphologie,* ed. Ferdinand Wienhandl (Darmstadt, 1967); *GL* 4 30; Waldstein, "Expression and Form," 75ff.
25. Jeffrey Kay, *Theological Aesthetics: The Role of Aesthetics in the Theological Method of Hans Urs von Balthasar* (Berne: Herbert Lang; Frankfurt: Peter Lang, 1975).
26. Hans Urs von Balthasar, *Herrlichkeit III, 1, 1: Im Raum der Metaphysik: Altertum* (Einsiedeln: Johannes, 1965), 32; my translation.
27. Waldstein, "Expression and Form," 99.
28. G. M. Hopkins, *Journals and Papers of Gerard Manley Hopkins,* ed. Humphrey House (London: Oxford University Press, 1959), 230. Italics added.
29. Ibid., 243.
30. Jacques Maritain, *Art and Scholasticism and the Frontiers of Poetry,* trans. Joseph W. Evans (Notre Dame: University of Notre Dame Press, 1962), 24ff.
31. Hans Urs von Balthasar, "On the Tasks of Catholic Philosophy in Our Time," *Communio: International Catholic Review* 20 (Spring 1993): 181; Martin Bieler, "Meta-anthropology and Christology," *Communio: International Catholic Review* 20 (Spring 1993): 133; E. Gilson, *Being and Some Philosophers.* 2nd ed. (Toronto: PIMS, 1952) 172ff.; Waldstein, "Expression and Form," 177–90; John F. Wippel, *Metaphysical Themes in Aquinas* (Washington, DC: Catholic University of America Press, 1984), 107–61.
32. Waldstein, "Expression and Form," chap. 2.
33. St. Thomas refers to the expressed form of a person in this sense as *anima forma corporis.*

34. The example of a mother's smile is particularly instructive on this point. For von Balthasar, the smile of a mother is a quasi-archetypal image expressing the boundlessness of human love that can actually appear in the form of a single gesture. See Balthasar, "A Résumé of My Thought," 471, and *Theo-Drama II*, 389; and Christophe Potworowski, "Christian Experience in Hans Urs von Balthasar," *Communio: International Catholic Review* 20 (Spring 1993): 110–11.
35. Waldstein, "Expression and Form," 49.
36. Gustav Siewerth, *Philosophie der Sprache* (Einsiedeln: Johannes, 1962), 11–36; Erich Przywara, "Bild, Gleichnis, Symbol, Mythos, Mysterium, Logos," *Analogia Entis II* (1962): 335–71.
37. Hans Urs von Balthasar, "The World of Images," 150.
38. Ibid., 145.
39. Ibid., 163.
40. Ibid., 159.
41. Siewerth, *Philosophie der Sprache*, 39–63.
42. Balthasar, "The World of Images," 149. Cf. Nicolaus Cusanus, *Compendium: Opera Omnia*, vol. XI/3., eds. K. Bormann and Bruno Decker (Hamburg: Heidelberg Academy of Sciences, 1964), chap. 8, N. 23.
43. "The World of Images," 149.
44. Ibid., 150.
45. Ibid., 152.
46. Ibid., 159.
47. Ibid., 154.
48. Ibid., 155.
49. Ibid., 160ff.
50. Siewerth, *Philosophie der Sprache*, 85–89.
51. Balthasar, "The World of Images," 168.
52. Ibid., 169.
53. Max Picard, *Der Mensch und das Wort* (Erlenbach-Zurich: Eugen Rentsch Verlag, 1955), 143–49.
54. Ibid., 154–61.
55. Peter Casarella, "Experience as Theological Category," *Communio: International Catholic Review* 20 (Spring 1993): 124–25.
56. Cf. Dionysius the Areopagite, *The Celestial Hierarchy*, II, 3. This notion is also related to Nicholas of Cusa's teaching about the descent of the Word into the silence of death (*ET* I, 136–37).
57. Krenski, *Passio Caritatis*, 273–76.
58. Michael Edwards, *Towards a Christian Poetics* (Grand Rapids, MI: Eerdmans, 1984), 217–37.

59. Balthasar, "God Is His Own Exegete," *Communio: International Catholic Review* 13 (1986): 280–87.
60. Rowan Williams, "Balthasar and Rahner," 29.
61. This view coincides with Gadamer's contention that everything that can be understood is language (1991, 475).
62. Paul Claudel, *Poetic Art* (New York: Philosophical Library, 1948), 86.
63. Jean-Luc Marion, *God Without Being: Hors Texte,* trans. Thomas A. Carlson (Chicago: University of Chicago Press, 1991), 139–82.
64. Balthasar, "God Speaks as Man," *Explorations in Theology I: The Word Made Flesh* (San Francisco: Ignatius, 1989), 82–85.
65. Ibid., 83.
66. Ibid.
67. G. M. Hopkins, *The Poetical Works of Gerard Manley Hopkins,* ed. Norman H. Mackenzie (Oxford: Clarendon, 1990), 120, poem 101.
68. Maria Lichtmann, *The Contemplative Poetry of Gerard Manley Hopkins* (Princeton: Princeton University Press, 1989), 82.
69. Ibid.
70. Hopkins, *Sermons,* 154.

4

An Exploration of the Notion of Objectivity in Hans Urs von Balthasar

Christophe Potworowski

The theology of Hans Urs von Balthasar is dominated by a movement from above. His whole thought is oriented by something that is received from above. Hence, his characterization of theology is "ana-logic." Closely related to this is his fascination with the unique. In short, the theologian is one who is

> overwhelmed by the Word of God in the way the beloved is overwhelmed by the declaration of the lover: "I love you because you are you"; or as one is overwhelmed by a great work of art—of Bach or Mozart, of Poussin or Dante—by something that is unmistakably unique and bears the imprint of grace.[1] (CT 80)

The focus on the unique is inevitably tied, for Balthasar, with an emphasis on objectivity. At first sight, this distinguishes his theology from those that have wholeheartedly taken the anthropological turn, inasmuch as the latter may imply an undue emphasis on the subject.

In an age when epistemological and hermeneutical questions are more burning than ever, what are the implications of this orientation "from above" for the practice of interpretation? More simply, what are the implications of uniqueness for hermeneutics? The question stands out even more sharply as we are no longer confident—in fact, we are quite suspicious—about anything that is not grounded in *us*, that is not firmly rooted in our own subjectivity. Anything that suggests an origin and a foundation other than ourselves sounds like a return to naive realism and to the ways of onto-theology, where truth was too easily turned into dogma (or rather dogmatism) and implied a denial of the necessary historical conditioning of all human assertions. Objectivity, in this large sense, seems to belong to a past age. Truth is now replaced by "perspective" or point of view. Can Balthasar's approach introduce something other than what Nietzsche once described as the "dogmatist's error"?[2]

The following pages explore Balthasar's notion of objectivity by examining three areas in which the ground of objectivity is laid out in complementary ways: in a phenomenology of the act of knowing, in the aesthetic experience, and in the dialogical situation. The three areas are preceded by an account of subjectivism, which provides a key element in the background against which Balthasar elaborated his theology. This is followed, finally, by a brief set of remarks on some implications of this notion of objectivity. This takes the form of a reflection on the relation between scriptural interpretation and holiness. Except for the last section, the emphasis throughout is philosophical rather than theological. The remarks that follow are quite preliminary. A complete and much more satisfactory treatment of objectivity would require a consideration of Christology and ecclesiology, and their trinitarian framework.

Balthasar mentions a number of times the need to overcome a certain "subjectivism" that is dominant in the religious sphere.[3] Again and again, he opposes to this tendency the primacy and the superiority of mission over psychology.[4] For now, let us just note the opposition to psychology and subjectivism. The importance of role and mission will be taken up later.

In more general terms, Balthasar believes that Western culture witnessed the forgetfulness of Being, and that this forgetfulness was in direct proportion to the rise of subjectivism. In the closing off of the ontological difference between Being and beings, and between Being and Absolute Being, in the space left vacant by the eclipse of Being, there arose the modern subject and, inevitably, the "anthropological reduction." The ground of human existence was now located in the human person: "Man is no longer a microcosm; with the growth of the natural sciences, he emerges as the author of those conceptions of the universe which in his reason he transcends. This is how Kant was to present him—bringing the Enlightenment to a close" (*LA* 25).

The same trend of thought continues in the claims of modernism at the turn of the twentieth century.

> The central proposition of the movement was the belief that the test of the objective, dogmatic propositions was their meaning and significance for the individual and their efficacy to fulfill and complete him,...whatever God in his grace reveals to him is to be measured and appreciated by the way it benefits, enlarges, completes and perfects the religious subject. (33)

Balthasar readily admits the presence of the subjective dimension on interpretation in the Christian past. The fathers of the Church noted again and again that a merely objective revelation is quite useless unless it is subjectively renewed and appropriated "as a dying and rising again with Christ in the Holy Spirit" (35). But this is quite different from locating the criterion of truth in the pious individual or measuring revelation according to the human need it fulfills.

Quite different from the above forms of the anthropological reduction, there is personalism, associated with the middle or late Scheler, which locates the ground of truth in the encounter with the "other." Yet even here, Balthasar says that the Christian revelation "cannot be reduced to a system based on a principle of dialogue" (39). However different the two persons in the encounter, they have the same nature: "Between man and God, however, the only language possible is the word of God...and not some vague knowledge of one another's existence"[5] (39). Anything else will involve a collapse of the difference and a necessary reduction.

Now, Balthasar's own approach can be further described by means of a contrast with that of the transcendental method and its account of the act of knowing. This is so especially because the aim of the transcendental method was precisely to bridge the gap between German Idealism and the position of St. Thomas.[6]

The difficulty Balthasar will have is the exclusive emphasis on desire as the fundamental characteristic of human existence. Being or any of its transcendentals, for Balthasar, cannot be defined primarily as the object of a desire or a tendency in consciousness.

Truth cannot be arrived at merely by considering the formal relation between a desire (*appetitus*) and the satisfaction it receives when encountering an appropriate object. It may very well be that it may satisfy an authentic desire to know, and I may very well be enriched by the knowledge of this object. But it becomes almost impossible to avoid the difficulty that the object will be exhausted as the desire is satisfied. The object tends to disappear as the desire is fulfilled, as the desire is the only foundation of the object as object.[7] The subject cannot bear the weight of the responsibility to constitute the object.[8]

A further problem arises, for Balthasar, if this approach makes the next step and links to desire the claims of the right to know. If the knower deduces from its structure that it can know more truth, it can go the further step and claim the right and the duty to know this surplus. In this perspective, where the desire to know dominates, there is no reason for a barrier to knowledge, and any such barrier would trigger a reaction of indignation. This is exactly the serpent's reaction in the face of the barrier to knowledge about good and evil in the book of Genesis. The serpent's cunning lay in claiming that all human knowledge is the result of the natural desire to know.

> The fact that this truth freely and exteriorly manifested is knowable in itself does not confer in any way the right to its effective knowledge. In short, the serpent develops a kind of anthropocentric theory of knowledge whereas the truth of the knowledge of this world is intelligible only on the basis of a theocentric theory. (*TL* I, 299–300)

It is thus not surprising that the first sin was precisely a desire to know more than is allowed, and that evil took the form of truth to disguise and hide itself. Here it is not so much the desire to know that is at fault because it is, after all, a natural desire. What is at fault is the way this desire seeks fulfillment and the way that truth is sought—without the fundamental attitude of service and obedience. Because it is creaturely, human knowing always has the intrinsic form of "welcoming belief" (*empfangenden Glaubens*) (301). The a *priori* of human knowing and of this welcoming belief is an "obedience of reason." Far from being against one's nature, this act of obedience follows from the creaturely character of human knowing, and if it is refused, it becomes an act contrary to nature.

The critical approach places the subject as absolute norm on the basis of its desire to know. The measure of knowing is sought within the knower and thus outside of love, thereby imposing a foreign measure on love. Here, sin consists in placing the measure of truth on a higher plane than the measure of love.

The above criticism of the critical approach is not arbitrary, Balthasar claims, as it is based on the structure of human experience. This structure reveals the simple fact of the receptivity of all human knowing. Our exploration of the philosophical elements in Balthasar's notion of objectivity thus proceeds in three steps. The first concerns his account of human knowing, found in a phenomenological treatment of the notion of truth; the second considers the aesthetic experience; and the third looks at the "original experience" of the dialogical situation. As in all exploration, the aim is to provide a map with the key features of the land.

Objectivity in knowing is based primarily on receptivity, service, and obedience, rather than control or mastery. The decisive attitude of the subject before the object of knowing is one of service. This attitude is at the root of all finite creaturely knowing.

Just as naive realism underestimates the moment of manifestation *(Erscheinung)* of the object toward the subject, so the critical theory of knowing tends to ignore it altogether. For Balthasar, on the other hand, this moment is crucial in the constitution of objectivity.[9] The critical approach tends to separate radically the subjective role from any role on the part of the object in the construction of the object of knowing. This is the separation of the *intellectus agens* from the *intellectus passibilis*. Balthasar's approach will relate the two, giving a slight primacy to the moment of passivity in knowing.

Knowledge, according to Balthasar, is primarily a service rendered by the subject to the object which intrudes, without invitation, onto the subjective field. The attitude of service is so fundamental in all knowing, that the one who is not so disposed with impartiality to welcome the object in the way the object wishes to reveal itself will thereby miss the first required condition for objective knowledge.[10]

The subject does not go about hungry for knowledge, looking for a possible object with which to engage in an act of knowing. It is rather the object that first manifests itself in the sphere of the subject, giving it for the first time the possibility of accomplishing an act of knowing. Only after this initial disposition can one speak of a will to know, a desire to know, in order to complete the description of human knowing.

What prevents human knowing from acting as an autonomous knowing independent of the object's manifestation is the consciousness of being preceded and surrounded by another *(cogitor ergo sum)*.

This is confirmed by what Balthasar calls the original phenomenon of the child's awakening consciousness through the smile of the mother.[11] Such is also the creaturely character of human knowing, making the attitude of service in knowing an act of obedience in accordance with one's nature. Otherwise, having to share the mission of truth and objectivity with the object's manifestation would be a violence perpetrated on the knower's autonomy. But since the consciousness of the knower is already constituted as one whose being is given, as one who is received, it will not be so difficult to conceive of truth as something received from another created being in the context of a dialogue (*TL* I, 298).

The subject is placed before an object that manifests itself to the subject, and that is dependent on the subject for its objectivity. The subject has a task of justice to fulfill vis-à-vis the object. The task is even better described in terms of love and in terms of a mission the subject is given (prior to the creative aspect of the act of knowing), to bring the object to its objective truth. Here, the fundamental attitude is that of obedience.12

The second step in our exploration concerns the aesthetic experience. The aim of this reflection is to recover an objective dimension in the language of Being. The importance of the aesthetic can quickly be established by means of a negative argument. In a world without beauty, or rather in a world such as ours that has lost the ability to see beauty, there is anguish and disgust, sadness and the inability to love. Chaos seems to reign. In a world without beauty, the good loses its power of attraction, the evidence that "it must be done." Why should I do good instead of exploring the fascinating possibilities of evil and of the dark side? Likewise, in a world no longer able to affirm the beautiful, truth loses its privileged status and is reduced to some syllogistic mechanism. Finally, Being itself loses it power of evocation for that which exists, just like the transcendentals. All that remains is a narrow portion of existence that is incomprehensible even to itself:

"The witness borne by Being becomes untrustworthy for the person who can no longer read the language of beauty" (*GL* 1, 19).

The emphasis here is on the perception of the unique, following Goethe's concept of form/figure (*morphe, Gestalt*). A similar idea is the notion of "inscape" introduced by Hopkins.

> When one experiences startling beauty (in nature or in art), then phenomena normally veiled are perceived in their uniqueness. What confronts us is overpowering, like a miracle, and only as a miracle can it be understood; it can never be tied down by the person having the experience. The appearance of its inner unfathomable necessity is both binding and freeing, for it is seen clearly to be the appearance of freedom itself.[13] (*LA* 44)

Something that I cannot guess at, "tie down," deduce, or explain from anything in me, appears before me. It is clearly beyond anything I can imagine, and yet it is perceived by me as having to be exactly thus and not otherwise. Balthasar calls this union of the "undiscoverable" and "highest plausibility" disinterested beauty. He clearly acknowledges that the experience of beauty, if and when it occurs, is situated within a network of subject-object relationships: mood, sensitivity, circumstance. So, it remains only a pointer, a signpost suggesting the direction for an understanding of the Christian experience. Still, it remains a valid pointer, bringing out similar emphases as in the account of knowing and, as we will see, in the dialogical situation (45).[14]

Balthasar does not wish to deny any use of the productive and creative imagination, only that imagination which implies exclusive control over its object by arbitrarily limiting what may appear to what is anticipated in one's horizon. That would ultimately be self-destructive. Neither love nor aesthetics, nor the understanding of the manifestation which is proper to them, can be "be subsumed under the categories of knowledge which imply control." None of the categories here are "products," and none can be reduced, "least of all [to] some person's need" (45). Imagination must rather be educated to see the world differently, following the direction suggested by the beautiful manifestation.

Thus, the key element received from a reflection on aesthetics, one we have already encountered in the account of knowing, is that of manifestation (Erscheinung). This is most explicit in the aesthetic experience of beauty where the heart of the issue lies in the relation between expression and interior depth, between the manifestation and the nonmanifested.[15] In the *Divine Comedy,* when Dante meets Beatrice, she speaks not of herself but of another. And yet, she is the Beauty that he encounters. This area of the nonmanifest depth belongs to the dimension of mystery in all beings, and particularly to infinite Being. It cannot be "bracketed-out" as some of the exact sciences want to do. Human knowing must include this dimension: "For it is only in this way that the figure which lies at the heart of the matter becomes legible as a figure of reality" (*GL* 1, 446).

Balthasar speaks of this in the context of "natural faith," in a similar way to the attitude of service and obedience mentioned earlier, as the necessary attitude to welcome and accept this dimension of mystery. Otherwise we do violence to reality. We close our eyes to its deeper dimension if we bracket the unknown on the basis of our perceived ability. "If our ruling idea is limited to what the cognitive subject is able to construe, then we wholly lose the phenomenon of objective self-manifestation, the self-revelation of the object from the heart of its own depths, and everything runs aground in shallow functionalism" (447). Balthasar applies this immediately to the manifestation of divine love in the revelation of the cross. The question of credibility arises which, for Balthasar, cannot be settled on the basis of anthropological reduction.

> The plausibility of divine love is not illumined by reducing it to or comparing it with what man has always recognized

> as love. Its plausibility comes only from the form of revelation itself. This form is so majestic that, without expressly demanding it, its perception exacts from the beholder the attitude of adoration. (*LA* 47)

Much more would need to be said on the aesthetic as introduction of a new notion of objectivity into theology, transcending the pitfalls of subjectivism, yet avoiding the violence of extrinsicism. An immediate example is the need for evidence in the area of credibility. Balthasar claims this must be objective evidence, "the kind that emerges from the phenomenon itself, and not the sort of evidence that is recognized in the process of satisfying the subject's needs" (*GL* 1, 64).[16] This does not mean that Balthasar disregards any subjective existential conditions, but it clearly indicates the limits he discovers in the spontaneous dynamism of the contingent subjective experience.[17] The thing of beauty stretches these limits and through its manifestation teaches the imagination to see more.

The third moment in our description of objectivity concerns what Balthasar calls the "original experience" (*ursprüngliche Daseinserfahrung*). It is usually presented in terms of intersubjectivity, as an instance of the dialogical principle, and where the human situation is illuminated in its fundamental structures, where there is an "epiphany of being." It thus functions as one of the privileged human experiences because it provides a context for access to the divine reality.

The human person exists only in dialogue with the neighbor. The example Balthasar constantly uses is that of the infant who is awakened to consciousness, or self-consciousness, by the smile of the mother. In the encounter between mother and child the horizon of unlimited being is opened to the child. The relationship with the mother, where the child is other than the mother yet at one with her, is source of goodness, joy, and truth. In light of this, all reality is experienced as one, true, good, and beautiful. All reality is bathed in the light which proceeds from this experience.

Thus, the original experience, which brings the child to consciousness, brings to light the four transcendentals (i.e., the one, the good, the true, and the beautiful) that are coextensive with Being. Balthasar notes: "We add here that the epiphany of Being has sense only if in the appearance *(Erscheinung)* we grasp the essence which manifests itself *(Ding an sich)*. The infant comes to the knowledge not of a pure appearance, but of his mother in herself" (*MW* 114).[18]

Balthasar stresses the original character of the experience. That is, its richness is simple: it cannot be broken down into separate components; it cannot be "decomposed"; and it cannot be reduced to something more original. In this sense, it represents a valid starting point for human reflection on existence. One cannot understand this experience on the basis of the "formal structure" of the human spirit or from "sensible impressions" that trigger a constitutive process of categories (which itself would be ordained to a dynamism affirming "being-in-general"). The experience can only be understood as a response of love to love. It is a response evoked by the mother, a response of an *I* to a *thou*.

The experience becomes a central point of reference for one's entire life. Everything that later in life will be seen as deficiency, disillusion, or nostalgic desire will have a derivative character in relation to this original experience and the absolute love it promised. It bears the character of a promise so that all of the subsequent experiences in life are seen, not so much as an addition to the original experience, but in terms of how much they are subtractions from the promised fulfillment. It acts as a normative criterion, either validating or rejecting various accounts of human existence. It becomes the basis for judgment.

In the beginning was the word of a loving *thou* addressed to an *I*. The *I* becomes conscious of itself. By giving itself, it discovers—*I* give *myself*. By coming out of itself *(ekstatic)* and advancing toward what is other than itself, in a world that offers him the necessary space, the *I* experiences its freedom, its knowing, and its nature as spirit. This is not experienced as something that could be produced from within but only as the result of a summons (*Anruf*) that did not originate with the child.

No part of this awakening is reducible to the *I*. To the extent the child responds to an invitation that could not possibly originate in the child's own being, the child would never think that it evoked the mother's smile. All of reality surrounding the *I* is present as an inconceivable wonder. The child is there, along with the surrounding space and world, not by the grace of the *I*, but by the grace of the *thou*. Along with the radical sense of contingency, the child experiences itself as the object of an "original favor," as having been granted permission to exist thanks to the gracious favor of a *thou*.

This experience of original favor, the summons and the permission to exist, cannot be accounted for through an *a priori* reason; that is, it is not dependent on anything in the child. The *I* cannot find a sufficient reason for this within itself. For if it could, there would be no *thou*, no summons, and being would be an illusion (*ET* III, 16).[19]

For Balthasar, only Christianity will provide the full realization for what is implicit in the experience of awakening consciousness, namely that Being and love are coextensive. As he says elsewhere, "What is meant by a 'person' only emerges in Christianity" (*TD* 2, 385). "At the most fundamental level, the dawn of self-awareness *in freedom* is not the realization that we are simply "there," even "there with others"[;] it is rooted in the fact that we are "gift" and "gifted" which presupposes a "giving" reality" (391). Throughout all this, it must be remembered that Balthasar refuses to operate from an abstract notion of being. His emphasis is on being as it concretely manifests itself.[20]

The parallel of this dialogical structure with the aesthetic experience is clear. The thing of beauty attests itself before us with an inner necessity which is not reducible to our aesthetic sense. And yet something more is brought out with this reflection on the dialogical character of human existence, something which was only hinted at previously. As expression of a hidden depth, the manifestation of beauty is never for its own sake but for the sake of engaging the beholder in a dialogue of freedom.

Along with beholding and being enraptured, there is the additional element of conversion or personal mission. This is clear when we say that one is never the same after beholding a thing of beauty. Where this is not taken seriously, where the aesthetic fails to reveal the ethical that lies within it, such rapture is degraded to mere fascination.

> Where a thing of beauty is really and radically beheld, freedom too is radically opened up, and decision can take place. But what is ultimate here is not my decision but that I hand myself over to the deciding reality and thus am resolved, decided, to let myself be marked by the unique encounter offered me. (*TD* 2, 31)

A classic illustration of how the aesthetic tends dynamically to the ethical is Dante's encounter with Beatrice referred to earlier. At the beginning of the *Inferno,* Virgil reminds Dante of this encounter in order to mobilize him. Without the memory of this encounter, Dante would remain in his crisis, paralyzed by the surrounding chaos, unable to fulfill his vocation. The pilgrimage of his re-education can then begin. In the *Paradiso's* second encounter with Beatrice, the meaning is clear. She is not there as a source of mere fascination, but as a source of courage for him to speak and write about the communion of saints that he has seen. In this sense, the relationship of Dante to Beatrice is far different from that of Paolo to Francesca.[21]

The consequences of the above approach become concrete quite quickly when we consider the interpretation of scripture. Balthasar contests the dominance of the historical-critical method and its absolute claims about objective knowledge in interpretation. What is the shape of interpretation when there is present "active indifference" of obedient reason, when the manifestation of the object's interiority before the subject is given priority over the subject's spontaneous desire? There is somewhat of a leap between the preceding reflections of an anthropological and philosophical order to the present remarks on scriptural interpretation. The relevant contributions on the nature of revelation, faith, grace, and church properly belong to any discussion of scriptural interpretation. The following paragraphs point to some of the elements of this discussion with particular reference to the role of spirituality and the objective status of mission (*GL* 1, 464).[22]

To begin with, there are no "bare facts" in theology, or in scripture, that could be considered in an intellectually neutral and detached way.[23] Historical-critical method breaks up the unity of the figure of scripture by "bracketing-out" what cannot be known. Hence, Balthasar laments the dualism between the Jesus of history and the Christ of faith created by the life-of-Jesus research spawned by the Enlightenment. He laments Bultmann's inability to conceive a Christ of history. For Balthasar, this can never lead to a vision of the phenomenon because the method is blind to the manifestation.[24] The form of Christian revelation must be approached in contemplation, that is, perceiving the hiddenness of the form in its manifestation. For this to happen, appropriation of the image and contemplation must join and become one. This implies a reversal of the usual understanding of contemplation as a consideration of something at a distance. Here, the one contemplating gives up his own standards and is assimilated into the standards of the image contemplated.

> The image unfolds *into* the one contemplating it, and it opens out its consequences in his life. It is not I who draw my consequences from what I have seen; if I have really seen it in itself, it is the object of my vision which draws out its implications in me. (*GL* 1, 485)

This involves a shift from seeing to being seen by the Word, from seeking to always being found by God. The model for this kind of response, contemplative obedience or active indifference, is a Mary's

Ecce Ancilla. In this context Balthasar makes reference to the letter-spirit relationship as understood by Origen, where the letter is "understood" to the extent it impresses its image in the life of the believer through the action of the Spirit. This is why, also, it is the saints who are the best interpreters of the scriptures because they give testimony of being grasped by God.

It now becomes clear that what Balthasar opposes to the dominion of subjectivism is the primacy of mission. Saints are living interpretations of scripture. Their lives are "lived gospel." Through them, through the action of their lives, the *forma Christi* becomes perceptible to others: "In them, Christian love becomes credible" (*LA* 97). Their whole lives are a pointing to the self-giving love as the origin of their lives.

Mission is objective. It is received from God as something which corresponds structurally and objectively to my being and which falls outside the arbitrariness of individual disposition.

> For each Christian, God has an idea that fixes his place within the membership of the Church; this idea is unique and personal, embodying for each his appropriate sanctity....The Christian's supreme aim is to transform his life into this idea of himself secreted in God, this "individual law" freely promulgated for him by the pure grace of God. (2*SS* 20–21)

Mission as sanctity or holiness is not something that one achieves through one's own effort, but it is a correspondence of one's being to the plan God has for us. This recalls the foundation of the *Spiritual Exercises* of St. Ignatius where we are told to "contemplate his life, to investigate and to ask in what kind of life or state his divine Majesty wishes to make use of us...and how we ought to dispose ourselves in order to arrive at perfection in whatever state or kind of life God our Lord shall propose for our election" (*Spiritual Exercises*, qtd. in 2*SS* 21–22).

The correspondence, finally, presupposes freedom. It does not suggest following a spiritual "blueprint" or an "anonymous universal law." On the contrary, Balthasar says, receiving and fulfilling a mission means freely realizing God's loving plan, and this not only presupposes freedom but is the very source of freedom: "No one is so much himself as the saint, who disposes himself to God's plan, for which he is prepared to surrender his whole being, body, soul and spirit" (2*SS* 21).

It is indeed to the concept of mission that we are led by an exploration of objectivity. A consideration of scriptural interpretation has shown that, once initiated, the interpretation of the Word becomes the Word's interpretation of the interpreter's existence. The movement of interpretation, through the beholding of the manifestation, tends dynamically to the mission of holiness. From the contemplation before a thing of beauty, we are called to become a thing of beauty before God. The attitude of service and obedience before the object's manifestation corresponds to the task of allowing the object its own objectivity within the space of my subjectivity. Such is the mission of truth and objectivity. The aesthetic experience brings out the structure and the laws of the relationship between form and expression, between beholding and being enraptured. It makes us attentive to the face of the *Thou* and the voice of the call. In the dialogical situation, the *I* is given permission to exist through a summons and becomes self-conscious as gift before the face of a *Thou*. Together, the aesthetic and the dialogical lead to mission as a central component in the rediscovery of objectivity.

Notes

1. Balthasar continues: "This approach cannot be described as 'extrinsicist,' to use an expression of the modernists."
2. *Philosophy in the Tragic Age of the Greeks* (Washington, DC: Regenery Gateway, 1962), p. 2: "...namely, Plato's invention of the pure spirit and the good as such....To be sure, it meant standing truth on her head and

denying *perspective,* the basic condition of all life, when one spoke of spirit and the good as Plato did."

3. See Peelman on this topic.
4. See *My Work,* pp. 31–32: "In each individual case, one must demonstrate the superiority of mission over 'psychology,' so that the whole project becomes a concentric onslaught against modern subjectivism and 'personalism' in the religious sphere." Elsewhere, he says, "For missions more than personal qualities are what individualize the Christian" (20). In the same piece, for example, he praises Reinhold Schneider exactly for this reason: "Nowhere else did I find in such a pure form what I sought everywhere, namely, the anti-psychological instinct, the native knowledge of roles, service and mission, a Catholic form that does not live in monastic fortresses and 'political Catholicisms'...but in the soul of those who have received commissions, whether these be kings or founders or simple laymen" (39–40).
5. This does not mean, clearly, that Balthasar rejects the dialogical principle. On the contrary, as we will show, he relies on it quite heavily but does not make it a basis for this theology.
6. See Waldstein's "Introduction to Balthasar's *The Glory of the Lord*" (*Communio: International Catholic Review* 14 [1987]: 12–33), especially pp. 15–17, where the author makes the same methodological step in introducing Balthasar's "objective metaphysics." See also Rowan Williams' chapter, "Balthasar and Rahner," in *The Analogy of Beauty,* edited by John Riches. The following remarks on transcendental method are not meant as a statement of Balthasar's position on Rahner's theology. That would require a much more particular treatment than the general one offered here.
7. See *Theologik* I, p. 252. This book reproduces a text originally published in 1947. Contrast this disappearance of the object with Ricoeur's notion of the "surplus of meaning" or the "iconic effect."
8. See Schmitz's 1992 plenary address to the *Catholic Theological Society* of America on this topic.
9. Cf. *Theologik* I, pp. 62–63.
10. Cf. *Theologik* I, p. 292.
11. See below on the dialogical principle.
12. Cf. *Theologik* I, p. 77.
13. Balthasar continues, giving an example: "If there is a finale to the 'Jupiter' symphony—and I cannot guess this, deduce it or explain it from anything in me—then it can only be as it is; its present form is necessary, every note is irrevocable—unless possibly Mozart would change it" (*LA* 44).
14. See *Love Alone* (1969), p. 45: "Just as in love I encounter the other *as* the other in all his freedom, and am confronted by something which I cannot

dominate in any sense, so in the aesthetic sphere, it is impossible to attribute the form which presents itself to a fiction of my imagination."

15. See *The Glory of the Lord* I, p. 442: "For what is manifest in a given manifestation is always, at the same time, the non-manifest....Along with the seen surface of the manifestation there is perceived the non-manifested depth: it is only this which lends the phenomenon its enrapturing and overwhelming character, just as it is only this which insures the truth and goodness of the existent."
16. See also p. 465: "The subjective condition of the possibility of seeing an object for what it is (a condition which can be very far-reaching) ought never to intrude upon the constitution of the object's evidence, or simply to condition this evidence and thus be substituted for it. In theology, even the most existential form of Kantianism must distort and thus fail to see the phenomenon."
17. Balthasar's comments on subjectivism and his critique of Kantianism and the critical approach focus on the generic dangers inherent to this viewpoint. They should not be seen as his last word about any particular expression of the transcendental method. His position on Karl Rahner is nuanced. His relation to the cognitional theory of Bernard Lonergan remains to be worked out. A first step in this direction is Mooney's *The Liberation of Consciousness*.
18. For a more complete treatment of this, see *Theo-Drama* II, p. 389.
19. "For if the 'I' could discover this reason, then the 'Thou' would not have addressed any summons at all, and all would be a dwelling of the 'I' in itself,...the world and love and knowledge would collapse in an instant, being would be an illusion, the contents giving fulfillment would be an empty law, [and] love would be at best an instinct, knowledge a mere function" (*ET* III, 16).
20. Cf. *My Work*, pp. 115–16.
21. For this and the previous example from Dante, and for their relation to the present reflection, I am indebted to Prof. Janine Langan of the Christianity and Culture program at the University of St. Michael's College.
22. See Georges Chantraine, "Exegesis and Contemplation in the Work of Hans Urs von Balthasar," in *Hans Urs von Balthasar: His Life and Work*, ed. David Schindler; and Brian McNeil, "The Exegete as Iconographer: Balthasar and the Gospels," in *The Analogy of Beauty*, ed. John Riches. Also, see Balthasar's article, "God Is His Own Exegete."
23. See *The Glory of the Lord* I, p. 125: "In theology, there are no 'bare facts' which, in the name of an alleged objectivity of detachment, disinterestedness and impartiality, one could establish like any other worldly facts,

without oneself being (both objectively and subjectively) gripped so as to participate in the divine nature (*participatio divinae naturae*). For the object with which we are concerned is man's participation in God which, from God's perspective, is actualized as 'revelation' (culminating in Christ's Godmanhood) and which, from man's perspective, is actualized as 'faith' (culminating in participation in Christ's Godmanhood)."

24. Cf. *The Glory of the Lord* I, p. 536, where Balthasar maintains against the dualist position that "in the theological domain, it is faith alone that can guarantee the full objective ('rational') knowledge of things as they really are."

5

Literature in the Drama of Nature and Grace: Hans Urs von Balthasar's Paradigm for a Theology of Culture

David S. Yeago

The terms *theology, literature,* and *culture* come together quite naturally when one considers the work of Hans Urs von Balthasar. In many respects a theologian's theologian, whose work plumbs the depths of the great mysteries of Christian belief—Trinity, incarnation, atonement—von Balthasar was at the same time deeply engaged with literature, being the translator of Claudel, Péguy, and Calderon, and a commentator on Bernanos, Reinhold Schneider, Dante, Hopkins, and others.[1] Von Balthasar's teacher and friend Henri de Lubac, himself not exactly a barbarian, wrote of him admiringly, "This man is perhaps the most cultivated of his time. If there is a Christian culture, then here it is!"[2]

But de Lubac's mention of "Christian culture" should not be taken too narrowly, for von Balthasar's literary and cultural interests were by no means limited to Catholic or even believing authors; they encompassed also most of the great pre-Christian and post-Christian writers of the West. His first major work, the three-volume *Apokalypse der deutschen Seele,* was a comprehensive survey of the eschatological theme in modern German philosophy and literature. His tour of Western thought on beauty in volumes IV and V of *The Glory of the Lord* includes insightful and sometimes luminous discussions of Homer, Virgil, and the Greek tragedians, as well as the great figures of the Renaissance and Romanticism. This comprehensive literary interest is perhaps nowhere more evident, however, than in the *Prolegomena* to *Theo-Drama,* the second part of his great trilogy.[3] This volume, which tends to overwhelm the reader with the range of its diversity, surveys with easy familiarity the whole corpus of Western drama and reflection on drama, from the Greeks to Pirandello and Thornton Wilder.

Certainly few theologians in this century have written *both* highly technical and creative treatments of trinitarian and christological doctrines, *and* informed discussions of Shakespeare, Shaw, Brecht, and Ionesco. To understand the full theological context of von Balthasar's engagement with literature, it is necessary to see how it hangs together with his larger account of the relationship of nature and grace, and the paradigm for a Christian theological engagement with human culture, including literature, which follows from that account.[4]

The theme of "nature and grace" became a standard topic in post-Reformation Catholic scholasticism, especially in the wake of the papal condemnation of the theologian Michel de Bay ("Baius" in Latin) in 1569. Over against the speculations of Baius, the post-Reformation tradition had a clearly defined agenda in its treatment of this issue: "grace"—the human creature's calling to a supernatural goal, and the provision of the assistance necessary to reach this goal—must be regarded as absolutely *"un-owed"* and *gratuitous* in relation to "nature." That is to say, nothing in the "nature" of any creature, nothing in what the creature is, lays any obligation on God, logically or morally, to call and assist that creature to a fulfillment (such as the beatific vision of God) that surpasses the creature's innate powers.

In the mid-twentieth century, Henri de Lubac launched an influential critique of the way this issue had been handled in post-Reformation scholasticism, which was soon taken up by other theologians.[5] De Lubac and those who followed him agreed with the post-Reformation writers about the absolute gratuity of grace, but argued that the way in which this point was typically asserted had disastrous, unintended consequences. The gratuity of grace was protected by an insistence that nature does not *need* grace, that created humanity is, in principle, wholly intelligible in itself without reference to grace. This went so far that many theologians saw it as part of their task to describe a counterfactual, but possible and imaginable, state of "pure nature" in which human beings would exist with their present natural endowments, but altogether without any orientation to a supernatural goal.

According to de Lubac, this approach made grace so entirely extrinsic to natural existence that it was hard to see any longer why we should be interested in grace, why we should regard it as the *perfection* of our humanity. Indeed, de Lubac regarded this theological "extrinsicism" as one of the roots of modern secularism and naturalism. Drawing on the Fathers, particularly Augustine, as well as the earlier Scholastics, he insisted that it is equally important for theology to insist *both* that grace is absolutely gratuitous *and* that created existence, whatever relative intelligibility it may have in itself, can nevertheless find no possible or even imaginable ultimate fulfillment apart from grace.

Theologians who accepted de Lubac's analysis of the problem differed in their accounts of how theology might say both these things coherently. Von Balthasar's proposal, worked out in detail in his long study of his neighbor in Basel, the Protestant theologian Karl Barth, is deeply determined by the principled *christological particularism* of his understanding of grace.

For von Balthasar, who was influenced here both by Barth and by his studies of the great seventh-century theologian Maximus the

Confessor,[6] Christian faith is centered on a particular person, Jesus of Nazareth, who is confessed to be of universal saving significance precisely *as* a particular person, in his singular, contingent concreteness. That is to say, Jesus Christ is not savingly significant because he symbolizes or mediates some more general truth, value, or dynamism; rather, it is just in the concrete *Gestalt* of his unique identity and the contingent singularity of his story that his all-encompassing redemptive significance is to be found.[7]

> Hence when we are attempting to grasp him, there is no place for abstraction, for disregarding particular cases, for bracketing off inessential accidentals at the historical level of his life, because it is precisely in this uniqueness that his essential, normative character lies....Thus theology in the strict sense of the word cannot do any abstracting at all; all it can do is display the normative content shining out from the irreducible fact. (*TH* 16–17)

According to von Balthasar, this discernment of all-embracing and unsurpassable meaning in the concrete contingencies of a singular human life is the very heart of Christian faith: the confession of Jesus of Nazareth as the *universale concretum et personale*;[8] the universal, that in relation to which all things find their ultimate meaning and fulfillment, the redeemer and judge of the world, coming on the scene as a particular person with a unique life story. "The *Logos* was made flesh, and dwelt among us, and we beheld his glory" (John 1:14).

In relation to the theology of grace, this means that von Balthasar must take "grace" primarily as a name for Jesus Christ. That is to say, the "grace" for which "nature" was created and in which it finds its fulfillment cannot be fully understood in terms of abstractions such as "a supernatural vocation and the help needed to attain it." Abstract terms such as these must be taken as, at best, second-order commentary on the reality of grace, which comes on the scene in concrete actuality in the figure of Jesus Christ and his obedience to his mission from the Father.[9] To say that nature is perfected by grace means, therefore, that the whole creation, and human beings as the foremost creatures, find the true purpose and goal of their existence in their historical encounter with the singular figure of the crucified and risen Jesus of Nazareth as their redeemer and judge.

This has crucial implications for von Balthasar's account of the *relationship* between nature and grace. If grace is irreducibly concrete and particular, then that relationship cannot be understood in abstractly theoretical terms, like those in which one might understand the relationship between sodium and salt or an acorn and an oak tree.[10] The kind of relationship in which a concrete figure gives meaning to a whole through singular, contingent agency is rather a *narrative, dramatic* relationship; the relationship of nature and grace must be, for von Balthasar, a *dramatic narrative configuration* rather than a general rule that could be described theoretically. Nature is ordered to grace much as the various characters, episodes, and themes of a complex dramatic narrative are ordered to the denouement in which the story "comes together" into a meaningful and unified whole.

From this perspective, of course, "nature" too must be redefined in dramatic-narrative terms. For von Balthasar, "nature" refers primarily to human beings in their contingent historical complexity; it is the concrete condition of creatures who are always already involved in the drama whose real resolution is Jesus Christ. Pressed by the logic of their own existence to ask questions which they cannot finally answer, they are nonetheless free to explore an open field of relative and penultimate meanings along their way, free also to go tragically astray. Thus von Balthasar thinks of nature in predominantly historical and cultural terms, as the *history* of human striving to imagine and attain a final meaning for human existence.[11]

"Pure nature" cannot therefore refer to some hypothetical state of affairs in which human beings would *not* be caught up in this dramatic complexity; rather, it describes abstractly the formal characteristics of human existence that make it possible for human beings to be implicated in such a drama.[12] More specifically, all the diverse and unpredictable dramatic situations in which human agents find themselves presuppose the characterization of human existence as *finite freedom.*[13] Only a creature who was both free and responsible—and at the same time finite, mortal, situated in the world in some limited, particular way—could be part of this tangled and tension-ridden story-line. All these various and unpredictable situations are just the sort of predicaments in which such a creature—and only such a creature—might get itself entangled.

It is by reconsidering the relationship of nature and grace as a dramatic-narrative configuration that von Balthasar is able to reconcile three claims that seem at first sight to be in some tension with one another: (1) grace is altogether gratuitous, in no sense "due" to nature by any logical or moral necessity; (2) nature nonetheless has no possible or imaginable fulfillment besides grace; (3) this ordering of nature to grace as its only thinkable fulfillment does not deprive created nature of a *relative* independence and significance of its own.

Von Balthasar understands the gratuity of grace in terms of its *narrative contingency.* In a well-crafted drama, as Aristotle pointed out long ago, both things are true: the plot is so constructed that it could have no other satisfying conclusion, and at the same time the conclusion is altogether surprising and unforeseen. In the same way, when the gift of grace is conclusively given in Jesus Christ, it can be seen that nothing else could draw the tangled threads of human existence into a meaningful resolution, while at the same time the shape of that gift could not be anticipated until it was actually given.

There is no contradiction in saying, about the denouement of a narrative, both that it was carefully prepared for from the very beginning of a story, and that it came as a great surprise. For the coherence of a narrative is of a different kind than the coherence of a syllogism. The latter sort of coherence is deductive; the conclusion is given in the premises, and needs only to be drawn out of them. The coherence of a narrative, by contrast, has room for freedom and thus for surprise. It is a coherence which is not already given at the start, but only in and with the story's resolution, when the climactic events actually occur and draw together the threads of the plot into a unity. The coherence of a drama is established from the end of the story, not at its beginning, although that *end* is aimed at by the playwright from the beginning.[14]

Since the coherence of a dramatic narrative is given only when its climax actually occurs in its contingency, it cannot be deduced or constructed from within the drama. The contingency of the resolution creates a logical gap between the preceding events and the coherence-granting conclusion; for the drama's characters (and for the audience, as it is drawn to identify imaginatively with the characters), the outcome of the drama is always a surprise, occurring freely, not dictated by any necessity inherent in the sequence of events to which it grants coherence.

Yet this freedom and contingency which characterize the resolution of a dramatic narrative and its consequent coherence do not imply that its author ever considered any other ending. Nor do they imply that another resolution could be imagined which would make equal though different sense of the elements of the plot. On the contrary, in a well-constructed drama, we would expect the elements of the plot to be carefully prepared to hang together uniquely well in the specific coherence granted by the story's specific resolution, even though that resolution cannot be anticipated until it actually occurs.

So von Balthasar writes, "And this is certain: from the standpoint of man, who receives grace as a totally gratuitous gift of God, any talk of its gratuity will necessarily and immediately entail speaking about how 'it could have turned out differently.'" Nevertheless, it is equally true to say, as it were from the author's point of view: "From all eternity God has willed one and only one thing: to open up his love to the human race" (*KB* 300). Thus one can say, "The certainty of the natural striving for the goal of our life and *gratuity* of grace do not rule each other out" (*KB* 296). One can say this because the relationship between nature and grace is not an abstract-conceptual relationship, but a narrative configuration.

This same perspective enables von Balthasar to account for the relative independence and meaningfulness of nature within its ultimate dependence on and orientation to grace. In dramatic-narrative perspective, the relative independence of nature is not only possible, but *necessary*, precisely as the context of the drama's denouement. The *final* coherence of the narrative is indeed given only with its resolution; but that resolution must have a context, a relationship to already-existing situations and characters that it embraces. "Grace is grace *for* a nature and *to* a nature" (*KB* 281).[15] The relative independence and significance of these penultimate elements of the plot are necessary for the sake of the *freedom* of the resolution, for the sake of the open space, the logical gap, between the beginning and the ending that distinguishes a story from a syllogism. Nature must have a meaning of its own that is not simply "read off" grace precisely so that grace can relate to nature in genuine dramatic freedom.

But this *relative* independence of nature within the dramatic configuration of nature and grace must not be absolutized. We cannot say that this relative meaningfulness is a sufficient motive for the creation of the world apart from the resolution of creation's story by grace. It is rather

> a realm of provisional meaning, that is not directly derivable from grace, but which rather serves as a presupposition for grace. We need not assert categorically that the significance of this realm is so great and so absolute that it suffices even for *God* as a reason for it to be called into existence for its own sake. (*KB* 300)[16]

The author has only one outcome in mind right from the start, the resolution which will come as such an unpredictable surprise at the end; for its sake, all the elements of the plot are posited, precisely in their relative independence.

Yet this relative and non-ultimate character of nature's significance apart from grace by no means prevents the characters, episodes, and themes of the drama from being "well-rounded" and complex in their own right, containing within themselves a wealth of provisional and partial meaning. Indeed, it is important that they in fact be so, precisely so that the meaning which is bestowed on the drama by its resolution may itself be as rich, complex, and satisfying as possible. The power of the drama's resolution is not diminished by the relative freedom and complexity of its characters, episodes, and themes; on the contrary, the former is magnified by the latter, for our surprise and appreciation and wonder are intensified when we see how the story's climax draws together—into a unity which we could never have anticipated, with such a profound wealth of new implication—all the threads of so complex and rich a plot.

Just so, Jesus Christ, the true consummation of the human drama, its judge and redeemer, is magnified by the richness and complexity which nature, and more particularly human historical existence, displays on its way to him. For von Balthasar, it should be noted, it is an elementary criterion of good theology that it communicate a kind of aesthetic wonder at the surprisingness and extravagance of the divine love; the reality of grace is apprehended appropriately only by theological reflection of a sort

> which allows the deed of God's love for us to appear more divine, that is, more radical, more perfect, but therefore also more incomprehensible, more unlikely. The criterion lies in a *maximalism* which (incomprehensibly) makes it possible to include even such aspects as would seem to human reason incompatible with the reality [i.e., of God's love in Christ]. (*WIS* 56)

Precisely so, therefore, nature must be allowed its own breadths and depths and heights of relative, provisional meaning. The "rounded" individuality and freedom of its characters, the intricate untidiness and dramatic tension of its manifold contingent situations, and the distinctive texture and complex development of its various themes are to be appreciated in their integrity. Theological reflection on nature must

> bring to light a breadth, fullness, and variety in the natural realm which then permits the work of grace to be fully valued; for grace needs the whole fullness in order to present itself[;] it penetrates, shapes, and elevates it, and brings it to its final realization. (*TL* I xiv)

The true depth and height of the grace of Christ, its genuine mystery as that love "than which a greater cannot be thought" (Anselm), can only be displayed when it is grasped as the resolution of a created story that is itself mysterious in its exuberant diversity and poignant allusiveness.

Thus, although human beings can neither anticipate the gracious resolution of their drama, nor find ultimate fulfillment apart from it, nature is far from being merely an empty space for grace to fill. On the contrary, through its temporal career humankind has accumulated a wealth of insight into the complexity and mystery of its own condition and a profound appreciation of its possibilities at once for greatness and disaster; even the exploration of blind alleys has not been fruitless. The event of grace must be all the more surprising, if it is to gather this rich confusion into a final and encompassing resolution.

Von Balthasar's theological account of nature and grace—in all its dialectical complexity—provides a distinctive paradigm for a reflective Christian engagement with the works and achievements of human culture, especially literature. We can get an initial sense of the shape of this paradigm by considering four implications of von Balthasar's understanding of nature and grace for a theology of culture.

In the first place, for von Balthasar, some reflective engagement with human culture, with literature, the arts, philosophy, and religion, is *necessary* for theology. But it is important to be clear about the specific kind of necessity involved. It is not, for example, that the mood of a particular culture, perhaps as reflected in its literature, is somehow normative for theological reflection, so that theologians would have to turn to the culture to discover the ground rules of acceptable theological discourse in that culture. Rather, for von Balthasar, the encounter with culture is necessary for *internal theological reasons,* for specifically *Christian* reasons.

As we have seen, in the dramatic-narrative configuration of nature and grace, grace can only be understood in its full dimensions in relation to the full unfolding of the drama of nature that it pulls together into a final and unsurpassably significant resolution. But concretely, for von Balthasar, "nature" is human historical existence, the reality of free and finite creatures groping splendidly and horribly and always unpredictably after the sense of their lives. It would be fair to say that von Balthasar takes literature and the arts, philosophy and religion, in much the same way: as the record of that grandly ambiguous groping, that persistent inquietude of heart which can neither suppress its questions nor give them final answers. It is *this* "attribute" to which "grace" comes in the particular life of Jesus of Nazareth; it is *this* story of which his crucified obedience is the utterly surprising and utterly fitting resolution.

In the context of von Balthasar's christological particularism, the axiom that "grace is grace *for* a nature and *to* a nature" is precisely equivalent to the New Testament's proclamation that Jesus Christ is *for us (pro nobis)* in his life, death, and resurrection. As the Nicene Creed states, it was "for us human beings and for our salvation" that the Logos "came down from heaven" to consummate the drama of creation as the particular man Jesus. Therefore, when theology turns to an attentive consideration of literature, art, and other significant works of the human spirit, this is only one way of following obediently the movement of

God's self-humbling, his *kenosis,* in Jesus Christ. It seeks a more profound understanding of the infinite significance of the concrete particularity of the incarnate Word by exploring the depth and height, the comedy and the tragedy, the beauty and horror, of the human existence which that particularity judges and redeems.

Second, von Balthasar's understanding of the encounter of Christian thought and human culture allows for a real, though asymmetrical, interpretive reciprocity between them. This distinguishes his thought, on the one hand, from a kind of Christian integralism for which Christian reflection has nothing to learn from the encounter with human culture, but has always-already "seen through" it in advance, since it already knows all it needs to know in Christ; on the other hand, this also distinguishes von Balthasar's thought from typically "liberal" approaches in which the meanings and insights present in human culture become the norm for the meaning and truth of Christian faith. For von Balthasar, the interpretive encounter with human culture can generate new understandings, new learning, precisely about the significance of that which is distinctively Christian, while at the same time the figure of Christ, in its concrete particularity, remains the center and norm of all meaning and significance.

For von Balthasar, the Christian confession of Jesus Christ as the Word made flesh, the *universal concretum et personale,* is incompatible with any view that makes culture's perceptions and standards of truth and meaning the normative context of interpretation, into which the figure of Christ must somehow be integrated. The advent of Jesus Christ in all its contingency is the arrival on the scene of "the finally valid *Logos*" which "surpasses, completes, and encompasses every other possible bestowal of meaning."[17] There can be, for theology, no more general "logos," no more universal, external standard of truth and meaning, to which Christian thought is accountable; the internal logic of the event of Jesus Christ is itself the final criterion. Thus any interpretive reciprocity between Christian revelation and human culture must be finally asymmetrical; it is nature which receives its meaning from grace and finds its truth in grace, and not vice versa.

But precisely because the fullness of Christ is boundless and inexhaustible, it cannot be understood as a static *datum* administered by the interpreter, who would then encounter human culture as one already in possession of all truth and meaning. On the contrary, Jesus Christ as the one "in whom are hidden all the treasures of wisdom and knowledge" (Col 2:3), is always greater, always more, than the Church or theology presently comprehend, and one of the ways in which this inexhaustible "more," this hidden treasure, continually comes to light is in the interpretive encounter of Christian thought with the imaginative life of the world. The encounter of the insights and achievements of human culture, of literature and art, philosophy and religion, with the concrete figure of Jesus Christ opens up new possibilities of understanding, precisely of Christ's own significance, possibilities which depend on taking the works of culture seriously and attending to them carefully.

This opening-up of new possibilities of Christian understanding thus constitutes a partial fulfillment of the "great promise" implicit in the mystery of Jesus Christ: "In the present we are never able fully to catch up with it or finish our work with it, and therefore [it] contains within itself the promise of an 'exceedingly great measure of the weight of the momentum of glory' (2 Cor 4:17)" (*GL* 7 114). This "weight of the momentum of glory" makes itself felt as the christological mystery proves itself competent, ever anew, in the most diverse situations, to take hold of works of human thought and imagination apparently external to it, correcting and reshaping though not negating them, and employing their distinctive resources to bring to light something of its own singular, yet inexhaustible, significance.

This is closely related to our third point: for von Balthasar, nothing in human experience and human culture is outside the interpretive range of the story of Jesus Christ, which is the universally and unsurpassably redemptive resolution of the whole drama of creation.

The Christian Church does, to be sure, have an "outside" but there is absolutely nothing which falls outside the story which the Church proclaims and on which theology meditates. All creatures are always already involved in that story, for in the intention of their Creator, Jesus Christ "is prior to all things and in him all things hang together" (Col 1:17).

This means that all human culture, all literature and art, all philosophy and theology, are in reality, knowingly or unknowingly, always involved in a drama whose true resolution is to be found nowhere else but in the particular flesh and blood of Jesus Christ. Therefore, what von Balthasar writes of the philosopher can be said equally well of the poet, the novelist, or the playwright:

> Insofar as the philosopher knows nothing of revelation (of God's Word) and looks out on a cosmos that is noetically and ontically saturated with moments of the supernatural, he will *also* be, at the very least—without knowing it—a crypto-theologian. The outlook of his reason will not be the outlook of a *ratio pura* but of a reason that already stands within the teleology of faith or unbelief. (*KB* 280)

In saying this, von Balthasar does not propose any kind of an imperialistic Christian "takeover" of non-Christian culture; his point is rather that because all people in reality inhabit a creation that is ordered to Christ, culture does not have to be explicitly Christian to be intelligible and interesting to Christian thought—positively or negatively.

The same point can be made the other way around: the figure of Jesus Christ has inexhaustible interpretive power in relation to all the phenomena of human existence. The particular person Jesus of Nazareth, precisely as a particular person, is self-identically the *Logos* of God, the one by whom and for whom all things were made, the meaning of all the possible meanings found in the created order. This implies that Christian thought should refuse in faith to entertain the possibility that it could encounter any phenomenon, any literature, any art, any philosophy, of which it could not, in principle, make a distinctively Christian kind of sense, a kind of sense constitutively centered in the figure of Jesus Christ.

It is probably important to point out that, for von Balthasar, this interpretation of human existence by reference to Christ by no means goes on exclusively or even centrally in the writings of theologians. Here as elsewhere he sees the *saint*, not the professor, as the paradigm theologian;[18] the demonstration of the inexhaustible significance of Christ takes place most centrally in the *concrete practice* of Christ's Church, and especially in the practice of the saints. For example, Mother Teresa's life "interprets" the phenomena of poverty and incurable disease by the figure of Jesus Christ incomparably more richly and more *adequately* than any essay by a theologian could possibly do. The theologian or critic can only hope to follow in the footsteps of the saints.[19]

Finally, because the encounter of nature and grace is a meeting of contingencies in freedom, the encounter of theological reflection with human culture cannot be governed by any general method or forced *a priori* into an invariant theoretical framework. In a dramatic-narrative configuration, both the developing plot, with its situations, characters, and themes, and the resolution that bestows on the drama its final sense and significance, are contingent, unpredictable, characterized by freedom and surprise. It is impossible to tell in advance of its occurrence just how the resolution of the story will relate to the various elements of the plot in their concrete diversity; one has to watch the story unfold and see.

Although von Balthasar does believe that there are indeed broad recurring patterns in the history of human culture,[20] his approach does not encourage the construction of Hegelian grand schemes in which cultural history is the predetermined interplay of embodied ideas. There is no way for Christian thought to know what it will find in the history of human culture, in literature, the arts, philosophy, and religion, without, so to speak, getting down on the ground and looking and listening. Nor is there any way to tell in advance of the actual interpretive encounter what Christian understandings may be generated when the phenomena of culture are read as part of the created story whose denouement is Jesus Christ. Culture is contingent, the work of finite freedom groping for the point of an existence that is always in reality on its way to Christ as its savior and judge; it is capable of great evil, of great error, but also of great wisdom and real discovery, although even its authentic insights will inevitably receive a new sense when they are interpreted by the incarnate and crucified *Logos* of God.

This last point has implications for the *practice* of theological reflection on culture. The Christian interpreter of literature and the arts, philosophy and religion, does not survey the scene from a great height, with a comprehensive theory ready at hand. Nor is the Christian interpreter one who has already "seen through" the works of culture in advance, as though the revelation of God's grace provided a systematic principle from which an *a priori* explanation of nature could be deduced. For the theological interpreter, according to von Balthasar, that which encompasses all things and bestows on them their ultimate significance, in judgment and mercy, is not a theory or a principle, but a particular person, who embraces all that is in the concreteness of his obedient witnessing, suffering, and dying. And the created story which he thus consummates is a rich and complicated story, with surprising and unpredictable twists and turns, abysses and sublimities, terrors and glories.

Thus what the Christian interpreter of culture needs most of all is not so much theoretical facility as a definite set of *virtues*: stubborn faithfulness to the Church's confession of Christ as the *Logos* incarnate, combined with patience in unraveling complexity, attentive respect for the particularities of both culture and the christological story, critical openness to unexpected possibility, and a kind of "contemplative receptivity in the face of the world's richness."[21]

As one approaches von Balthasar's interpretive practice, his actual readings of works of literature, it is important to understand the theological context of his lifelong engagement with the legacy of Western thought and culture. That engagement was part of a larger reflective enterprise, governed by a disciplined and distinctively Christian mode of vision and imagination in which the interpretation of culture was integrated with both theology and the practice of the Christian life.

If this is understood, then it becomes clear that von Balthasar's relevance to the enterprise of the Christian interpretation of literature and culture is not bound by the limitations of his own interpretive practice. It is possible, of course, to find von Balthasar's readings of particular literary texts wanting for various reasons.[22] It is likewise possible, in our present climate of opinion, to be put off by his exclusively European focus and his relentlessly aristocratic, "high-culture" literary tastes. But von Balthasar's theological vision transcends these boundaries, and offers a paradigm that may well be illuminating for those with very different interests and concerns. It repays consideration in its own right for the remarkable way in which it integrates commitment to Christian distinctiveness with an open and questioning approach to the whole range of humanity's hopes and dreams and imaginings, convinced that nothing whatsoever falls outside the shining of the light of Christ.

Notes

1. See Balthasar, *Gelebte Kirche: Bernanos and Nochmals—Reinhold Schneider*; on Dante and Hopkins, see *The Glory of the Lord* III.
2. Henri de Lubac, "A Witness of Christ in the Church: Hans Urs von Balthasar," *Hans Urs von Balthasar: His Life and Works*, ed. David Schindler (San Francisco: Ignatius, 1991), 272.

3. It is important to note, however, that von Balthasar's interest in drama is not only literary; a concern with the staging of drama, with theater, is also crucial to his purpose.
4. In what follows, I have drawn extensively on my doctoral dissertation, "The Drama of Nature and Grace: A Study in the Theology of Hans Urs von Balthasar" (Yale, 1992).
5. See Henri de Lubac, *Augustinianism in Modern Theology.*
6. See von Balthasar, *The Theology of Karl Barth and Kosmische Liturgie.* An earlier abridged translation of *The Theology of Karl Barth* by John Drury omits much of von Balthasar's own theologizing on nature and grace. On christological particularism in Barth, see Bruce Marshall, *Christology in Conflict*; on Maximus, see my article "Jesus of Nazareth and Cosmic Redemption" in *Modern Theology* 12.2 (April 1996).
7. On the crucial notion of *Gestalt* in Balthasar's theology, see *The Glory of the Lord* I.
8. Balthasar, *TH* 92.
9. "And when [theology] makes use of general truths, propositions and methods (as happens in all its branches), it must be careful that everything of this kind always subserves the contemplation and interpretation of the unique" (*TH* 17).
10. "If the historical factum of God's Incarnation in Christ is the meaning and goal not only of worldly history but also of nature and creation as a whole, then the necessity of intraworldly history and nature rests on a decision which cannot be reduced to any sort of general norm (*allgemeine Gesetzlichkeit*)" (*KB* 335).
11. To say this is not to deny, of course, that von Balthasar also provides a metaphysical account of created being and humankind's place within it, but this metaphysics is consonant with an understanding of human nature in historical-cultural terms. See Rowan Williams, "Balthasar and Rahner," in *The Analogy of Beauty,* ed. John Riches (Edinburgh: T. and T. Clark, 1986).
12. See *KB,* 282–92.
13. See *Theo-Drama* II.
14. "The order of grace takes absolute priority over the order of nature in the order of intention (*in ordine intentionis*) and the created order takes relative priority over the order of grace in the order of executing the divine plan (*in ordine executionis*)" (*KB* 302).
15. Translation altered.
16. Translation altered.
17. See *Theo-Drama* II, 115–16. The text as cited is my translation from the German.

18. See "Theology and Sanctity" and *Two Sisters in the Spirit.*
19. On a very different plane, but following the same logic, the work of Christian writers and artists is likewise an encounter with human culture that takes on a more-than-theoretical density.
20. For example, the recurrent alternation between "Neoplatonic" and "Stoic" answers to the "aporia of roles"; cf. *Theo-Drama* I, 481–648.
21. Williams, "Balthasar and Rahner," 24.
22. See, for example, Martin Simon's argument that von Balthasar gives altogether too Christian a reading of Hölderlin, in "Identity and Analogy: Balthasar's Hölderlin and Hamann," in *The Analogy of Beauty,* ed. John Riches, 77–104.

6

Balthasar's Aims in the "Theological Aesthetics"*

Aidan Nichols, OP

The sheer bulk of *The Glory of the Lord*; the variety of sources—both theological and philosophical—on which it draws and the diversity in time of their origin—Hellenic, Hellenistic, Roman, biblical, patristic, medieval, early modern and modern; the lack of any clear argumentative development in the six volumes (seven in English) as a whole; the abundance of Balthasar's illustrative material and his seeming inability to stop himself from running after hares (a difficulty compounded, no doubt, by the circumstance of owning his own publishing house and so encountering no externally enforced limits either of length or of expense): all these factors help to explain the discouragement of readers when faced with the Herculean labor of actually reading this monumental work. There is, accordingly, a problem in the "reception" of Balthasar: the message of *Herrlichkeit* as a whole is not getting through. In this essay I propose to fill this gap by asking, What did Balthasar intend to achieve in writing *The Glory of the Lord*?

What, in other words, are the aims of the *Theological Aesthetics*, supposing—as is surely natural—that we treat the text as evidence for those aims. Artists may sometimes surprise themselves by their work, and we can perhaps regard Balthasar as a theological artist who is trying to extend the Christian vision of the world by a creative manipulation of traditional ideas, sources, and themes. But on the whole we regard the artifacts artists leave behind—on canvases or in print—as evidence for our reading of their intentions, though naturally conflicting interpretations of such intentions can arise, in which case appeal may be made to anything they may have said autobiographically about what they were doing. Nothing I shall say about the aims of *Herrlichkeit* will be gainsaid by Balthasar's own, very brief, account of what he was about, as that is found in, above all, four short overviews of his theological production written under the titles "Reckoning" (*"Rechenschaft"*), in 1965; "A Decade On" (*"Noch ein Jahrzehnt"*), in 1975; *Epilogue* (*Epilog*), in 1987, and finally, in 1988, "A Retrospective" (*"Ruckblick"*), published in the year of the newly nominated cardinal's death.[1]

Balthasar's first aim in the early sections of the first volume of *Herrlichkeit* (referred to by the volume numbers of the English translation throughout) is to show us why we need such a thing as a "theological aesthetics" at all. Why should we want to invite such a creature into the house of theological culture in the first place? For his part Balthasar wants to make us aware what a strange question this is: what has happened to us, as human beings first of all, and then as Christians, that we do not see it as something sublimely obvious that the biblical revelation—like, it should be added, everything else—is somehow related to *beauty*.

There was a time, Balthasar proposes, when everything that was real, everything that stood up to the measure of truth—all that is *ens* and *verum*, as the Scholastics would say—was experienced in some fashion as beautiful. And to go back long before those terms—*being, truth, beauty*—and their interrelations were formulated by the Christian thought of the Western Middle Ages; to return, in fact, to the fountainhead of the Western experience of humanity in ancient Hellas, the Greeks seem to have encountered the world as transfigured by a godlike radiance which touched events, people, and things: at least Balthasar believes so, in line with a long German tradition of reverential interpreters of the Greek experience, from the poet

Hölderlin at the end of the eighteenth century, to the philosopher Heidegger in the middle of this one. What a contrast with the typically modern experience of reality that takes, so Balthasar says, a somewhat jaundiced view, essentially one of a world where all is brute facticity until meanings are projected on it by ourselves.

Certainly the Greeks ran together the concepts of the good and the beautiful: the two formed a differentiated unity, the unity of *kalokagathia*. When the good ceases to be related to the beautiful, Balthasar points out, goodness loses its self-evidence. In other words, people start asking, Why be good, why follow the good, why admire the good? Just to say that a life is good, or that some piece of acting exemplifies a virtue, is no longer (for moderns like ourselves) to draw forth the response, So it must be wonderful! For that earlier sensibility, through recognizing beautiful goodness, people were at once aware of the love-worthiness of something—it could be the pattern of a life, or some natural nonhuman reality, or an artifact like the vase apostrophized by John Keats in his "Ode on a Grecian Urn." In each case people were struck by the radiance that shone out through some form. And this, explains Balthasar, would always have been pertinent to truth, to the real intelligibility of things, for that real intelligibility is always in some way incarnate, even if it be only in the sounds of language. At all levels of reality we have to do with spirit expressing itself through form, and earthly beauty is the paradigm.

Clearly enough, all this is philosophically important. But Balthasar wants us, by means of it, to take hold of something else. What he is really driving at, in this lament over the loss of beauty from the world at large, is something specifically evangelical, to do with the Gospel of Jesus Christ. Our capacity to perceive what he calls "the primordial phenomenon of the beautiful" is a necessary condition for our being evangelized, for receiving the Gospel. Becoming, remaining, and growing as a Christian depends on our enjoying access to the wondrous beauty of a unique form, Jesus Christ, as given us by the God who is the primal Creator of images and remains so in his communication with us in revelation. The re-Christianization of Western civilization depends on a few people at least (at any rate to begin with) getting this message. Thus, although Balthasar speaks of form in connection with the forms of nature and such human life-forms as marriage (which he considers, incidentally, a very instructive case since it suggests how biology can condition but not explain form, and how the materials a scientist might investigate can be animated, therefore, by a form that in itself is not material), and though he also—and this comes closer to his central concern—looks at how the saints are key forms for the Catholic Christian precisely because the image of their lives is engagingly lovable, nevertheless, his real focus is Jesus Christ himself, whom he wants to present as summing up the entire many-sided yet ultimately unitary form of God's self-revelation in salvation history. Everything in the Old Testament leads up in one way or another to this form, just as everything in the New Testament Church issues out of it.

So in this Christ-centered but by no means exclusively biblical fashion, Balthasar would recover for us, as a theologian, the "lost transcendental" of beauty—alongside *ens* and *verum, pulchrum*—and more especially beauty's biblical correlate (one can hardly just say "biblical equivalent"), *glory*. By this means Balthasar aims at nothing less than the wholesale transformation of Catholic theology in its two main branches. And what are those two branches? They are, first, fundamental theology, which says what revelation is and how we come to find it credible; and second, dogmatic theology, which explores revelation's content, the various truths about the triune God, Christ, salvation, the Church, human destiny, and that of the cosmos: truths which revelation puts forward.

Now Balthasar is aware that this is going to strike people as a somewhat unusual project. After all, one may well ask, Why do you accept the Christian faith and by that faith, what is it that you believe in? But one does not expect to get the answer, I believe because it's beautiful, and what I believe in is the beauty of God. Such replies might well sound self-indulgent and mawkish, or superficial and dilettantish. So he now has to show that working out a theological aesthetics is not an unprecedented enterprise for a Christian thinker. What, I think, Balthasar really aims to do here is to meet the objections he expects from serious-minded Protestants. Because of their strong insistence—an insistence Balthasar, in fact, echoes—that revelation is something different and unconditionally new, something that stems from beyond culture, beyond society, (i.e., it is not just human reactions to the world dressed up as something special, but really is the very word of God in human guise), such people might well feel that all this beauty-stuff—with glory being the biblical version of the beauty that is found in nature, people, and art—is simply too tangential to the scriptural revelation to be a suitable perspective in which to view its contents. Really, Balthasar cannot show the contrary until he has finished *Herrlichkeit.* But in this first volume he at least can demonstrate awareness of the problem.

He agrees that once we begin thinking in aesthetic terms we have a tendency to glorify the world, not God. Taking stock of the way things satisfy the aesthetic judgment of human beings and so delight their faculties can lead the world to pride itself on its loveliness, such that the object of marveling—of what both Aristotle and the Gospels call *thaumazein,* being lost in wonder at something—is displaced from God to the world, a world which is not just nature, the direct divine creation, but a world of nature humanly transformed, a world (in great part) of cultural artifacts, and thus an extension of ourselves. That way lies idolatry. But, Balthasar points out, if that displacement happens, cannot revelation, with theology at its service, point this out? And in any case, divine judgment on the world as the work of so many would be the narrowest, most mean-minded kind of Protestantism. Humankind does not always mean condemnation of the world: to think divine judgment can also mean the assumption of what is human into the new life of grace, as when Jesus told a scribe who questioned him: You (though you have not yet come to faith in me and my message) are not far from the Kingdom.

It would be wrong just to presume that the role of grace is always to snap whatever links there may seem to be between natural beauty and supernatural glory. Appealing to a celebrated term in Catholic philosophy and theology, could there not be *analogy*—neither complete identity nor total dissimilarity—between the beautiful in creation and the glorious in the re-creation or new creation? Could there not be, in this respect as in others, analogy between the natural world and the world of God? Does not theology have to admit that the values in the world around us can and should be ascribed in a pre-eminent way to their ultimate Source, God? Can theology deny that the redemption and final consummation or transfiguration of the world must reflect and at the very least equal the artistry with which God made the world in the first place? Can it eliminate from the resurrection-faith of the first Christians the conviction that the very glory of God, exceeding all natural beauty, was manifested on this earth through the form of Christ's risen flesh? Such biblical writers as, in the Old Testament, the authors of Ecclesiasticus and Wisdom, and, in the New, Paul and John, can surely be described as setting out contemplatively to explore the marvel of the saving work of God in, respectively, Israel and Jesus Christ. And that is the cue for Balthasar to move on to the offensive, and propose that all theology that neglects what is beautiful in revelation will finish in a dead end, incapable of permanently inspiring anybody, or fructifying anything in an abiding way. All the great theologies of the Church have been in some sense beautiful creations, something Balthasar will try to convince us of by judicious selection in the second and third volumes of *The Glory of the Lord*.

None of this is to say, however, that marrying talk of the beautiful to revelation is easy or straightforward. The historical materials in volume one of *Herrlichkeit* are designed to show us some of the pitfalls that can occur. Only in volumes six and seven, the concluding biblical volumes, shall we see how Balthasar thinks this marriage should be celebrated, though a number of important hints are dropped in the metaphysical volumes, four and five, where he describes how the glory of being—the wonderfulness of reality in its global meaning—has been perceived by pagans, Christians and post-Christians, and so gives us a feel for specifically evangelical beauty, for the difference in these matters which the biblical revelation makes.

But meanwhile I must explain what Balthasar is aiming at in the remainder of his prolegomena to *Herrlichkeit,* after calming, to his own satisfaction at least, the fears of those who consider the aesthetic to be opposed to the moral and so, *a fortiori,* to the religious. In saying that the revelation given in Christ is credible because it is in an unsurpassable fashion worthy of our love, and sweeps us off our feet by its beauty, Balthasar aims to bring together fundamental theology or apologetics and dogmatic theology or doctrine, and moreover to bring them together in the closest union that the teaching of the Catholic Church will allow. In standard manuals of apologetics in Balthasar's young manhood and middle age, fundamental theology was based on rational argument for the existence of God, and for the idea that human beings could receive a communication from the side of God were one offered them, along with historical arguments that such a communication had actually happened in Jesus, as proved by the signs which attended his life (miracles, the fulfillment of prophecy, his moral perfection). The gap between such argumentation and actually believing in biblical revelation was then closed by appeal to something happening deep within us, when interior grace begins to illuminate our minds and attract our wills so that, by means of the arguments and evidences, we are brought to something greater than any rational or inferred conclusion—namely, to faith in Christ. In this way the "standard believer" comes to accept as truth the teaching (about the Trinity, the identity and saving purpose of Jesus Christ, and so forth) that Christ, his apostles, and the Church he founded propose to us—namely, via doctrinal truths, and then, in themselves quite separate from the grounds we have for believing them, via apologetics. Balthasar, by contrast, wants to make our initial perception of the beauty of doctrine—of the picture Jesus paints of the triune God in his saving design, not only in words but in gestures—the main factor in our conversion to belief in Christ in the first place. Getting a first glimpse of the form of Christ begins a process of enlightenment that adapts our powers to God's self-revelation, such that when we set all this down on paper it turns out that apologetics is really incipient dogmatics, and dogmatics is just matured apologetics.

Now I said that Balthasar wants to recast the relation of fundamental and dogmatic theology, the study of how we find revelation credible and what it is we actually find ourselves believing when we do so, by turning that interrelation into the tightest union *compatible with the official teaching of Catholicism.* That qualification is important. Suppose what would happen had Balthasar simply identified apologetics with dogmatics *tout court.* He would have ended up with some kind of fideism. Such fideism could be of a Protestant kind, where, as in Reformation dogmatics, nature and rationality are regarded as so corrupted by the Fall that they provide us with no ground to stand on in assessing the claims of revelation. It could be a theory where, as in the twentieth-century Protestant Neo-Orthodoxy of Karl Barth, a more subtle case can be propounded. That case would propose that since nature and rationality—all beings and all our powers of reflection on being—are from the outset christocentrically ordered by God, and that they are destined to find their consistency, stability, and integrity in Jesus Christ, the Word Incarnate, and in him alone, with the result, once again, that there is nowhere outside dogmatics that will support us in reviewing revelation's claim. Alternatively, such fideism could be of what is increasingly called a postmodernist kind, where the history of metaphysics and the attempt to find a foundation for our rational procedures are said now to have collapsed, thus opening a way—according to the Christian-theological version of postmodernism—for the doctrines of Christology and, especially, the

Holy Trinity to triumph as the only available justification for such themes as the need to respect others in their otherness and particularity on which, so it is said, the universalizing claims of metaphysics and philosophical rationality have foundered. But Balthasar is not a fideist; he leaves a place for reason vis-à-vis faith, for nature vis-à-vis grace, for the common being studied by metaphysicians vis-à-vis the gift of new being which is grace (the first volume of his trilogy, *Theologik* I, shows as much), though for reasons internal to his project in the theological aesthetics he downplays rather than accentuates these distinctions in this context.

For Balthasar aims to show that the light which illumines us in faith does not just break forth in our minds in a purely subjective way, even though this be a change in our subjectivity caused by God himself. More importantly, this "light" breaks forth from within the revelatory form which is Jesus Christ, as we begin to encounter this form and see it as making an impact on us, beautifully ordered whole of saving goodness as it is, and ultimately as stunning us, since in the final analysis it is nothing less than God's own self-revelation. The power of this Christ-form, what the Church's faith, in keeping with the Scriptures, calls the Holy Spirit, can catch up that desire for transcendence, that desire to be and to be with something more than we are which is inscribed in our nature (Pascal remarked that only what transcends us can satisfy us) and turn this needy desiring of ours into a mighty drive that carries us toward the reality of God now thrown open to us in Christ Jesus. In other words, the subjective evidence for revelation is, at its highest, the way this form, Jesus Christ, is compellingly radiant, and all other features—like the role of miracles, prophecy, and the moral perfection of Jesus as a self-proclaimed envoy of God—must find their bearings within that context and that alone. What we are dealing with in theological aesthetics is the study of how we come, enraptured, to see God, the world, and ourselves in relation to God and the world with new eyes, thanks to our perception of the form of God's self-disclosure. It is because Balthasar aims to show us that the Christ-form in all its objective novelty and originality has the power to change our understanding of the world and our habitual sensibility in this way that he adopts a reserved attitude toward the historical-critical method as applied to the Jesus of the Gospels, with its necessarily somewhat-reduced and minimal conclusions about the Jesus of history, and argues instead that the real Jesus is found only by looking through the lens of the New Testament canon as a whole, guided in so doing by the liturgy and teaching of the Church born from his Spirit.

In volumes two and three of *The Glory of the Lord* Balthasar reassures us that we are not the first to tread this path. All twelve of the figures he exhibits to us in those volumes, from Irenaeus of Lyons in the second century to Charles Péguy in the twentieth, have passed this way before. The purpose of Balthasar's twelve "studies in theological style" is to show how rich are the ways that the "glory of the Lord," delineated abstractly in the opening volume of *Herrlichkeit,* has been beheld and described. Two criteria were at work, he tells us, in his choice of "stars" with which to study the sky of his theological world: intrinsic excellence and historical efficacy. These will be "a series of Christian theologies and world-pictures of the highest rank." However, they will not be supernova exploding unobserved, so much as theologies which "have illuminated and shaped Christian culture through the centuries" (*GL* 2, 13). In point of fact, Balthasar claims that these criteria coincide: in this domain there can be no real efficacy without true excellence. Balthasar does not aim to bring these twelve theologies into any sort of systematic unity by treating them as building blocks for a synthesis larger than themselves. But he does expect us to grasp their harmonies, the way they echo, or at least fit in with each other, like instruments complementing one another in an orchestral score.

That metaphor of the symphony of theologies is actually his own, for he takes their harmony to prove that (in his words) they "all play from the same score which both transcends and embraces them." He does not conceal the fact that the centers of interest of these writers—five "clerical stylists," i.e., Church doctors working in Greek and Latin, from Irenaeus to Bonaventure, and seven "lay" or vernacular writers, from Dante to Péguy—are very different. But this is not, he says, a problem. It is perfectly natural that one theology will center its sense of glory on God himself (so that all else is lovely only insofar as he shines forth in it); and another on his revelation in its mediating role in his regard (so that beauty belongs primarily to God's self-display in creation and salvation); and a third theology center on Jesus Christ as, in his two natures, "the synthesis of God and the world" (here, where redemption in the Son takes center stage, it is the beauty of suffering love which, above all, strikes and overwhelms the observer); or, yet a fourth on the Spirit of Christ, poured out on humankind from Father and Son as the gift of a share in their glory—whereupon the focus shifts to the theme of transfiguration. And this plurality of centers of interest, which can coexist happily as so many perspectives in mutual collusion, is mirrored, Balthasar goes on to explain, in the variety of styles in which these theologies, with their distinct foci, come to expression. Here too he feels no need to retract his claim that a correspondence exists between the glory of revelation and its imitative expression in theological beauty. The divine freedom, in its choice of vehicle in the history of the Church's tradition, is not likely to be *less* free than its human counterpart, and we know it is typical of human artistic expression that the beauty an artist creates comes about in freedom: great art conveys at one and the same time the impression of disciplined necessity (no detail, we feel, can be other than it is) and yet sovereign freedom (the whole need not have been at all). So why not accept that the living revelation of God is not just possessed of form, but can actually create form—that revelation can call forth in history a vast array of great theologies whose inner form it inspires.

It is these "inner forms" (rather than the outward stylistic qualities that are their sacrament) that Balthasar will try to capture in these dozen monographs that follow, on finishing which we can, I think, fairly allow him to have made his point, wander off though he may and does. The cumulative effect of these substantial essays, on writers from Anselm to Pascal, from Dante to Hopkins, is to persuade the reader that there have indeed been many and varied practitioners of theological aesthetics in the Church.

Not by chance, however, does Balthasar end with the French poet, social critic, and lay theologian Péguy: volumes two and three reach their climax in this figure. In Péguy's theological aesthetic better than anywhere else (better even than in the Fathers, of whose work he finds Péguy's to be the extension) Balthasar locates elements he will take up in the final volumes of *Herrlichkeit* on Old and New Covenants when he will speak in his own voice. First, Balthasar, like Péguy, will give a key role to the experience of Israel. Second, following Péguy, he will take the relationship of Old and New Covenants as decisive for aesthetics, for here the dialogue between God and Israelite man in the covenant, the Law, the prophetic word and the cultus gives way to a divine "self-showing" *(Sich-zeigen)*, "self-speaking" *(Sich-sagen)*, and "self-giving" *(Sich-geben)* in human bodily form. And so third, with Péguy he will treat the transcendence of Christ's Godhead as emerging from the visibility of his human figure. Certainly, Balthasar wants us to drink from the ancient springs of patristic thought and of the medievals who were the continuators of the Fathers. Not for nothing is he a representative of the movement of patristic *ressourcement* in the mid-twentieth-century Church. Certainly, too, he wants us to take seriously the theological contribution made by poets, novelists, and dramatists. Not for nothing, again, was he the translator of Claudel's odes, the commentator on Bernanos's novels, the interpreter of Reinhold Schneider's theatre—and got his fingers rapped by more high-and-dry Scholastic theologians for treating the works of these writers as authentic lay theology, authoritative voices of Christian experience under grace. But above all Balthasar is, like Barth, a biblical theologian, for whom Scripture is the supreme source, the true soul of theology.

So why in volume four does Balthasar turn to look at the "metaphysics of antiquity"? If not just to make a display of his classical learning where the mythology, philosophy, and religious thought of the ancient world are concerned, what purpose does this serve? The answer is that it illustrates the element of theological aesthetics that is drawn from general religious metaphysics, from the sensibility and thinking of humankind at large. And this is important not only because it constitutes a preamble of faith, a preparation for the Gospel, a demonstration of how there are features of being at large and humanity at large which alert us to the theological aesthetics the Gospel will commend. Appealing to the pagans is even more important for enabling Balthasar to show how—to grasp revelation is to grasp revelation's going beyond all that the mind of man has conceived, all that the heart of man has imagined. On the one hand, the Church needs all the help she can get in the task of refreshing our sense of the splendor of being, helpful preparation for our grasp of biblical glory as this is, and Balthasar has never been averse to drawing such help from pagan sources. On the other hand, and more primordially, the appeal to the classics is a sign not of weakness but of strength. Balthasar does not turn to Greece and Rome—which stand here for all experience outside the biblical covenant—out of fear that the revelation to Israel and, in Christ, to the Church will prove to be really rather parochial. On the contrary, so vast is the sweep of that revelation that it requires theologians to seek out that other immensity to which it is addressed, what Balthasar calls *Geist:* the human spirit open of its nature as it is to the being of all that exists. And what Balthasar tries to show, in inadequate yet cumulatively impressive ways, is that the mythology, philosophy, and religion of the ancient world point to the fundamentally divine nature of beauty, beauty's quality as an epiphany of the divine—divine not simply as inserted into the world from above but as welling up from below, from the wellspring of creation. Accordingly, the Church's earliest thinkers felt no need to disengage a purely revelational view of beauty from the philosophical. They found that, in an integrated account of being, the beauty of the world and God's better beauty, grace, do not compete but collaborate.

What Balthasar would like us to see is the way the Church consolidated an all-embracing aesthetic inherited from antiquity: first, from a period dominated by myth, where the human being encounters *to on*, what is in, above all, the form of dramatic images; then, second, from a succeeding age where wisdom predominates as the nascent discipline of philosophy begins to produce instead *concepts* of reality; then, third, an epoch of renewed religiosity (with Virgil in the West, Plotinus in the East) when concepts are relativized through a pointing to *mystery*. And all that is valuable in all of that, says Balthasar, was captured by the Church's single greatest divine, St. Thomas Aquinas, when he presented the beauty of finite dependent being as reflecting the glory of the infinite subsistent being from whom it receives everything it has. It is the Thomas who knows how infinitely the divine Essence transcends common being yet for whom that common being is no commonplace thing but something irradiated by glory. It is the Thomas who grasps, moreover, that revelation does not nullify a natural theology but raises and completes it as the glory of the Son elevates by his saving grace the beauty of the world. It is *this* Thomas whom Balthasar places at the axis of metaphysics, ancient and modern. Aquinas's thought is the classical and climactic moment that should serve as a paradigm for the whole enterprise of linking philosophical and biblical aesthetics on which Balthasar is engaged.

And why is that? It is because of the way Thomas shows being as always in process of pouring itself out into the things that are. The glory of being that flows into beings from their source is not unconnected with what we can call being's simultaneous poverty. Being keeps back nothing for itself and has no final resting place save in the actual beings whose act of existing it provides. So, in its self-dispossessing glory, being finds its fulfillment in the self-emptying Son of God, who in the incarnation, divested himself to the point of death on the cross, just as, similarly, being finds its ultimate explanation in the mystery of the Holy Trinity revealed by Christ where the persons pour themselves out for each other in the very act of constituting themselves as who they are.[2]

Balthasar must now show *negatively* how we came to decline from this perception through the sad fate of metaphysics in the West, and, more *positively*, how through coming to the biblical revelation with new eyes we may be able to recover the perception of glory again.

Already within a century of Thomas's death, the Franciscan Scotus and Thomas's fellow-Dominican Eckhart have let the side down. For Scotus, being has just the same rather boring meaning in beings that it has in God. The key Thomistic notion of divinely gifted nonsubsistent being as the foundational reality at the heart of all beings, flaring out epiphanically in its selfless reflection of God its Creator, is now abandoned. Being becomes an idea that is at once supreme, for it applies to both God and creatures in exactly the same way (something Aquinas would not have dared to assert), and yet is also almost meaningless, for being is now reduced to a mere registering of this or that's existence. So for Balthasar, Scotism anticipated the contemporary scientific outlook at its most banal. What exists are data or facts of which, if he exists, God is simply the largest and most important. In Eckhart, by contrast, being becomes identical with God and creatures lose their full reality. This might seem to be a gain for God, and no doubt Eckhart thought it so, but if God expands to be the reality of everything (he is the All, I am nothing), this cannot but call in question his glory, which now has virtually no "space" left in which to manifest itself. So Eckhart—on Balthasar's genealogy of thought—prepares the way for Idealism where reality in its intelligibility becomes a single infinite process neither Uncreated nor created or, if you prefer, both at the same time from different standpoints, and so ends up in the abolition of God. As Nietzsche would cry, God is dead, we have killed him—killed him by the progression of our thinking.

How then did people react to the discovery, whether post-Scotist and so ultimately "scientistic" (i.e., pseudoscientific) or post-Eckhartian and so ultimately Hegelian, that the world has no splendor coming to it in (literally) glorious objectivity from beyond itself? They might try desperately to return to the world of antiquity in the hope that a touch of glory might still be bathing the pagan cosmos, and this is the strategy we find in the Renaissance, in classicism, and in the early Romantics. However, once the infinite God of the biblical revelation had shown up the deities of the ancient pantheon as less than God, there was no real going back. Sooner or later people would find themselves faced with a more radical decision: either nihilism or, in Balthasar's words, "surrender to the sign, in all its purity, of the glory of God's love revealed in Christ" (*GL* 5, 48). Here we have a typical trait of Balthasar's thought. The world is irredeemably post-sacred. Through the history of thinking and the feeling which thinking brings in its train, the world has become irreversibly secular (we can think of our own situation where economic and technical innovation, not God, are central to culture)—unless, that is, the Gospel be rediscovered. No other religion than Christianity can meet our need, for none other can return glory to being by portraying being as the fruit of the absolute love that the Christ of the incarnation and cross has revealed the Trinity to be.

However, Balthasar does not want to persuade us that the history of religious thought since Aquinas is just the story of a two-track disaster leading by two convergent routes, then, to the stupefying either/or question, nihilism or the Gospel? For, in his opinion, another kind of experience of glory which also drew from the pagan world and notably from its tragic heroes, and was as authentically Christian as that of Thomas (Thomas not so obviously all-embracing) proved able to develop in a surprising place. Displaced from the life of the cosmos at large, glory took refuge, so to speak, in the hearts of God-filled persons, which is what Balthasar has in mind in speaking, as he now does, of the "metaphysics of the saints." If European Christendom turned away from *esse* (being) in its cosmic manifestation, this had the unexpected advantage of leading people to emphasize the importance of a more immediate—if also somewhat isolated and thus vulnerable—relation with God, which, owing to forgetfulness of *esse*, was a world where the God of glory seemed absent and thus a tragic world where evil might well appear to have the last word. There was at any rate a compensating possibility of giving greater emphasis to such themes of the Gospel as patience, endurance, suffering out of love—in a phrase, the theme of abandoning oneself to God. And what Balthasar tries to show, by setting forth for us the spirituality of a host of figures from the Rhineland mystic John Tauler to the French Jesuit Jean-Pierre de Caussade, is that the self-abandoned person who relies totally on God—the saint—is a kind of personalized version of *esse* in its outpouring, a personalized version of the way that for Thomas Aquinas being in its dependence on God only consolidates itself in giving itself away to beings. The saint, not the cosmos, in other words, now becomes the epiphany of glory.

What is Balthasar talking about? He is talking about the way in which, beginning in the late medieval period, a picture of what it is to be a saint emerges—a portrait of selfhood as what he terms "total self-giving prodigality," consciously modeled on not only the incarnate atoning Savior but the Holy Trinity itself. The mystics think of the individual as finding his or her identity—being him- or herself—only ecstatically, through going out *(ek-stasis)* in contemplation toward God and in apostolic service toward one's fellow men or women, which "apostolic" ecstasy shows precisely the fruitfulness of the original "contemplative" ecstasy toward God. The mystical saints, therefore, exhibit a form of throwing themselves lavishly just as does, on the Thomistic view, being itself. What Balthasar would have us see in volume five of *The Glory of the Lord* is that the mystics not only guide us to the heart of the biblical revelation but in a sense "solve" the problem of metaphysics. As he writes by way of comment on the Flemish mystic Jan Ruysbroeck, the behavior "and experience which flow from this encounter with God is not only the supremely free bestowal of God's grace and thus the center of theology. It is also what gives meaning and fulfillment to spiritual nature and is consequently the center of metaphysics."[3] Christian philosophy as lived is summed up in holy fools: Don Quixote of Cervantes, Prince Myshkin of Dostoevsky's *The Idiot.* Perfect fools: this is where in our postmedieval Western tradition theological aesthetics takes up its abode.

And yet Balthasar also recognizes that we cannot simply leave the cosmos as a more or less meaningless stage on which meaningful human acts are by exceptional people occasionally performed. It is not enough for the self-giving glory of God to manifest itself at these few scattered points; we need to know as well that it really is the universal foundation of the whole world and its history.

And that is why in the concluding volumes Balthasar turns again to the Bible in the hope that—since we now grasp what is at stake in theological aesthetics—we can read Scripture afresh. If we do so in the light of these concerns, we shall perhaps see how through the New Testament's amazing consummation of the Old, the mystery of all creation, man included, received its definitive interpretation as the hidden presence of absolute love, to which—in its luminous, bountiful, and exuberant character—beauty's qualities of clarity, integrity, and proportion by analogy belong. See too how the recipients of God's self-revelation—ourselves—receive thereby the call to make the divine visible in charity, the specifically Christian love of neighbor which is, as Balthasar puts it:

> something quite distinct from a good and morally upright model for interpersonal conduct. [This love] occurs always as the focal point, as the demonstration and realization of a love which itself wholly transcends man, and thus also as an indicator of that love which man cannot ascribe to himself since it has long since showed itself to him as that which is ever greater than himself.[4]

"Ever-greater," *je grosser, semper major*—that refers to the inexhaustible, self-dispossessing energy of the triune love, which was pointed to in the prophets of the Old Covenant, those servants in whom YHWH expressed his burning passion, but at the turn of the ages was actually manifested, beyond all human expectation, in the mission of the Son, whose incarnation, death, and descent into hell flesh out for us in the art of a divine narrative the very essence of the Holy Trinity, the absolute love which God is and in which Christ's glory too consists, as the Easter mysteries tell us each year in the liturgy of the Church. The incarnation and atonement—this is the message of the closing volumes of *Herrlichkeit*—resolve the central issue of all aesthetics: how an infinite significance can be found through a finite vehicle, and *what* a significance it turns out to be! In Jesus, the image of God which for Israel is man, and the glory of God which for Israel is God himself, come wondrously to coincide, and the unfolding of Jesus' story—his life, death, and resurrection—exhibits to us what that is going to mean if God's glory really is his unconditional love now freely exposing itself in vulnerable fashion to a sinful world.

And this is how Balthasar himself sums up the aim of *Herrlichkeit* at large in his essay "*Rechenschaft.*" The goal of the theological aesthetics was

> to let us see the revelation of God that his lordliness, his sublimity, what Israel calls *kabod* ("glory") and the New Testament *gloria,* can be recognized under all the incognitos of the human nature [of Christ] and [his] Cross. That means [Balthasar concluded] God comes not primarily as our teacher or as our purposeful redeemer but *for himself*—to show forth and radiate out what is splendid in his eternal triune love in that disinterestedness which true love has in common with true beauty. (*MW* 62)

In E. M. Forster's novel *Howard's End,* we read: "'But this is something quite new,' said Mrs. Munt, who collected new ideas as a squirrel collects nuts and was especially attracted by those that are portable."[5] This essay may have included some nuts, but how far they can be carried into the wider wood of American or British culture remains an open question. Balthasar himself, in *Epilog,* questioned how much use his entire trilogy of aesthetics, dramatics, and logic was going to be to a Church that is often as activist and unthoughtful as the culture it inhabits. He offered his theology, he said, as in the spirit of someone putting a message in a bottle and throwing it overboard from a boat in mid-ocean. That such a bottle land and someone find its message is, he commented, something of a miracle, adding, *Aber zuweilen geschehen solche,* "But sometimes such things happen" (*Ep.* 8).

Notes

* After its presentation at Marquette University, this chapter first appeared as "Von Balthasar's Aims in the Theological Aesthetics," *Heythrop Journal* 40 (October 1999), pp. 409–23. Copyright Trustees for R. C. Purposes and Blackwell Publishing.

1. See respectively *Mein Werk: Durchblicke,* pp. 62–69; 76–77; *Epilog,* pp. 45–52; and (once again) *Mein Werk,* p. 94.
2. Andre Leonard, *Pensées des jommes et foi en Jesus Christ. Pour un discenement intellectual chrétien* (Paris: Namur, 1980), 251–74, 277–88.
3. Ibid., p. 68.
4. Ibid., p. 649.
5. E. M. Forster, *Howard's End,* ed. O. Stallybrass (London: Edward Arnold, 1973).

7

Hans Urs von Balthasar and the Traditions of Christian Humanism

Virgil Nemoianu

By its very nature the field of the humanities belongs to the traditions of harmony, spirituality, and hope, not to the kind of antifoundationalist negativity that prevails nowadays in the academic world (in America and elsewhere). The humanities were "invented" in order to nurture the ecology of the human race; they were never meant to be yoked to the linear advance of merely utilitarian goals. The humanities have always seen as their highest goal the quest for a reconciliation—a "federal" one if you will, one based on subsidiarity—between the need for human solidarity and inclusiveness on the one hand and the dignity of individual, concrete persons, situations, and facts on the other.[1] An opening toward the *possibility* of transcendence was "always-already" (to speak with the deconstructionists) part of the whole project.

How does one go about teaching Christian humanism in the face of inevitable opposition? To begin with, such an opposition should not be unexpected: it accompanies any cross-disciplinary endeavor. Christian humanism seems more closely related to fractals and turbulences than to the firm geometries of Euclid and the causalities of Laplace. In other ways, however, it is nothing but reclaiming the basic inheritance of the world as it is: the natural and organic connection of worthwhile cultural work with the religious roots and vistas of the human being. It is the current separation that is artificial, not the other way round. I will provide an outline that is on purpose vague, flexible, and broad. I will also choose, as will be seen forthwith and as my very title indicates, one of the greatest thinkers of our century as a model.

What later came to be called "Christian humanism" seems rooted in the very earliest stage of a movement that perhaps was not even describing itself as Christianity at the time. It is no exaggeration to say that these roots stem from the Gospels of Luke and John. The Lucan text is clearly addressed to a more cultivated and rationalistic public than the other Synoptics; it is, much more than the others, the "Roman" version among the founding accounts of Christianity. In its turn, John is a highly intellectual text; it clearly aims for a combination of the spiritual, the symbolic, and the factual. Even Pilate's notorious question—"What is truth?"—with its disabused, ironic, slightly weary tone (not necessarily a mean-spirited, perhaps not even a hostile, question), is also one of the beginnings of Christian humanism, not least because of its skeptical connotations. A skeptical strain that does not gain hegemony, but is not fully suppressed either, announces itself here. Thus Christian humanism is already a matter of Evangelical interest.

In turn, it is highly appropriate to add that the Old Testament is the indispensable background for any Christian humanism (and that it was so understood over the centuries.) This is the case because its underlying assumption is Jehovah's passionate and immediate interest in human affairs, his involvement with a particular chosen group of people, his punishments and benefactions, or, more generally and simply, his continuing presence among his beloved people. Thus Johannine and Lucan discourses follow naturally and simply from biblical precedents.

The other chief mechanism and impelling motive for Christian humanism is more obvious yet. At least some of the early Christians had expected Jesus' Second Coming as near at hand, together with the general renewal or rebirth of nature and society. When it became clear that this was not the case, and that it was more prudent to interpret the Holy Spirit as an abiding presence of long duration, it became imperative to construct an alternative framework for handling the world and its culture—or cultures.

Historically, things seem to have happened in the following way. One of the strong, widespread, and unspoken arguments against early Christianity was the argument from snobbishness. Christianity was seen by the imperial establishment and by large parts of the upper classes as a quaint and modest doctrine, devoid of those enlightened and sophisticated qualities that fishermen, peasants, and houseslaves could never aspire to. This was actually a quite powerful (and, indeed, sincere) argument for many Roman citizens and Mediterranean intellectuals who feared that the triumph of Christianity would endanger the aesthetic amenities, the social balances, and the interactions with nature that had been formerly assured by different variants of polytheism.[2]

It was not at all absurd to argue that Christianity was ill-equipped to cope with the complexities of the world and that its message was simple, naive, and linear. Emperor Julian ("the Apostate"), a highly interesting and complex figure, but also a major persecutor of the Christians (AD 361–63), exactly illustrates this state of mind. Julian and others felt that the texture of a whole civilization, its security, and its delights were threatened. I am convinced that the emergence and the stunning spread of the Neoplatonist doctrine was precisely a response constructed (rather deliberately) by pagan antiquity to the challenge of Christianity. Neoplatonism supplied the demand for an ideological vision that was philosophical and rational, and yet could subsume a variety of religious forms and preserve the need for a lively dialectic with the aesthetic and natural realms. It might be seen as the adequate response to a challenge.

Granted, by that time, the beginnings of a Christian philosophy and theology were already in place; even some rudiments of Christian art can be noticed (c. AD 270, the year of Plotinus's death). Thus, to confine myself to just one example, Christians could boast the allegiance of somebody of the stature of Origen, certainly a powerful and abundant intellectual by any standards. Nevertheless, it all happened as if Christianity had collectively decided to pick up the gauntlet and meet its adversaries on their own ground. Soon after the establishment of Neoplatonism, we witness what is probably the most formidable century of Christian intellectual achievement, all around the Mediterranean, fueled by Africans and Greeks, Latins and Syrians, Egyptians and Dalmatians, in a truly cosmopolitan spirit.

I refer to the period approximately between AD 350 and AD 450. Simultaneously St. Jerome was translating the Bible into Latin, and using the most advanced philological methods then available; St. Athanasius was playing a decisive role in formulating the Profession of Faith; meanwhile, perhaps the first great Church orator, St. John Chrysostom, emerged. Toward the end of this period St. Augustine began to acquire his reputation, while in Milan, St. Ambrose was displaying his extraordinary managerial power combined with spiritual depth. Out of this amazing group I would single out, however, the Cappadocians (i.e., St. Basil the Great, St. Gregory Nazianzen, and St. Gregory of Nyssa) because more than anyone else they engaged their polytheistic rivals on their own terrain. In a bold strategic move they actually *appropriated* Neoplatonism, which was the "*Summa*" of the ancients, so to speak; they turned the tables on it and Christianized it (GL 252–81).[3]

In time this action was to become the most typical and fundamental gesture of Christian humanism: to respond to the world by taking it over, by embracing it, by showing that all that is beauty, intelligence, and goodness is *not* alien to Christianity, or incompatible with it. On the contrary, the argument went, everything that *is* beautiful and harmonious, all wisdom and all objects of curiosity, are already parts of the divine design, are already prepared by Divine Providence to enrich human existence and human options.

In the case of Neoplatonism (an appropriation that culminated with Dionysus the Pseudo-Areopagite and Maximus the Confessor) things happened roughly as follows: Plotinus and his followers had constructed an image of the historical universe as both centralized (in its origin) and decentralized (in the growing distances of layers of materiality from their remote origin). The history of the universe was also both linear (evolutive) and circular (created by a "Big Bang," but yearning for a return to that very same point of origin). Christian thinkers jumped to the possibility of choosing elements out of this description of the universe and thus reorganizing it. Over time, features such as the primacy of Beauty (and/or its equality with Truth and Goodness), the validation of localism and subsidiarity (without abandoning unity), the metaphysics of "descent" and grace, and others became fixtures in Christian theology (particularly in its Eastern branches). They also laid the foundations of future Christian humanism.

It may puzzle the student to note that for the next thousand years or so Christian humanism does not seem to have been very prominent. Up to a point this is a mere impression, but in another sense it has some obvious explanations. Christian humanism tends to appear more strongly and prominently when Christianity is challenged, thus the great flowering of Christian culture through most of the Middle Ages in the West, but also in large parts of the Middle East (the realm of Byzantium): the cathedrals and the philosophical systems, as well as Christianity's impact on the social structures. (It is inside religious frameworks that we discover the first outlines of health insurance, old age benefits, and unemployment benefits as a substitute for duties which until then had all fallen almost exclusively on the shoulders of family and other blood and tribal kin.) One German scholar (Gerhard Nebel) spoke about the *kairos* of Christian art (the moment of maximum vicinity between the divine and the artistic): the historical moment when, simultaneously yet independently of each other, the Romanesque style was devised in the West while the art of the icon appeared in the East (c. AD 800–1100). In the history of Christianity this was truly the age of Christendom.

Nevertheless, even in this special age, the signs of a continuing intersectional and borderline flourishing of Christian humanism (as opposed to purely and completely Christian accomplishments) remained vivid in figures such as Albertus Magnus, an enormously encyclopedic mind, or, earlier yet, the formidable Hildegard, the abbess of Bingen in the Rhineland, with her ability to be at the same time a composer, a painter, an author of mystical vision, and a sage whom kings and emperors sought for advice. More generally I tend to think of at least two movements of the Middle Ages, that of the great women mystics and that of the Franciscans, as being Christian-humanistic in some of their most important features. The women mystics brought together the sentimental and the rational, better than many others at the time (although the movement developed around the Abbey of St. Victor in the twelfth century is good evidence that such goals were not gender constricted). The Franciscans belong to Christian humanism because of their involvement with nature and eventually with the beautiful (St. Bonaventure in particular).

Louis Bouyer, himself one of the great Christian humanists of our own age, wrote in 1959 a book titled *Erasmus and His Times,* which is to this day as good an introduction to Christian humanism as any I know; a similarly good book is the one by Henri de Lubac, (later Cardinal Lubac) about Pico della Mirandola. The figures examined in these two studies may well represent the peak of Christian humanism: Erasmus, Pico della Mirandola, St. Thomas More, and, slightly before them, Nicholas of Cusa. They include popes and cardinals: Eugene IV, Nicolas V, Pius II (Aeneas Sylvius Piccolomini), Paul III (Alexander Farnese), Pole, Contarini, Barberini, Bessarion, and others. Protestants (particularly in the seventeenth-century Church of England) developed their own Christian humanism, informed by the sweet erudition of Donne, Marvell, and Izaak Walton.

A narrower and more precise use of the term would confine Christian humanism to the sixteenth century, often presented by historians as almost anti-Christian, or at least as a departure from Christianity. Many commentators argue that the Christian idiom was just a thin protective layer hiding what was in effect a farewell to the past of "Christian mythology." This theory is not supported by the biographical evidence and the written works of key figures such as Erasmus, Thomas More, and Pico della Mirandola. More was ready to put his head on the block for his beliefs, Pico went so far as to approach Savonarola toward the end of his short life, and Erasmus stubbornly and ingeniously pursued a mixture between personal independence (and cagey doubt) and a refusal to abandon Catholic tradition and community. With brilliance and philosophical depth, Cusanus had already demonstrated ways in which radical skepticism and intensely honest faith/obedience can enter into a fruitful dialogue: and this was the model chosen in one way or the other by many pontiffs and cardinals of the sixteenth century. In essence, during the Renaissance we witness a reinscribing of the Cappadocian gambit: an appropriation of the best cultural achievements of the ancient world, of Platonism in particular, as well as a dramatically heightened presence of the Church in the world of culture. The humanism of the Renaissance was in many ways elite-oriented, as opposed to the much more broadly popular sweep of medieval efforts. On the other hand, Renaissance humanism strongly affirmed Christianity's capacity to be inclusive and to reclaim areas of the historical past (and of the present) in which its *universality* could shine forth again.

At bottom the humanism of the Renaissance can be defined as an attempt to explain how the "two revelations" overlap and intersect, and come to support each other. (A similar attempt is found later in the writings of the Romantics.) God reveals himself, yes, through the Scriptures, but also through his works, through nature, through other religions, even when those might be deemed incomplete or unclear. Nevertheless, the essence of their message is ultimately analogous to that of Christianity. All religions are engaged in a common endeavor, that of speaking with God and about God. This argument was later put forward with particular eloquence and philosophical talent by both Catholics and Protestants such as Malebranche and Leibniz.[4] The latter gave us what is today still the best fusion of rationality and faith. The former talked with wonderful eloquence about the connection of belief with the book of nature and how the two are geared to one another. Both of them would deserve detailed treatment.

This is as good a place as any to bring up the issue of "universalism." The history of Christianity can be read in fact (sociohistorically) as one of broadening inclusiveness. A local, small, and highly coherent subbranch of Judaism expanded in an effort initiated by Paul of Tarsus and others and continued through the end of the patristic age until it turned into a Mediterranean-wide body of doctrines and visions, Graeco-Roman primarily, but with significant Eastern accretions. A tough propagandist such as St. Clement of Alexandria was already speaking of the mysteries of Eleusis as a kind of prefiguring of Christianity. A second phase (from c. AD 800–900 on) primarily saw tribes of Germanic, Slavic, and Celtic descent joining with this combination. (Both Orthodoxy and Protestantism might be seen as exercises in consummating this wedding).

The next stage, though apparently slow in getting off the ground, began around 1500–1600 and aimed at a globalization of Christianity; perhaps Matteo Ricci's experiments with Confucian religious traditions will be seen some day as those of a major precursor and farsighted thinker.

Many humanists (Erasmus, della Mirandola) lobbied actively for universalism, for ecumenical attitudes, for a variety of forms of dialogue with other religions, and designing unifying schemes or scenarios. Missionary work was not often (or primarily) an oppressive kind of imposition. In fact, many of our first non-Western dictionaries come from missionaries; many missionaries tried to understand and to present local cultures in a good light, and on several continents (such as South America and the Indian Subcontinent), interesting syntheses between local traditions and cultures and Christianity enjoyed longer or shorter durations.

By now it was also becoming clear what the undergirdings of Christian humanism were. People were beginning to understand what has become clearer to us now: that there are certain fundamental or structural commonalities between humanistic culture and Christianity that bring them together objectively, irrespective of the wishes and plans of writers, artists, and intellectuals. Some of those seem to be the following:

Both explore, in essence, the relational nature of divinity. Unlike the strict ("binary") connection of polytheistic or rigidly monotheistic visions of the divine, Christianity's concept of the Trinity posited from the very beginning a tremendous abundance of mutual activities inside God's nature: processes and dialectics, reciprocal engendering, sacrifice and giving, and—not least—a great variety of relations with the created world. On a closer look, "cultural production" was in its turn trying to do the same: stake out a territory of freedom, openness, and creativity. Or, even better, it was trying to imitate on a finite scale the infinite creative and gratuitous freedom of God. Culture could be seen as the faithful imitation of God. A humanity created in God's "image and likeness" was following the God of Genesis: incessantly creating, as a free gift, new faces and possibilities of the universe in architecture, music, verse, or philosophical speculation. The humanity of Christian humanism was one that was trying to supplement in its modest way the majestic gestures of original Creation.

Furthermore, Christianity could serve as a cultural model owing to a rather unique feature. The most crucial and indispensable part of its message and belief was not given in one indisputable and bluntly unambiguous text. The Christian Bible contains no fewer than four separate accounts of the central event of the incarnation, birth, actions, sacrifice, and resurrection of the Second Person of the Trinity. These accounts provide a multitude of overlappings, angles, eyewitnesses, and reverberations of eternity, but also secondhand accounts, summaries, and reconstitutions, as well as already in-built hermeneutical materials. The supernatural power of the narrative must needs explode, Christian humanists believed, any capture in the simplifying categories of earth-bound reason and representation, hence the need for a prismatic or kaleidoscopic account. This very special kind of description brought Christianity close to the modes of operation of literature, for example, with its ambiguity, dynamic processes, and its lack of closure and unified meaning.[5] No less suggestive culturally was the nature of Holy Tradition, the continuing work of the Holy Spirit. Briefly put, there is in that particular part of the Church's life a special connection between stability and expansion, between growth and continuity, that never ceases to amaze the observer. This, of course, as much as anything else, could serve as a model for the pursuit and the shaping of the beautiful and of intellectual speculation in the secular world on the basis of common outlines.

Other commonalities could be easily enumerated. Suffice it to say that they were all wrapped up in two large realities on which nobody cast doubt and which, I think, are still valid. The first was that *any* kind of human society must contain as an indispensable feature a kind of opening toward transcendence; the relationship between the human person and God is constitutive and unavoidable, no matter what channels of communication or religious idioms are employed. The second was the equally incontestable fact that culture in the realm of the West, and indeed on all continents, was derived from and connected with religion: architecture to temples of worship; drama to religious ritual; universities to the acquisition of sacred knowledge; music, sculpture, and painting to the praise of the divine; indeed, science and economy themselves perhaps to categories generated by divine narratives. By the end of the eighteenth and the beginning of the nineteenth centuries, such views were crystallized and widespread and, surprisingly, accepted not only by religious persons but also by skeptics, agnostics, or lukewarm believers.

Therefore, it was around this date that Christian humanism finally took on its current form. This was due in large measure to Chateaubriand, who invented an idiom at the boundaries of the theoretical and the purely literary in which the great harmonies of the world could be spoken and highlighted. In his *Genius of Christianity* (1802) the beautiful emerges as an indispensable key to any grasp of the true and of the good, not the other way round. His example was followed by many Romantic and nineteenth-century writers and thinkers, not only in France, but also in Germany and England, and even in Russia and in Eastern Europe. The amazing appeal of Chateaubriand derived from his ability to turn the privileging of nature (the great innovation at the end of the eighteenth century!) into an argument for sacrality, and to legitimize the spheres of the emotional and the aesthetic as valid replacements for those of the rational and the social.

Chateaubriand was, of course, not alone. Many German and some English Romantics (e.g., Coleridge) worked toward forging this alliance between the beautiful and the world of religion. The Swiss Alois Gugler, today virtually forgotten, argued that biblical writing was the prototype of any sublime expression. The Catalan Jaime Balmes engaged directly the philosophies of history of his time, and his contemporary Donoso Cortes argued that politics derives from (or is wrapped in) theology. Cardinal St. Klemens Maria Hofbauer gathered around himself in Vienna a dazzling circle of intellectual and artistic stars. The Oxford Tractarians, whether they remained Anglican or turned toward Rome, revamped the whole moral-religious landscape of England for almost a century. The apologetical writings of Hannah More smashed all best-seller records then known in the Anglo-Saxon world. Schleiermacher reinvented hermeneutic analysis starting from religious principles. Lamennais, Ozemas, and Gorres demonstrated how crucial religious concepts could still remain operative in the context of obsessive social and national preoccupations.

It would be idle to deny the crisis of Christianity in the twenty-first century; the perception that we have entered a "post"-Christian age has become generalized. While this is usually seen as a dangerous and ambiguous place to be, it is also rather evident that "post" can be read not only as indicative of rupture, break, and rejection, but also as signaling descendance, filiality, succession, and continuity. It can be argued that *without* the organizing force of Christianity the main cognitive activities and the social dynamics of the modern age would have been entirely different from what they are, and perhaps impossible. Thus nobody can overlook the enormous resurgence of original intellectual thought and artistic creativity associated with the names of Romano Guardini, Joseph Pieper, Jacques Maritain, Henry Bremond, Jean Danielou, Lubac, Lonergan, Rahner, Claudel, Péguy, Chesterton, Waugh, Flannery O'Connor, and Walker Percy on the Catholic side; and Eliot, Auden, C. S. Lewis, Barth, Tillich, Niebuhr, Vladimir Solovyov, Lossky, Florensky, and Sergey Bulgakov, not to mention Unamuno, Simone Weil, Berdyaev, and Leo Chestov—all these are only a small number among those connected closely or remotely with Christian humanism.

It cannot be emphasized strongly enough that parallel phenomena can be noted inside Judaism and Islam, synchronically, with many structural analogies and, more than once, some cross-influences. Meanwhile, the vigor of religions outside the sphere of monotheism is equally notable. More generally, there is a continuing and efficient presence of religion in virtually all the societies of our globe. Any conscientious instructor will not fail to point out these connections.

It is here that I would highlight the name of Hans Urs von Balthasar (1905–88). His work offers a kind of *summa* of this revival of Christian humanism in the early twentieth century. He tried to bring together the insights of most of the above-mentioned thinkers. Balthasar provided historical outlines of the Catholic tradition in culture, and he strove toward constructing a kind of explanatory system for ordering the rather individualist views of many of his predecessors.

Significantly, his system resorted to the values of the aesthetic, the dramatic, and the symphonic in order to communicate a tentative synthesis of Christian humanism to the twentieth century.

Balthasar's work begins with the study of Germanistics. His first major work was *Apokalypse der deutschen Seele* (1939) and had three volumes, only one of which is in print, or more generally available. Why this work and why this period? Balthasar goes to the roots of modernity, the period 1780–1830, when Europe was transformed and when the foundations for a speedy global transformation were laid. Technological and industrial revolutions were carried out at the same time as the generalization of urban life, the emancipation of the individual and the loosening of organic ties of community and solidarity, and political upheavals on a rarely experienced scale. The vitality of an alienating and analytical rationalism was accompanied by spiritual crises, by a rush toward democratic and egalitarian modes of governance, the domination of nature, and as I said, globalization of horizons. Romantic poets, idealist philosophers, statesmen, revolutionaries, and many ordinary folk perceived this knot of crises as a massive trauma and a shattering challenge to traditional ways of life. Most Europeans recognized enormous opportunities for freedom, progress, and prosperity, but they were also afraid of disruption, of a thinning of the very substance of their emotional and imaginative existence (later this was called a "loss of being"); they feared the dangers of life without roots, attachments, or rich meanings and passions.

Therefore an earnest and profound debate ensued in those years, and a staggering multitude of responses and solutions were generated and proposed. These ranged from enthusiastic approval of the new to its wholesale rejection, but there were also ingenious and thoughtful compromises and combinations. It is no exaggeration to say that the "age of Goethe" (the *Goethezeit*) has remained to this day a veritable reservoir of ideas and visions for the subsequent ages, including our own. Liberalism, conservatism, utopianism, socialism, and nationalism, such as we were to know them, were conceived in those decades. In the following two centuries, other parts of the world (Russia and Eastern Europe, Latin America, and many sections of Africa, Asia, and of the Islamic world) were forced to come to terms with the pervasive, emancipatory trauma of "modernity" and all of its joys, sufferings, and dilemmas. Each country or culture tended to replicate the ways of thinking and living pioneered in those crucial decades—favorably or in the guise of opposition.

Small wonder that the intellectual and cultural life of the period 1780–1830 received close scrutiny and was treated in scholarly or imaginative fashion by people as different as G. Lukacs, Thomas Mann, or M. H. Abrams. Hans Urs von Balthasar surpasses these, I am convinced, by the depth of his philosophical analysis and by his overwhelming erudition. He points out the inevitable collapse of the Romantic project from its noble Promethean humanism into doubt, morbidity, and the apologia of death. At the same time Balthasar does not hide his enthusiasm for the enormous achievements of Goethe, Schiller, and their contemporaries. He was convinced that the concern for organic wholeness, the exploration of the right balance between reason and imagination, and the emphasis on the social goodness of cultural beauty so eloquently advocated by these poets and philosophers must be adopted and expanded.

Thus the young Balthasar came to believe that it would be fruitful to reverse the steps of Goethe, Humboldt, and their contemporaries. Whereas these great minds had tried to institute cultural humanism as a replacement for religion, Balthasar proposed to recuperate for Christianity the best insights of the *Goethezeit.* Since, in his opinion, the great systems and visionary images of that age had originated in an imperative religious need (howsoever dimly perceived!), he strove to bring them back where they rightfully belong, namely into the family of Christian humanisms, and to reconfer upon them a spiritual grace that they deserve but are always on the verge of losing.

Does this grand design not remind us immediately of something? Is it not a good parallel to the "appropriation" of Neoplatonism by the Cappadocian and other early Christian Fathers? Is it surprising that so much of the work of the mature Balthasar was concerned with patristics and that he was seen (with Lubac) as a patristic continuator, rather than a disciple of the Middle Ages?

The work of Balthasar was enormous, comparable in size to that of the greatest figures of Christian theology, from Chrysostom, Augustine, and Aquinas to Rahner. One biographer calculated that, until 1975, just the major works amounted to almost eleven thousand printed pages. If we add the major works of the other thirteen years and the numerous *opuscula* and articles, we will come closer, I think, to twenty thousand. (Another bibliographer counts, until 1977, sixty-two volumes; almost five hundred articles, reviews, and introductions; seventy-one translations; and twelve anthologies). Among these stand out, clearly, the works on patristics: monographs and/or anthologies on Maximus Confessor, Origen, Gregory of Nyssa, and others.

Balthasar's activity was prodigious by any standards.[6] He was influenced by his Jesuit instructors, by Henri de Lubac and Erich Przywara, by the mystic and hermeneut Adrienne von Speyr. He initiated the publishing house Johannes Verlag and the quarterly *Communio* that now appears in twelve languages (each with slight variations). He not only theorized but founded "secular institutes" and may have been the inspiration behind the important Italian Catholic movement "Communione e liberazione". He was active in Church affairs, critiquing the preconciliary Church, but expressing strong reservations on some postconciliary interpretations of Vatican II that reverberated well and loudly in the minds of John Paul II, of Cardinal Ratzinger, of bishop Kasper, and many others. He was a university instructor, a priest, a converter of major cultural figures, a translator of talent. He was active in ecumenical dialogue, a friend of Karl Barth's, a careful commentator on Martin Buber, and an awardee of the Great Mount Athos Cross by Athenagoras, the Patriarch of

Constantinople. His knowledge of world literature and music was overwhelming. He ended up by being elevated to cardinalship, an honor that he did not desire and, ultimately, did not (formally) obtain, because of his demise.

The two great syntheses that crowned Balthasar's scholarly life are *The Glory of the Lord* (*Herrlichkeit,* 1961–68) and *Theodramatics* (*Theodramatik,* 1975–81). The general idea is that the numinous ought to be approached not primarily from the point of view of the good or the true, but rather from that of the beautiful, for without the beautiful, the good and true cannot exist.

At every step, Balthasar finds similarities between literature and religion as they seek, and express, the truth. For instance, the distinction between *lumen* and *figura* (the divine and the historical) in theological discourse is seen as analogous to the dialectic of inspiration and shape (or *Gestalt*) in literary utterance. More importantly, the dialectic of subjective and objective in religious truth can be understood by reference to the same process in literary authorship and reading. Subjectivity organizes and crystallizes the objective reality that is its target and center, while the objective reality (unknowable though it may ultimately be) channels and steers subjectivity. Like aesthetic knowledge, religious knowledge and experience entail forms of collaboration of rationality with irrationality, chaos, and silence. Without the shaping provided by its aesthetic component, Christianity would not have coalesced into a stable historical reality.

To drive home this point, Balthasar looked at the issue also in its dynamic. Thus the first volume of *Theodramatic* was devoted exclusively to the theory of drama and to theatrical categories, theatrical literature, and the investigation of performance techniques. He applied immediately these theatrical mechanisms to salvation history and the trinitarian economy, as well as to the relationship between the human and the divine. Dramatic functions were used to illumine, organize, and explain in human terms the functioning of the transcendent. For example, Balthasar discussed the relationship between person and mission by referring to the relation between dramatic character and the art of acting. Elsewhere Balthasar resorted to the triangular relationship author-actor-director (shades of Goethe's *Faust*!), as well as the audience-production-horizon triad, to clarify the nature of trinitarian divinity as one that was neither abstract, nor purely mythical-immanent (as in animist religions). The "dialogic" principle (a prominent tenet of contemporary literary theory, in the version of Mikhail Bakhtin) or the investigation of *topoi* such as *theatrum mundi* or the "holy fool" also are integral to Balthasar's arguments.

To simplify some of the complexities of Balthasar's labyrinthine theory, we can distinguish three definitions of the role of the beautiful in faith. The first is quantitative and historical. There were several successive embraces of the world by the Church in its incarnational *animus*, and thus successive layers or versions of religious humanism came about: in late antiquity, in the Middle Ages, in the post-Tridentine and high-Jesuit era, and so forth. All these are precious and have to be rediscovered continuously.

The second definition of the role of the beautiful in faith is to recover religious truth and methodology from the inner workings of aesthetic itself, particularly of music (the "symphonic" nature of truth was one of his most famous and widely adopted phrases).

The third definition of the beautiful is the mediating role of aesthetic culture, which has always had one leg planted in the world of the rational and the pragmatic, the other one firmly in the realm of the mysterious and the metarational. It can thus serve as an appropriate (and usually quite willing) incarnational vehicle for the highest transcendental designs. After all, it is not absurd to argue that among all kinds of human action, it is aesthetic culture that best resembles the discourse and the ends of religious search and hope. It is endowed with the resources of abundance, multiplicity, substance, nuance, and presence that cannot be equaled by any of the "social sciences" with their reliance upon reduction, simplification, streamlining, numerical power, and binary modes of argument.

When all is said and done, what is then the nature or design of Christian humanism? One short way of putting things in perspective is to say that, for the Christian humanists, culture is seen as a kind of tumbling ground for the spiritual, the social, the historical, and the psychological. For them the human being individually and the human species collectively act as a key, as the intersectional *locus* where all areas of the cosmos can meet. At this crossroads, Christian humanists believe, culture actually behaves as an enormous mediating force between the creaturely and the divine. According to them, aesthetic culture is that which seeks to articulate the opening toward transcendence that appears as a human constant in all human societies known to us.

Aesthetic culture can do so because, more obviously than other human activities, it is an imitation of creativity (the essence of the divine, in accordance with the description provided by the book of Genesis.) The great majority of the Christian humanists do not shy away from uncertainty, nor do they bemoan it; rather they seem to receive it in a joyful spirit, whether on the metaphysical level, or in matters political and ideological. They accept imperfection and the ephemeral endeavor of human efforts without lassitude or resentment. If God is seen as primarily the creator, the builder, *imitating* the fundamental gestures and behaviors of God must be the proper human vocation.

Along with this constructive experimentalism, courage is seen as a key Christian virtue. This follows naturally from the strain of doubt (sometimes prominent, sometimes barely perceptible) in Christian humanist writings. A close reader will be struck to discover in these writings that hope gains an ever-so-slight precedence over faith and charity: but hope without courage would be sheer irrationality—and the tradition described in this essay is always rational.

Is there a friction or conflict between Christianity (or religion in general) and the modern world? The question is legitimate and sometimes quite topical. I think we can speak about *two* kinds of friction or clash. One of them is rather destructive: it is taken by a variety of currents that we tend to call "fundamentalist." According to these, modernization (as mentioned above: rationality, urbanization, industrial and postindustrial modes of production, empirical and analytical kinds of judgment, democracy and equality, and higher standards of living) represents a great danger to the spiritual essence of mankind. Modernization, these currents maintain, tries to supersede divine creation and replace it with "human" (actually diabolical and negative) constructions. Actually such an antimodernism was shared by two or three of the large totalitarian experiments of the twentieth century.

A second kind of opposition ought to be seen as creative, a form of constructive criticism. It notices the drawbacks (or dangers) of the Enlightenment tradition and of its globalist consequences, but it tries to repair them and to propose complementary solutions. According to this line of thinking (to simplify a little), Christianity (and, again, virtually any religion) can well remain a "stumbling block" to the world, adopt an oppositional behavior inside society, remind it of its own ideals, and goad it toward them. However, this second kind of opposition does not immobilize itself into absolute adversity and negation. Rather, it returns to its own salvational purposes: it tries to embrace and enhance the structures of matter and society, not to block or to eliminate them.

Fortunately for us, this second attitude is often encountered not only inside Christianity and Judaism, but also in many other religions. In Chateaubriand's above-mentioned book, a longish list of commandments (taken from different religions) is cited, with the intention to show that the biblical Ten Commandments have more emotional depth and subtlety than their equivalents in other religions. Ironically, readers are struck not by the contrast, but by the similarity between these tables of different religions. And, by the way, C. S. Lewis (in his *Abolition of Man,* 1947) deliberately uses similar comparisons to emphasize the common religious fund of humanity. In many of his works, Vladimir Solovyov tried hard to discover not only the common ground of the branches of Christianity, but also commonalities with features of ancient and Eastern religions. Sir James Frazer, the "Cambridge Ritualists," Eliade, Kerenyi, Campbell, Turner (most of whom cannot be considered Christian or perhaps even religious) endeavored nevertheless to throw light on the common features of mankind's languages of communication with transcendence.

Mystics, visionaries, and dogmatics have their own justification, ecclesial not less than existential, but they are less often Christian humanists. On the other hand, monasticism is not necessarily (and historically has not proved) contrary to this positioning toward the religious. Sociohistorically, monasticism began as an alternative, utopian mode of communitarian life. Nevertheless, rather soon, many monastic communities turned to the preservation of skills and knowledge, no less than to innovation in matters economical and technological. Their hostility toward a violent and stagnant world (e.g., in the ninth to the twelfth centuries) was a tenacious and well-reflected response and was definitely informed by a patient, farsighted vision. It remains to be seen whether similar circumstances will be repeated.

The implosion of the Communist experiment signals, at the very least, the weaknesses of *any* exclusively secularist socioeconomic mode. Does it also warn us of the collapse of the capitalist-democratic mode? This may be an exaggeration, but it is not entirely impossible. Even leaving aside apocalyptic scenarios we can still begin to reflect on how a *renewal* of our world, one founded on the premises of the eighteenth century, might come about. In that case it is precisely Christian humanism that might remind us of the *spiritual* roots of the Enlightenment, which later came to be cavalierly ignored.

In the countries in which Communism had reigned, the breakdown of the Communist alternative model was not followed by paradisial conditions, as was expected by many: far from it! Deep scars were left, as well as pervasive disorientations. The process of recuperation has been exceedingly slow. Vaclav Havel, one of the most important moral consciences of our time, compared the process to the painful depressurization of a prisoner released after many years of penal servitude. In turn, a broad reconfiguring of the Western mode of life might become inevitable—whether under some kind of collapse, or in the midst of the dire need for self-rethinking.

At that point, Christian humanism certainly, monastic communities possibly, might find a new (and highly relevant) sociohistorical role. The feeling of loss, disorientation, and estrangement will create (as it already does) a need for an articulate mediating force. Inside God's freedom, plausible structures and patterns will be (perhaps already are) in great demand. The supply for that demand is often shoddy, sometimes downright deleterious (irrational or exploitative cults, secular or spiritualist, politically left or right). It is *absolutely essential* to have on hand a supply of forces for recuperation of life and thinking, individual persons, modes of functioning—perhaps an Isaian "remnant." The potential for healing, nurturing, reconstruction, and bridge-building of the categories of Christian humanism may well prove invaluable in the future, even more than in the past.

In most (and the best) of Balthasar's work, as well as in the tradition(s) here described, Christian humanism appears not as an isolating and dividing force. On the contrary, we can regard it as a hope-filling and meaningful energy of unification and growth, one that seeks interaction with other religions and other horizons of thinking. In my opinion, *any* renewed humanism would have to choose as part of its foundation certain forms of sacrality recognized by most or all civilizations and sought after by people from all societies and ages. We can trust that such a new humanism would be broader, more democratic, less elitist, and devoid of certain earlier kinds of imposition (even well-intentioned ones). Biblical, Aristotelian, and Confucian categories of ethical command would be connected with it. At the same time, the thinking of contemporary figures—Michel Serres, Frederic Turner, Emannuel Levinas, René Girard, Paul Ricoeur, Jean-Luc Marion, and many, many others—would fit in with it.

We know that we live in an age of accelerated modernization. This is an age of great hope and progress, but also one of asperity and even cruelty, of great dilemmas for the ecology of culture. Are smaller societies and languages going to disappear with all their customs and rich traditions? Are most of them going to be swallowed up and assimilated into one totalizing and homogeneous informational culture? This would be (most of us will agree) a sad and dangerous event. Precisely here, in the ecological salvation of society, in the rescue of the secondary, of the marginal, and of the heterogeneous, literary and cultural productions can have a beneficent role. Christian humanism finds itself inevitably in the forefront of these discussions, because the Judeo-Christian tradition was and still is, more than others, intimately interwoven with "modernization": partly fostering it, partly struggling with it. It is also the case that the principle of *subsidiarity* was engendered inside this religious tradition. This principle can be applied quite successfully not only in the sociopolitical sphere, but also in the literary, the cultural, and the religious. Subsidiarity can allow us to entertain a framework of global-informational structures, even while cultivating our private religious and literary-cultural gardens. In this horizon, values as different as charity, courage, indeterminacy, hope, honor, and temperance can coexist fruitfully and interact to the general interest.

Notes

1. See Chantal Millon-Delsol, *L'Etat subsidiaire* (Paris: Presses Universitaires de France, 1992).
2. Many of the arguments of this first section are more fully developed in my "Neoplatonism si cultura romana," *Revista de Istorie si teorie literara* 43 (July–December 1995): 261–71. The current article is based upon three other previously published articles of mine: "Christian Humanism through the Centuries," *Image* 16 (May 1996): 1–10; "The Beauty of Balthasar," *Crisis* 11 (April 1993): 42–46; and "Voice of Christian Humanism," *Crisis* 6 (September 1988): 36–40. Part of my argument was also presented as a position paper at a conference on humanism in Santiago de Compostella, Spain, in July 1997.

3. See also Endre von Ivanka, *Plato Christianus. Ubernahme und Umgestaltung des Platonismus durch die Vater* (Einsiedeln: Johannes Verlag, 1964).
4. See Lochbrunner Malebranche, "Entretiens sur la metaphysique, sur la religion, et sur la mort," in *Oeuvres*, 2 vols. (1696; repr. Paris: Gallimard-Pleiade, 1992), II:649–1042; also G. W. Leibniz, *La Theodicee* (1710; repr. New Haven: Yale University Press, n.d.). Cf. C. D. Broad, *Leibniz. An Introduction* (Cambridge: Cambridge University Press, 1975), pp. 148–72. Cf. *Malebranche et Leibniz,* ed. Andre Robinet (Paris: J. Vris, 1953). In fact this was a philosophical *topos,* if we think that coming from a different direction, Francis Bacon was judging similarly in his *Advancement of Learning* (1605) and was eloquently defending the idea of the two revelations (scriptural and natural). In a sense medieval thinkers such as St. Thomas had already laid the seeds for this mode of thinking.
5. It is important to note that here also Judaism (through kabbalah and midrash) was acting as a forerunner and/or parallel. A unified text (the Torah) became the object of a multiplicity (infinite in principle) of interpretations. This procedure had sound theological foundations: it was meant to prove convincingly the infinite multidimensionality of God and his sayings. Additionally, the interest from the point of view of literary and literary-critical angles must be immediately obvious.
6. Some of the most prominent works on Balthasar's thinking are Aldo Moda, *Hans Urs von Balthasar: Un'esposizione critica del suo pensiero* (Bari, Italy: Ecumenica, 1976); Manfred Lochbrunner, *Analogia caritatis: Darstellung und Deutung der Theologie Hans Urs von Balthasar* (Freiburg: Herder, 1981); Edward Oakes, *Pattern of Redemption: The Theology of Hans Urs von Balthasar* (New York: Continuum, 1994).

8

Balthasar's Critique of the Historical-Critical Method

Edward T. Oakes, SJ

In a book published in 1994 called *Scripture, the Soul of Theology,* the noted Scripture scholar Joseph Fitzmyer accused Hans Urs von Balthasar of "ranting" against the historical-critical method. The next year Fitzmyer gave an interview in the Jesuit weekly journal of opinion *America* that was centered on the contents of this book.[1] His charge of ranting seemed substantial enough for the interviewer to ask him to explain the justice of the accusation, to which he replied: "I am not sure I can remember all the things he [Balthasar] said that made me refer to his 'ranting,' but he has a number of articles in which he is impatient with people who use the historical-critical method."

Father Fitzmyer's response to the question is indicative of how Balthasar is often perceived by those whose acquaintance with his writings is, in fact, slight and who know him simply by reputation alone. Consider, for example, Father Fitzmyer's response to the interviewer's question: first, he conveniently forgets which writings of Balthasar's actually contain these fulminations, and then he subtly alters the charge from "ranting" to *impatience* (and moreover not with the method itself but "with *people* who *use* the historical-critical method"), which can either mean that he identifies as a "ranter" anybody who is impatient with any practitioner of the historical-critical method *tout court—or,* when he is asked to justify his accusation, that he backpedals and changes the terms of the charge and suddenly begins talking about "impatience": a much different word and attitude.

Father Fitzmyer's book, where this charge first appears in print, cites an article where he thinks this ranting takes place, but he gives no quotes from the allegedly offending piece so that the reader might come to an independent assessment of the charge, based on Balthasar's own words. In fact, the article Father Fitzmyer cites is called *"Exegese und Dogmatik,"* and appeared in 1976 in the German edition of *Communio.*[2] But far from being one long "rant" against the historical-critical method, the article is a careful and balanced assaying of the impact of historical-critical exegesis on dogmatic theology, as the title of the article in fact implies. And indeed, so far from a "rant" is this article that Balthasar actually says within the first two pages that "theology will have to reflect on this [that is, the challenge of history-of-Jesus scholarship] quite explicitly if it does not want to build its house on sand."

Father Fitzmyer's rhetorical violence to the plain sense of the text of Balthasar's essay[3] highlights a forensic difficulty that anyone must face in the current climate of scholarship when dealing with the topic of Balthasar's critique of the historical-critical method. For there is no doubt that Balthasar *has* a critique to deliver, that he looks askance at both the method and its current practice now gloriously reigning in the world of biblical scholarship; moreover, he can definitely be "impatient," to use Father Fitzmyer's word, with certain practitioners. But if all of this—or indeed any of it—is to count as "ranting," then dialogue is finished, because first of all *any* criticism of the historical-critical method will be ruled out of court, and second Balthasar will come across as some rear-guard obscurantist blocking the way to a fair-minded appraisal of the positivism and sheer load of facts that have been unearthed by historical scholarship.[4]

It will therefore be my task to present Balthasar's critique of the historical-critical method in all its nuance and *subtlety*—and subtle it is. It has nothing in common with the turn-of-the-century campaign of the anti-Modernists against biblical scholarship. Moreover, the sources from which it draws to make its critique can sometimes surprise by their postmodern provenance.

Here I am thinking of Nietzsche in particular, that philosopher who is often taken to be the "founding father" of the perspectivism and radical relativity of truth-claims that are the foundation, so to speak, of that school of antifoundationalism which goes under the name of postmodernism. In fact, it was the burden of one of the chapters of my recent book on Balthasar, *Pattern of Redemption*, to highlight how indebted Balthasar was to Nietzsche, from the time of his doctoral studies on. In any event, I would like to begin my treatment of Balthasar's critique of the historical-critical method with a quotation from Nietzsche that exactly sets the context for Balthasar's own views. In his book *Untimely Meditations*, sometimes translated as *Observations Out of Season*, Nietzsche says the following:

> Anything that constrains a man to love less than unconditionally has severed the roots of his strength: he will wither away, that is to say, become dishonest. In producing this effect, [the academic discipline of] history is the antithesis of art: and only if history can endure to be transformed into a work of art will it perhaps be able to preserve instincts or even evoke them. Such a historiography would, however, be altogether contrary to the analytical and inartistic tendencies of our time, which would indeed declare it false.[5]

Here, admirably set forth in just two or three of Nietzsche's famously eloquent sentences, we have the whole Balthasarian program: the absolute norm of love, against which *all* scholarship must be judged; the valuation of art over the academic discipline of history; and the insistence that *real* history will plumb the inner depths of our being rather than bury those selfsame depths under a truckload of footnotes. As Peter Berkowitz says in his wholly admirable book on Nietzsche, "In Nietzsche's view, his age betrays distressing symptoms of a general malady: too much of the wrong kind of history. He declares his meditations untimely because while his contemporaries take pride in their 'cultivation of history' he views their preoccupations with the past as a crushing burden and a consuming disease."[6] And despite Nietzsche's intense aversion to Christianity, he could not help but notice how Christianity, this deeply historical religion, was undermining its own power and reality by approaching its history with the wrong method: "History that merely destroys without any impulse to construct will in the long run make its instruments tired of life: insipid and unnatural.... For a time one can take up history like other studies, and it will be perfectly harmless. Recent theology seems to have entered quite innocently into partnership with history, and scarcely sees even now that it has unwittingly bound itself to the Voltairean cry: écrasez—uproot the infamous thing!"[7]

To avoid this mortal danger to the Church, Balthasar adopts not only Nietzsche's diagnosis but also his prescriptions for a cure. Let us begin with a central Nietzschean motif, one that we have already seen him use in *Untimely Meditations*: the valuation of art over history. This insistence that art is more of a window into the divine than the positivity of history ever can be will—as everyone with even the most superficial knowledge of Balthasar's work realizes—become the starting point of his own theological trilogy, which begins with art and aesthetics and only then moves on to questions of action and truth.

But *why* is it that art should be valued over history? Does Balthasar perhaps follow Aristotle's opinion that poetry "is something more philosophic and of greater import than history, since its statements are of the nature rather of universals, whereas those of history are singulars?"[8] Quite the contrary! For Balthasar it is because art is *more* concrete and singular than history—in the sense of an academic discipline—that it offers a better access to the reality of Christ, who is for Balthasar by definition the *concretissimum,* the most concrete reality of all.

This is indeed why he can develop his aesthetical theology at such length: seven volumes in all, because of his theory of concretion. In Balthasar's Christology, Jesus Christ is by definition the paradox of absolute concretion: when Christians encounter in the Gospel of John the claim of Jesus to be "*the* Way, *the* Truth, and *the* Life," this represents for them a claim to what Balthasar calls "absolute singularity": the paradox is so total as to be, in effect, incomprehensible, rather as if one whitecap atop a wave were to claim to be the whole sea and the seabed on which it rests. How is that claim to be understood?

For Balthasar that claim can only be understood by analogy with other realities we recognize as "relative singularities," the first of which he chooses is a work of art. And in his description of a work of art, it becomes clear that what Balthasar is looking for in concretion is, so to speak, an intensification of reality so that the "singularity" becomes a prism through which one can look out at the totality of the world through the concrete work of art. Just as when one falls in love one sees in the beloved the whole of life's meaning, so too when one looks on a great work of art, a masterpiece, one sees *in* it and *through* it a whole world of meaning, condensed, impacted, and ready for explication.

Before getting into this issue in more detail as Balthasar will apply it to theology, let me first highlight what I think he means, by quoting from Harold Bloom's *The Western Canon,* where he makes a remark that I think exactly expresses Balthasar's own view of what constitutes a "relative singularity." Bloom is speaking here of Shakespeare and of his centrality in the canon; his justification for this judgment will remind any reader of Balthasar. Bloom says:

> Here they [the professional resenters who attack the canon] confront insurmountable difficulty in Shakespeare's most idiosyncratic strength: he is always ahead of you, conceptually and imagistically, whoever and whenever you are. He

> renders you anachronistic because he *contains* you; you cannot subsume him. You cannot illuminate him with a new doctrine, be it Marxism or Freudianism or DeManian linguistic skepticism. Instead, he will illuminate the doctrine, not by prefiguration but by postfiguration, as it were: all of Freud that matters most is there in Shakespeare already, with a persuasive critique of Freud besides. The Freudian map of the mind is Shakespeare's; Freud seems only to have prosified it. Or, to vary my point, a Shakespearean reading of Freud illuminates and overwhelms the text of Freud; a Freudian reading of Shakespeare reduces Shakespeare, or would if we could bear a reduction that crosses the line into absurdities of loss. *Coriolanus* is a far more powerful reading of Marx's *Eighteenth Brumaire of Louis Napoleon* than any Marxist reading of *Coriolanus* could hope to be.[9]

One of the fascinating implications of this passage is that there is no way of verifying the judgment Bloom makes here except by saturating oneself in the canon and seeing—by direct insight, as it were—how true this is. This is what Balthasar means by his insistence that great works of art establish their own norms for longevity to which it is the task of hearers/viewers/critics of that work to conform:

> A great work of art [says Balthasar] has a certain universal comprehensibility but discloses itself more profoundly and more truly to an individual the more attuned and practiced his powers of perception are. Not everyone picks up the unique inflection of the Greek in a chorus of Sophocles, or of the German of *Faust, Part II,* or of the French in a poem of Valéry. Subjective adaptation can add something of its own, but that objective adequacy which is able to distinguish the noble from the commonplace is more important. (WC 21–22)

This begins to get us near to the substance of Balthasar's critique of the historical-critical method. There is a danger that lurks inside this method that we may, speaking generally, call the Hegelian danger. The great danger that the Hegelian perspective on history can conjure up is the illusion that his dialectic of history *explains* how and why a certain event, whether historical or artistic, occurred; by making historical events seem like the inevitable outcomes of the process of the self-realization of Absolute Spirit, Hegel gave the impression of inevitability to history. Its astonishing contingency was gone and in its place was a script of inevitable outcomes. It was this aspect of his philosophy of history that prompted Schopenhauer to one of his most famous sneers: he told Hegel in Berlin that the only thing missing from his philosophy of history was an "ontological argument" for Herr Krug's pen. But for Balthasar both

> art and history are fundamentally, astonishingly inexplicable: Great works of art [he says] appear like inexplicable miracles and spontaneous eruptions on the stage of history. Sociologists are as unable to calculate the precise day of their origin as they are to explain in retrospect why they appeared when they did. Of course, works of art are subject to certain preconditions without which they cannot come into being: such conditions may be effective stimuli but do not provide a full explanation of the work itself. Shakespeare had his predecessors, contemporaries and models; he was surrounded by the atmosphere of the theater of his time. He could only have emerged within that context. Yet who would dare offer to prove that his emergence was inevitable? (WC 20)

The objection to the Hegelian outlook in no way is meant to yank a work of art from its historical context. Quite the contrary: the particular moment in which a masterpiece appears is an essential element to its concretion. For what it offers is a prism both to its own time and, paradoxically, to all subsequent times. But it is precisely the illumination it casts on all later times that means its context cannot control it; rather it illuminates its own times far more than those times explain the work:

> At most we can point to or guess at the propitious moment—the *kairos*—but never what it is that flows into it and gives it that lasting form which, as soon as it emerges, takes control. It *speaks the word.* Its unique utterance becomes a universal language. A great work of art is never obvious and immediately intelligible in the language that lies readily available, for the new, unique language now emerging before us is its own interpreter. It is "self-explanatory." For a moment the contemporary world is taken aback, then people begin to absorb the work and to speak in the newly minted language (hence such terms as "the age of Goethe," or "age of Shakespeare," etc.) with a taken-for-granted ease as though they had invented it themselves! The unique word, however, makes itself comprehensible through its own self: and the greater a work of art, the more extensive the cultural sphere it dominates will be. (WC 21)

To understand how this insight will form the basis of Balthasar's more direct critique of the historical-critical method, it might be of help to recall another remark of Bloom's in *The Western Canon,* who makes it clear that, *pace* Father Fitzmyer, it is not the *historical*-critical method *per se* that does violence to the text, but rather the assumption of the critic to have got control over the text by contextualizing it. Or as Bloom puts it more polemically:

> Precisely why students of literature have become amateur political scientists, uninformed sociologists, incompetent

> anthropologists, mediocre philosophers, and overdetermined cultural historians, while a puzzling matter, is not beyond all conjecture. They resent literature, or are ashamed of it, or are just not all that fond of reading it. Reading a poem or a novel or a Shakespearean tragedy is for them an exercise in contextualization, but not in a merely reasonable sense of finding adequate backgrounds. The contexts, however chosen, are assigned more force and value than the poem by Milton, the novel by Dickens, or [the tragedy] *Macbeth* [by Shakespeare].[10]

This is the central challenge for any critic of any text, but it pertains above all to the text of the Bible. For here it is not just a question of avoiding an attitude of superiority to the authors, which would be absurd. But more crucially it entails a willingness to be judged by the text in what theologians call a "super-eminent" way. Do we allow the claim of Jesus to address us over and above the historical-critical archeology that describes how this claim has been handed down to us? In other words, once we trace that history of how that claim came to be embedded in the text, have we thereby dispensed with hearing that claim addressed to us? To understand what I am driving at here, let us listen to this important programmatic challenge in Balthasar's polemical manifesto, *A Short Primer for Unsettled Laity*:

> Closely connected to the plurality of biblical ways of access to the mystery of revelation stands the contribution made by exegesis to its understanding. Since, taken abstractly in itself, it [exegesis] is a neutral philological science, it can be practiced by a believing or an unbelieving scholar, but of course in a very different spirit. Jesus demands a radical Yes or No to his person and claim. What is "neither hot nor cold" is spat out. Someone who wants to "bracket" this claim "methodologically," even if he does

> so only provisionally, in order to wait and see if this claim had really been made and, if so, if it was made rightly, exposes himself to the danger of a neutrality which is forbidden by the object and falsifies it. (*SPA* 47)

But here it must be stressed that this critique is leagues removed from any kind of anti-Modernist obscurantism that rejects historical-critical scholarship *in toto*. And this can be proven, ironically enough, in the very essay that Fitzmyer cites as his "proof" of ranting. Balthasar not only accepts for the sake of argument but explicitly adopts in *propria persona* the most radical conclusion of recent history-of-Jesus scholarship: that Jesus mistakenly expected the end of the world to be imminent, perhaps even to be linked to his own death—which, however, still caught him by "surprise," so to speak. Let us hear how Balthasar summarizes this scholarship and simultaneously makes it his own:

> The horizon of a genuine human being—and Jesus was one—is necessarily finite. Now a rather large number of texts, however, show undeniably that Jesus expected the arrival of the kingdom of God and with it the end of the world in the very near future: "some of those standing here" will experience this event before their death. The device of shifting this "apocalyptic imminent expectation" away from Jesus and attributing it primarily to the primitive Church just doesn't work. Every means has been tried in order to read into some texts the supposition within Jesus himself of an "interval" between his death and his Second Coming, without striking success, *we think*, since one is dealing there with late levels of tradition or interpretations or ecclesiastical adjustments, so as to explain the delay of the *Parousia*. Was Jesus then mistaken, and—what is almost worse—did he mislead the primitive Church to its unequivocal imminent expectation? Many,

> *and not just liberal exegetes,* flatly concede this in view of the textual evidence. (Ex 385)

But far from being an embarrassment for Balthasar, he not only accepts these results but insists that they will, properly interpreted, be of immense use to the dogmatic theologians, even going so far as to claim that genuine exegesis will free dogmatic theology "from many illusory problems and lead [it] back to its true object" (Ex 392). The reason Balthasar is so insistent upon this point is that he has his own theodramatic reasons for holding that Jesus saves precisely because he must face the future with the same sense of darkness that all the rest of us do. For Jesus to have some kind of Thomistic, hypostatic "gleaning" of the future by virtue of his status as the incarnate Logos of God would be to rob his theodramatic participation in God's drama of salvation of its specifically human dimension. Let us hear how Balthasar describes this christological logic that dovetails so well with current exegesis:

> The ultimate horizon, says the dogmatic theologian, out of which [Jesus] speaks is not the general apocalyptic of his time but the tremendous mandate of his Father to accomplish the atonement of the whole world with God, to "be finished with" the world, to reach the end of the world—as John puts it, to take away the sin of the world. He does not have to know in advance how this will be possible; enough that "the hour" of the Father will come, which no one ("not even the Son") knows; enough that the "hour of darkness" will soon come; and this is what provokes the end and brings the solution: "God made him to be sin," "in order to have mercy on all," says Paul. It is judgment and salvation at once, and this through Jesus' fate ("I must be baptized with a baptism of fire"). Once again, he does not have to know anything about the cross; nay, he *should not,* in order to achieve full obedience, know anything precise about it;

> the exactly spoken prophecies of the Passion could well be *vaticinia ex eventu*. But something horrible for him is coming, through which he will attain the end of the world: *that* he knows. And how extraordinary it is that this horror looming over him does not force him to any kind of apocalyptic haste: he projects an ethic for believers that is not an "interim ethic" for a short time that is left but sounds as if all time was available to live it. That too is an expression of his perfect obedience, that he lives in the presently given day and leaves worry for the morrow to his Father. The only thing that is important is that each day be filled to the brim with doing the will of the Father. To *that* end he presses on, to the approaching "hour" of the Father—which will simultaneously be the hour of total darkness of the Father's total absence from him. (Ex 390–91)

With this perspective Balthasar is even willing to be so bold as to claim that dogmatic theology can "lift" exegesis, so to speak, out of the culs-de-sac and blind alleys to which it often leads itself. In other words, the relationship between dogmatic theology and historical-critical scholarship can be mutually beneficial. For just as the results of recent history-of-Jesus scholarship has finally liberated Christology from the Monophysite temptation that has always plagued it since the Council of Chalcedon, so too dogmatic theology can benefit historical theology by radicalizing the meaning of the "end of the world" in Jesus' own horizon of consciousness *precisely because dogmatic theology is itself now freed of Monophysitism:*

> Notice that what the dogmatic theologian is saying here is absolutely anti-Monophysite. Jesus was no superhuman being who looks out over all time. His horizon was "economically" confined to his mission to be fulfilled in obedience. But again on the other hand, this confinement is also

> not [just] the general-anthropological one common to all human beings or the common confinement of Jews of Jesus's time, (which for that era of history would have been the apocalyptic expectation). Rather Jesus's horizon is completely unique (conditioned by the hypostatic union of God and man), because only in a human mission can he get to the end of the (old, sinful) world. (Ex 392)

Now historical-critical scholarship is able to be instructed by dogmatic theology in this way because this is *precisely what the word "end" means* in this context. But this meaning can only be discovered inside a discipline of history that has become "art" in Nietzsche's sense, that is, one that does not cut it off from the deepest wellsprings of being, wellsprings which indeed one encounters only in the concrete finitude of one's own existence hurtling toward its own end.

But how can historical-critical scholarship admit, according to its own restrictive methodology, the basic premise of dogmatic theology: the hypostatic union, out of which dogmatic theology makes its results available to the historical scholar? To make this transition the historical scholar must first admit a fundamental distinction about the text and the event to which it refers. This, of course, the historical scholar does all the time, for the whole intent of the method is to distinguish the narrative of an event from the event itself (*wie es eigentlich gewesen*). The dogmatic theologian can have no quarrel with that method *per se*, since obviously no historical narrative can exactly reproduce *any* event. But the dogmatic theologian must insist that the first and primary event to which the whole of Scripture gives testimony is the event of what *God* was doing to reconcile the world to himself in Christ, who is himself the definitive Word of his Father.

In other words, one must be able to distinguish between what Balthasar calls the *gezeugtes Wort* and the *bezeugtes Wort*, a play on words that is not available in English but which means the *begotten Word* and the word that *testifies* to that Word.[11] Revelation, *proprie dicta*, applies only to the Logos of God who became man for our sake; the testifying word of Scripture, then, only bears witness to that Word that has primacy. And just as in the famous Zen koan to the effect that the finger that points to the moon must not be confused with the moon, so too the word of Scripture is not to be identified outright with revelation.[12] But this distinction does more than just short-circuit fundamentalism—it also establishes the central justification for a specifically *theological,* as opposed to a merely historical-critical, interpretation.

Balthasar's argument here is fascinating and we will do well to follow it in detail. First of all, because of that distinction between (begotten) Word and (testifying) word, we see exactly how Jesus "fulfills" the Old Testament and then gives rise to the New Testament. And note again that Balthasar most emphatically does *not* understand that fulfillment in the naïve, precritical fashion of old-school apologetics. According to this precritical school, Moses and the prophets foretold the coming, centuries in advance, of a Messiah to be born in Bethlehem and to suffer and die for the sins of the world.[13]

What historical-critical scholarship has subsequently made clear to all is that the narratives of Jesus' life and death were shaped *by* those same Old Testament passages, which in a stroke removes that style of apologetics. What happened was that the evangelists *retrospectively* shaped their narratives *after* they had felt the full impact of the life, death, and resurrection of Jesus as a total *Gestalt,* or pattern. And then this pattern magnetically shaped, as it were, the disparate "iron filings," that is, assorted Old Testament passages that had never previously been linked before, especially Suffering Servant with Messiah.

But far from opening up a "crisis" of apologetics for theology, historical-critical analyses of the narrative strategy of the evangelists actually tell us how Jesus fulfilled the Old Testament, but only when seen from the dogmatic perspective. Old Testament images, then, are like fragments, or iron filings, which coalesce around their intended center and converge into a form only with the appearance of that Form—Jesus Christ—who is their magnetic attraction, as it were, without whom they have no coherence. But like the "saints" of the Old Testament, the images and roles inherited from this time must remain open and expectant, and do not carry within themselves the ultimate meaning of their referent. They find fulfillment only retroactively. On this basis, Balthasar can then propose three rules by which a theologian may formulate a new *argumentum ex prophetia,* one that will hold up as valid in face of the historical-critical method:

> 1. The individual forms which Israel established in the course of her history converge together upon a point that remains open and that cannot be calculated ahead of time on the basis of their convergence or their mutual relationship, especially since they stand in opposition to one another so often.
>
> 2. The midpoint is occupied in the fullness of time by one who lives this midpoint, although his primary mission is not to construct and conceive of his existence as the fulfillment of the various (and hitherto irreconcilable) individual forms of Israel.
>
> 3. When this midpoint is interpreted subsequently, one sees, in this later stage of reflection, that the midpoint retains its place as midpoint through the crystallization of the periphery around it, and that it is only through this crystallization that the periphery acquires the point of reference that gives it form. (*GL* 6, 403–4)

One of the great tensions that affect any attempt to construct a "theology of the Old Testament" is the conflicting nature of the images that cluster around the vaguely formulated hopes for the future as expressed by the prophets and narrators of the Old Testament, leaving what Gerhard von Rad calls "an extremely odd theological vacuum."[14] No line drawn from one image leads naturally into another but remains hovering in an unpatterned confusion, so that, Balthasar says, "the Messianic idea does not adjoin the idea of the Son of Man, nor does the idea of the Son of Man lead naturally to that of the Suffering Servant, etc." (*GL* 6, 404). But this only becomes obvious and clear *ex post facto*:

> The type of "Isaac's sacrifice" or "Job's night of abandonment by God" or "Elisha's multiplication of bread" or "the Passover Lamb" or the "Suffering Servant," etc., is in each case in the same immediate relationship to the antitype [Christ] as is every other type. This naturally does not mean that the images can be abstracted from their context in salvation history and taken as something existing in themselves. For they bear their meaning only as [part of the] history that has happened between God and Israel, and it is only thus that they form an analogy to the definitive event of Christ. But precisely as types, they stand in a time of promise which is qualitatively different from the time of fulfillment. (*GL* 6, 407–8)[15]

In Christopher Morse's lapidary phrase, "one may say that the personal identity of God as Promisor is 'one and the same' but that the keeping of a promise adds something new to the making of it."[16] And in Christ this is super-eminently true, Balthasar says, for he treats the cluster of Old Testament expectations with a sovereign freedom that fulfills these expectations precisely by going so far beyond them: "It is not his task to compete with the Old Testament images on their own level or even to pile them up to trump them. If his life is to be the breaching of the Old Testament boundary, then the event that is his life can only be, for the world, something obscure, since it is an eschatological event" (*GL* 6, 405).[17]

What, for example, are we to make of that strangely taken-for-granted assertion throughout the New Testament that Christ died and rose from the dead "in accordance with the Scriptures" (1 Cor 15:4 and elsewhere)? Such a statement, which can be found embedded in the earliest strata of the kerygma, would be incomprehensible if the early Christian community had not interpreted the Christ-event first in terms of itself and only then in terms of the preceding scriptural matrix. Such a statement, Balthasar insists, "presupposes, beyond all individual quotations, a total vision of the relationship between Old and New Covenants" (*GL* 6 406). And it is this total vision that is the key to the New Testament understanding of that frequently invoked verbal form "it was necessary that...," "it had to be that..." It is, so to speak (and obviously speaking anachronistically), an "Anselmian" understanding of necessity, that is, an aesthetic one: "The necessity of what *de facto* happened ('Must not the Christ suffer this [kind of death] and thus enter into his glory?' [Lk 24:26]) is unfailingly deduced [by New Testament writers] from the way the formless images take on form" (*GL* 6, 406–7).

First of all, the way that Christ gives form to the unpatterned assemblage of Old Testament images is not a matter that can be adduced from a neutral examination of the evidence: Christ gives form and crystallizes the prior fragments of Old Testament imagery precisely because he stands in a qualitatively different relation to them, as promise to fulfillment, and so as such stands outside of deducible history: "It is, of course, only on the theological level—that is, with the eyes of faith—that it is possible to see this whole relationship in its objective correctness, and not with the eyes of the historian or psychologist of religion who abstracts from faith" (*GL* 6, 408).[18]

As Balthasar beautifully puts it, Jesus "fulfills not only the Word of the Father coming down from heaven, but equally the word stored up for him in history and the tradition of [Old Testament] Scripture" (WST 13). This is, in other words, a case of *distinguer pour réunir,* of distinguishing to reunite. But the same holds true for the distinction between the historical-critical determination of the meaning of a text and a so-called "theological" interpretation of the same text. Far from being a meaning "added on" to the text, a theological interpretation is simply the acknowledgment of Scripture's inspired status. And *that* status is no obscurantist refusal to admit error in the inspired writings (as Balthasar rather tartly, or perhaps amusingly, notes: "Many a book is free from error without thereby being inspired" [WST 21]), but simply an acknowledgment of its theological inexhaustibility:

> The perfect correspondence the Son effects between expression and content does not imply that the content, which is divine and indeed God himself, does not surpass the expression, which is [formulated] in created terms. Christ's divinity cannot be wholly comprehended through his humanity, and no more can the divine sense of Scripture ever be fully plumbed through the letter. It can only be grasped in the setting of faith, that is to say, in a mode of hearing that never issues in final vision, but in a progression without end, a progression ultimately dependent, in its scope, on the Holy Spirit. Faith, the foundation of all our understanding of revelation, expands our created minds by making them participate in the mind of God, disclosing the inward divine meaning of the words through a kind of co-working with God (1 Cor 2:9–16). For this reason it is the saint, the person most open to the working of the Spirit, who arrives at the closest understanding. The saint will not do what the ordinary person, so dominated by original sin, does almost unawares, yet with such desperate persistence: confine the meaning of God's word within human bounds, admitting its truth only to the extent that it corresponds to human forms of thought and ways of life, and content himself with the meaning he has managed to elicit at some time or other, as if it were the final one.... The idea that one has understood a passage of Scripture finally and completely, has drawn out all that God meant in it, is equivalent to denying that it is the word of God and inspired by him.... Inspiration involves a permanent quality, in virtue of which the Holy Spirit as

> *auctor primarius* is always behind the word, always ready to lead to deeper levels of divine truth those who seek to understand his word in the Spirit of the Church, the Spirit she possesses as Bride of Christ (WST 21).

This view actually dovetails very nicely with the best of recent theory in literary criticism, which insists that the meaning of a text is not some hard nugget called the "intent of the original author" waiting to be retrieved by the panning-for-gold skills of our exegetical gold-rushers. On the contrary, meaning always involves a listener as well as a speaker, a reader as well as a writer. As the Reformation scholar at Duke University David Steinmetz puts it so well, "the meaning of historical texts cannot be separated from the complex problem of their reception and the notion that a text means only what its author intended it to mean is historically naive....To attempt to understand those original meanings is the first step in the exegetical process, not the last and final step."[19]

Notes

1. Thomas H. Stahel, "Scripture, the Soul of Theology: An Interview with Joseph A. Fitzmyer, SJ," *America*, May 6, 1995, p. 8–12.
2. *"Exegese und Dogmatik," Communio: Internationale katholische Zeitschrift* 5 (1976): 385–92; the quotation at the end of this paragraph is from p. 386.
3. Whose examples could be multiplied. For example, in the same article, Balthasar openly avers that "exegesis and dogmatic theology need each other." And even when he admits that dogmatic theology has become confused under the intimidations of historical scholarship, he does *not* recommend their divorce; on the contrary, he claims that theology "has been freed by genuine exegesis from many illusory problems and led back to its true object" (392).
4. There are so many citations that one could pull from Balthasar's writings to prove the injustice of the Fitzmyer charge that one must necessarily be arbitrary in citing any one in particular, but let this one suffice: "Let us not overlook at the beginning what a great *enrichment* in understanding of Scripture the modern research has brought us; where only a two-dimensional plane seemed to be at hand before, research has opened to

us at least one other, third dimension. The texts become living in an entirely new manner through the historical limitations and variations appearing in them. They begin to speak in a way in which they could never speak earlier, and they carry on a conversation among themselves which is at least comparable to the ecumenical dialogue." This is from the chapter "The Multitude of Biblical Theologies and the Spirit of Unity in the Church," in Balthasar's *Convergences: To the Source of Christian Mystery*, trans. E. A. Nelson (San Francisco: Ignatius Press, 1983), 77.

5. Friedrich Nietzsche, "On the Uses and Disadvantages of History for Life," *Untimely Meditations*, trans. R. J. Hollingdale (Cambridge: Cambridge University Press, 1983), 95: "Jedem, den man zwingt, nicht mehr unbedingt zu lieben, hat man die Wurzeln seiner Kraft abgeschnitten: er muss verdorren, nämlich unehrlich werden. In solchen Wirkungen ist der Historie die Kunst entgegengesetzt: und nur wenn die Historie es erträgt, zum Kunstwerk umgebildet, also reines Kunstgebilde zu werden, kann sie vielleicht Instincte erhalten oder sogar wecken. Eine solche Geschichtschreibung würde aber durchaus dem analytischen und unkünstlerischen Zuge unserer Zeit widersprechen, ja von ihr als Fälschung empfunden werden" ("Vom Nutzen und Nachteil der Historie für das Leben," *Unzeitgemässe Betrachtungen*, from *Nietzsche Werke: Kritische Gesamtausgabe* III/1, 292). German makes a distinction between *Historie*, the academic discipline, and *Geschichte*, the events of history; although under the influence of Bultmann these two words also distinguish all the thousands of unimportant details that make up the past *(Historie)* from the truly historic—that is, decisive—events of history *(Geschichte)*. Needless to say, not every author writing in German maintains the distinction in every sentence, but Nietzsche is obviously referring to the academic preoccupation (obsession?) with all of the positive facts of history that can be dredged up by professionalized research.
6. Peter Berkowitz, *Nietzsche: The Ethics of an Immoralist* (Cambridge, MA: Harvard University Press, 1995), 29.
7. "Historie aber, die nur zerstört, ohne dass ein innerer Bautrieb sie führt, macht auf die Dauer ihre Werkzeuge blasiert und unnatürlich: denn solche Menschen zerstören Illusionen, und 'wer die Illusion in sich und Anderen zerstört, den straft die Natur als der strengste Tyrann.' Eine gute Zeit lang zwar kann man sich wohl mit der Historie völlig harmlos und unbedachtsam beschäftigen, als ob es eine Beschäftigung so gut wie jede andere wäre; insbesondere scheint die neuere Theologie sich rein aus Harmlosigkeit mit der Geschichte eingelassen zu haben und jetzt noch will sie es kaum merken, dass sie damit, wahrscheinlich sehr wider Willen, im Dieste des Voltaire'schen *écrasez* steht" (*Untimely Meditations*,

p. 292). Of course, Balthasar would not use the word "illusion" in precisely this sense, so the quote cannot quite be taken over wholesale; but at least this quotation points out that Nietzsche's critique of Christianity as an illusion is much more nuanced than Freud's, who tends to fall into the same jejune positivism than animates so much of the historical-critical method. See, above all, Nietzsche's remark that "even we godless anti-metaphysicians still take our fire, too, from the flame lit by a faith thousands of years old, the Christian faith, which was also the faith of Plato: that God is the truth, that truth is divine" (*The Gay Science,* trans. with commentary by Walter Kaufmann [New York: Vintage Books, 1994], section 344).

8. *Poetics,* 1448b, 10–19.
9. Harold Bloom, *The Western Canon: The Books and School of the Ages* (New York: Riverhead Books, 1994), 24. Central to Bloom's thesis here is Shakespeare's innovation of the soliloquy: "We all go around now talking to ourselves endlessly, overhearing what we say, then pondering and acting upon what we have learned. This is not so much the dialogue of the mind with itself, or even a reflection of civil war in the psyche, as it is life's reaction to what literature has necessarily become. Shakespeare...adds to the function of imaginative writing, which was instruction in how to speak to others, the now dominant if more melancholy lesson of poetry: how to speak to ourselves" (46).
10. *Western Canon,* 487. Earlier Bloom says, "The flight from or repression of the aesthetic is endemic in our institutions of what still purport to be higher education. Shakespeare, whose aesthetic supremacy has been confirmed by the universal judgment of four centuries, is now 'historicized' into pragmatic diminishment, precisely because his uncanny aesthetic power is a scandal to any ideologue. The cardinal principle of the current School of Resentment can be stated with singular bluntness: what is called aesthetic value emanates from class struggle. This principle is so broad that it cannot be wholly refuted....Myself the son of a garment worker, I have been granted endless time to read and meditate upon my reading. The institution that sustained me, Yale University, is ineluctably part of an American Establishment, and my sustained meditation upon literature is therefore vulnerable to the most traditional Marxist analyses of class interest. All my passionate proclamations of the isolate selfhood's aesthetic value are necessarily qualified by the reminder that the leisure for meditation must be purchased from the community" (22–23). But that having been granted—and plain honesty compels one to admit such obvious advantages of status and class entailed in being a professor—the aesthetic remains as its own self-explanatory realm. And once more for

Bloom Shakespeare provides only the most obvious test case: "A Marxist or Foucault-inspired historicist can insist endlessly that the production of the aesthetic is a question of historical forces, but production is not in itself the issue here. I cheerfully agree with the motto of Dr. Johnson—"No man but a blockhead ever wrote, except for money"—yet the undeniable economics of literature, from Pindar to the present, do not determine questions of aesthetic supremacy. And the openers-up of the Canon and the traditionalists do not disagree much on where the supremacy is to be found: in Shakespeare. Shakespeare is the secular canon, or even the secular scripture; forerunners and legatees alike are defined by him alone for canonical purposes. This is the dilemma that confronts partisans of resentment: either they must deny Shakespeare's unique eminence (a painful and difficult matter) or they must show why and how history and class struggle produced just those aspects of his plays that have generated his centrality in the Western Canon" (23–24). And later Bloom says, "I am not at all certain what the metaphor of 'social energies' stands or substitutes for, but, like Freudian drives, such energies cannot write or read or indeed do anything at all. Libido is a myth, and so are 'social energies.' Shakespeare, scandalously facile, was an actual person who contrived to write *Hamlet* and *King Lear.* That scandal is unacceptable to what now passes for literary theory" (487). The phrase "historicized into pragmatic diminishment" nicely captures the effect on the churches of this current obsession with life-of-Jesus research—which, *pace* Fitzmyer, is definitely not the same thing as saying historical research into the historical figure of Christ is illegitimate.

11. See *TD* 2, 106–30.
12. "In this distinction we part company with many Protestants. Scripture is not identical with revelation. And although it is truly God's word, it is so only in the mode of testifying to his revelation. Scripture is in fact only the mode of God's self-witness in words, while there are besides other modes of his self-witness" (Balthasar, "The Word, Scripture, and Tradition," *Explorations in Theology,* Vol. 1: *The Word Made Flesh* [San Francisco: Ignatius Press, 1989] 11–26; quotation here, 11).
13. One need only think of Pascal's *Pensées* or of Isaac Newton's retirement from natural philosophy to devote himself entirely to research into the New Testament's fulfillment of the prophecies of the Old Testament (primarily the Book of Daniel). Pascal even goes so far as to say that "Moses [was] the first to teach the Trinity, original sin, the Messiah"! And for Pascal all the later prophets are equally univocal: "If a single man had written a book foretelling the time and manner of Jesus's coming and Jesus had come in conformity with these prophecies, this would carry

infinite weight. But there is much more here. There is a succession of men over a period of 4,000 years, coming consistently and invariably one after the other, to foretell the same coming; there is an entire people proclaiming it" [Blaise Pascal, *Pensées,* tr. A. J. Krailsheimer (Harmondsworth: Penguin, 1966), 126, 129; Brunschvicg #752, 710; cited henceforth by these Brunschvicg numbers, abbreviated B].

14. Gerhard von Rad, *The Message of the Prophets,* trans. D. M. G. Stalker (New York: Harper & Row), 349.
15. Von Rad also considers the case of Jeremiah: "One thing stands out—both the passages in which Jeremiah holds converse with God and those in which he alone is the speaker always shade off into darkness, the impossibility of the prophet's task.... One is haunted by the impression that the darkness keeps growing, and eats ever more deeply into the prophet's soul.... It is a darkness so terrible, it is something so absolutely new in God's dealings with Israel, that it constitutes a menace to very much more than the life of a single man: God's whole way with Israel at this point threatens to end in some kind of metaphysical abyss. For the sufferings concern not just Jeremiah unofficially, as it were, as a private individual, about experiences common to all men. In every instance these confessions grow out of his specific mission as a prophet: what lies behind them is a call to serve in a quite particular way, a relationship of particular intimacy with YHWH, and therefore they have in the highest degree a typical significance for Israel" (Von Rad, *The Message of the Prophets,* 172–74). This clearly illuminates a great deal about the life and mission of Jesus, but it is equally illuminated by *it,* because of the retrospective light thrown on the life of Jeremiah by the nature of Jesus's own trinitarian mission. Except in the light of the cross, it would have been impossible for Von Rad to further write: "If it is only with Jeremiah, and not earlier, that the earthly vessel broke, the reason is primarily that the prophetic office assumed by Jeremiah was far greater in its range and depth than that of any of his predecessors. In proportion, he also required the continuous support of God. At the same time, however much we attempt to place Jeremiah in the correct historical framework of his age, and this is essential, a great deal remains that we cannot explain. It is still Jeremiah's secret how, in the face of growing skepticism about his own office, he was yet able to give an almost superhuman obedience to God and, bearing the immense strains of his calling, was yet able to follow a road which led ultimately to abandonment.... Again, if God brought the life of the most faithful of his ambassadors into so terrible and utterly uncomprehended a night and there to all appearances allowed him to come to utter grief, this remained God's secret" (175).

16. Christopher Morse, *The Logic of Promise in Moltmann's Theology* (Philadelphia: Fortress Press, 1979), 116.
17. Also consider here the words of Von Rad: "The realm of the dead remained an indefinable third party between YHWH and his creation. Apart from isolated questionings, it was not a subject of real interest to faith....Should we not see in this theological vacuum, which Israel zealously kept free from any sacral concepts, as one of the greatest theological enigmas in the Old Testament?" [*Old Testament Theology,* trans. D. M. G. Stalker (New York: Harper & Row, 1965), 350). This is one of the central reasons that Jesus so completely transcends Old Testament expectations and so radically reconstitutes the cluster of Old Testament images into a new pattern of redemption.
18. James Barr introduces a welcome breath of common sense into this discussion when he points out how theological convictions also precede exegesis *de facto*: "The question is not whether we can eventually arrive at theology [through exegesis]: the student begins with theology. Theology is there before exegetical knowledge is there. On the whole, people do not build up theological convictions on the basis of exegetical work already done: on the contrary, they have their theological convictions before they do any serious exegetical work. The theological student proceeds from the general to the particular. He knows the centrality of justification by faith before he begins the study of the Pauline letters. He knows the importance of the Virgin Birth before he studies the evidence in the various Gospels on that subject. He has his view about the historical accuracy of Scripture before he begins to study the differences between Kings and Chronicles. Students do not spend years studying the biblical evidence before they make up their minds whether Paul was right about justification by faith, or whether Jesus was the Son of God in reality. They are sure of the great dogmatic principles before they begin; only because they are sure of these principles do they enter upon the study of theology at all. People's faith is founded upon the general, dogmatic, principles much more than upon the detailed biblical material" (James Barr, "Exegesis as a Theological Discipline Reconsidered and the Shadow of the Jesus of History," in *The Hermeneutical Quest: Essays in Honor of James Luther Mays on His Sixty-Fifth Birthday,* ed. Donald G. Miller [Allison Park, PA: Pickwick Publications], 1986, 11–45; here, 12–13). Such common sense is not just refreshing, but helps liberate this discussion from the impression one often gets from certain professional exegetes that theologians are "trespassing" on their territory. Quite the contrary, as Barr points out: "Thus theological exegesis is not something

produced by an extension from nontheological exegesis, but is a dialectical relation between the text and theology" (19).

19. David C. Steinmetz, "The Superiority of Pre-Critical Exegesis," *The Theological Interpretation of Scripture: Classic and Contemporary Readings*, ed. Stephen E. Fowl (Oxford: Blackwell, 1997), 36.

9

Hans Urs von Balthasar's Theo-Drama: A Contribution to Dramatic Criticism

Ed Block, Jr.

One of the strongest arguments for the relevance to literary criticism of Hans Urs von Balthasar's *Theo-Drama* is stated at the end of the Preface to volume one:

> In the theatre man attempts to a kind of transcendence, endeavoring both to observe and to judge his own truth, in virtue of a transformation—through the dialectic of the concealing-revealing mask—by which he tries to gain clarity about himself. Man himself beckons, invites the approach of a revelation about himself. (*TD* 1, 12)[1]

The focus in this passage is the theater, but the horizon of *Theo-Drama* is nothing less than the whole of drama. His purpose in the *Prolegomena* is "to get a view of the dramatic elements inherent in revelation itself" (*TD* 1, 23). What is needed for the twentieth century, he says (and, of course, even later) is a dramatic theology (*TD* 1, 25–50, 122, 125–31). Balthasar's focus in the *Theo-Drama* is clearly theological. It is his immense culture and erudition, however, which also make this theological work a fruitful source of reflection and application for those interested in the relationship of Christianity and literary criticism.[2] Study of the *Theo-Drama* has the potential to renew dramatic criticism. Though there are untold riches for the literary critic in almost all the volumes, it is particularly with the *Prolegomena* that this essay will be concerned.

To bring into focus the issue of Balthasar's literary critical relevance, I would argue that *Theo-Drama* gives new meaning and force to the claim that drama—perhaps more than other genres—illumines existence through an ecstatic involvement and "surrender" of all participants: author, actors, director, and audience. This ecstatic involvement opens the participants to the meaning of existence, a vision of the transcendent, and an intimation of the Christian mystery. It is likely that Balthasar's ideas about drama originated as early as his 1939 "Afterword" to a translation of Paul Claudel's play, *The Satin Slipper,* and were in fact shaped by reflection on the ecstatic self-surrender of the chief characters in that play. Elaborated within a larger theoretical perspective, many of the ideas in that "Afterword" became central to *Theo-Drama* (see "*Nachwort*").

Balthasar's theoretical reflections and examples in the *Prolegomena* remind us of the cultic origins of drama and the mythological creative matrix out of which artistic—particularly dramatic—language emerges. Balthasar situates his discussion by pointing out the unique form that a revelation of Being takes. Such revelation occurs within the mythological attitude he had discussed in "Revelation and Beauty" (in *Explorations in Theology*), where his subject was not drama *per se* but the larger issue of beauty. There he had commented upon an observation of German poet R. M. Rilke:

> For the beautiful is nothing else than the onset of the terrible, which we only just endure, and we admire it, because it calmly disdains to destroy us." *This* beauty has its own

> proper historical moment, a time when the primitive, simple terror of the numinous begins to weaken, when the stage of philosophical speculation about "the divine," secure and disenchanted, has not yet been reached—the stage when the beautiful is domesticated. (*ET* I, 106)

Locating the original appeal of drama within this mythological moment, *Theo-Drama* keeps the numinous possibility of revelation before us, even as it makes us more attentive to the unique particularities of specific dramatic works.

To demonstrate my claims about the relevance of *Theo-Drama* to literary criticism, I shall first discuss the twin foundations of Balthasar's aesthetics: the analogy of being and a dialogue model of understanding. I shall then briefly outline his theory of drama and some of its salient features. These will include Balthasar's view of the author, actor, director, and audience relation; his conception of horizon, situation, and finitude; and finally his preliminary resolution to the problem of role and mission.

Balthasar's aesthetics, developed in numerous essays and the monumental *Herrlichkeit (The Glory of the Lord)*, assumes a model of understanding founded in the analogy of being and a conception of human understanding as dialogue. In "A Résumé of My Thought," Balthasar articulates his idea of beauty within an overall philosophical perspective.

> I have thus tried to construct a philosophy and a theology starting from an analogy not of an abstract Being, but of Being as it is encountered concretely in its attributes (not categorical, but transcendental). And as the transcendentals run through all Being, they must be interior to each other: that which is truly true is also truly good and beautiful and one. A being *appears*, it has an epiphany: in that it is beautiful and makes us marvel. In appearing it gives

> itself, it delivers itself to us: it is good. And in giving itself up, it *speaks* itself, it unveils itself: it is true. (471, 472)

Encompassed forth in this abstract statement are a number of insights. First, for Balthasar the preeminent case of a being who *"appears"* is Christ. He is the model or prototype of such an appearance. But also implied is the fact that other beings can effect a similar manifestation. Any work of art participates by analogy in this appearance of Being.

In his essay "God Speaks as Man," Balthasar relates the analogy of being specifically to language: "Man's spiritual speech presupposes the speech of nature, and the speech of revelation presupposes for its part the speech of God's creation...which persists through each individual existence and the whole historical course of peoples and cultures" (*ET* I, 84–85). This passage implies that the revelation of Being is reflected in, as it is mediated by, "the speech of nature." Hence a close attention to the revelations that occur in the world will yield not only an awareness of beauty, goodness, and truth, but a sense of their author and origin as well. Language deserves attention because it bears within it a share of those revelations.

Of the way in which the analogy of being applies to drama, Balthasar says simply: "The analogy between God's action and the world drama is no mere metaphor but has an ontological ground" (*TD* 1, 19). *Theo-Drama,* then, thanks to Balthasar's own analogical thinking, assumes a fundamental—though necessarily paradoxical—likeness between the finite world and the incommensurateness of the supernatural. His play with analogies is Balthasar's way of suggesting the nature of aesthetic experience and its analogical relation to revelatory experience. Because of Balthasar's way with analogy, we can reverse the direction of his stated goal for *Theo-Drama:* "to get a view of the dramatic elements inherent in revelation itself" (*TD* 1, 123). That is, we may look to his theodramatic theory in order to find and highlight the revelatory elements in drama.

The second major foundation of Balthasar's *Theo-Drama* is the principle of dialogue. While it is examined at great length in the final chapter of the *Prolegomena* (and will be the focus of my concluding remarks), it is sufficient at this point to refer to two earlier statements of the issue. In *Science, Religion, and Christianity,* Balthasar had claimed with some boldness that "inter-subjectivity is the crux of all philosophy" (38). Elaborating this idea, again in "A Résumé of My Thought," Balthasar asserts:

> Now man exists only in dialogue with his neighbor. The infant is brought to consciousness of himself only by love, by the smile of his mother. In that encounter the horizon of all unlimited being opens itself for him, revealing four things to him: 1) that he is one in love with the mother, even in being other than his mother, therefore all being is one; 2) that that love is good, therefore all being is good; 3) that that love is true, therefore all being is true; 4) that that love evokes joy, therefore all being is beautiful. (470, 471)

Resembling the accounts of the origin of consciousness offered by some recent psycholinguists, this formulation amounts to a summary of Balthasar's fundamental philosophical assumptions, and upon this foundation Balthasar builds his theodramatic aesthetics.

Theo-Drama rests upon the conviction that each dramatic experience is both unique and universal. What Balthasar means by the unique revelation of the work of art is clear in this passage from *Love Alone:* "When one experiences startling beauty (in nature or in art) then phenomena normally veiled are perceived in their uniqueness. What confronts us is overpowering, like a miracle, and only as a miracle can it be understood" (43). In a critical climate which seeks to explain the work of art deterministically, Balthasar defends the unique, unexpected, and yet paradoxically inevitable quality of the work of art. The production of a great play is the epitome of this paradox in that its action and denouement have both the inevitability and the surprise that derive from uniqueness.

In discussing the production and performance of a play, Balthasar quotes Charles Péguy approvingly to the effect that "a play should explode in the year of its birth" (qtd. in *TD* 1, 301).[3] Balthasar is aware of an obvious tension here. How can a play from the past continue to "explode" with a sudden, unique revelation for the many "presents" in which it might be produced? And how does a play, whose duration is longer than a "moment," sustain the experience of revelation? These questions Balthasar seeks to answer as he analyzes how drama is an "illumination of existence" and as he discusses in specific terms the "dramatic elements" which work together to make revelation in the theater possible.

Not a systematic theory of drama like Aristotle's, nor a taxonomy after the fashion of Northrop Frye's *Anatomy of Criticism,* Balthasar's *Theo-Drama* is a rethinking of the tradition of drama in a manner that resembles the thinking of Heidegger.[4] To afford the opportunity to observe, judge, and thereby achieve a kind of revelation about self and existence, *Theo-Drama* considers the central questions which drama asks or raises: Who Am I? What is my role in life? What meaning or ultimate significance do my actions have? Though other genres of literature also raise these questions, Balthasar argues that it is preeminently in drama that such questions have their maximum force. Put into the mouths of characters who acquire a life of their own, the questions have the power to challenge accepted ways of thinking and open up horizons that stretch to the infinite. In this fashion, drama, as "the dialectic of the concealing-revealing mask," invites revelation. Insofar as we may care to define it, Balthasar's theory of drama is mimetic, but not naively so. It is more in the fashion of Peter Szondi's *Theory of the Modern Drama,* whose debt to Heideggerian thought is as apparent as Balthasar's own. Balthasar's theory is more flexible than Szondi's rather narrow semiotic approach, however, in that it reserves an important place for revelatory transformation. Action, rather than mere perception, is the goal of drama (*TD* 1, 66).[5] Balthasar's theory of drama is also, however, deeply aware of the half-revealing, half-concealing quality of any aesthetic experience. Revelation requires receptivity and is never guaranteed. It also arises from concrete experiences. We see Balthasar's awareness of these qualities as early as the aphorisms of *The Grain of Wheat* (*Das Weizenkorn*). Their insights about the paradoxical nature of understanding and revelation ring with a maturity which anticipates his later work: "One can behold all things in a dual fashion: as fact and as mystery," he says (*G* 30). For Balthasar, to behold things as mere facts leads to the alienation of modern life. "Only one who has a sense for symbolism has entree to the world of the Gospel, whose instruction is always concrete" (*G* 31). To understand the revelation of drama, as of scripture, requires a "sense for symbolism."

Although Balthasar finds "a real analogy between revelation and the beautiful, both the natural revelation of mythology and the supernatural revelation" (*G* 106), he is careful to distinguish drama from religious cult. From its cultic origins, however, drama retains the element of mystery. The space of drama is "the dangerous borderline where magic and revelation cannot be told apart" (*TD* 1, 260). But this borderline situation has a familiar dialogical structure that prevails in drama to this day.[6] "By the time of Aeschylus the dancing area for the mimic chorus and the special raised stage for the divine epiphanies were separated from one another. Yet the two belong to each other like question (or provocation) and answer" (*TD* 1, 260). Greek drama was a place for revelations, a place where the divine and the human worlds confronted one another. But there is a further danger here:

> There is a certain hubris involved in showing the point of encounter between the human question and the divine answer in an event performed by human beings. This hubris will always be there in the background in all theatrical performance, awakening in the spectator a tense

> expectation that he will learn something revealing about the mystery of life. (*TD* 1, 260)[7]

Like the audiences of ancient Athens, Balthasar reminds us, theatergoers today continue to expect some "revelation," some "solution" to the problems of existence. In mythological ages, human beings speculated about and invented structures for encountering the transcendent. As Balthasar's observations on the cultic origins of drama show, the history of drama is a rich and complex record of those efforts, speculations, and structures.

One of Balthasar's major contributions to a renewed understanding of drama is his integrated conception of what author, actor, director, and audience contribute to "the phenomenon of theatre." Surveying what he calls the "three elements of dramatic creativity" (author, actor, and director), his rereading of the tradition yields insights into the relationship, tensions, and significance of these three necessary components of drama. Though he only hints at the connection, the relation of the author, actor, and director is also—for Balthasar—an analogy of the trinitarian relation among God the Father, Jesus Christ, and the Holy Spirit.

It is the paradoxical nature of self-giving (or *Hingabe*) which is the key to what each creative element contributes to the realization of the play, just as it is, according to Balthasar, a key to understanding what theologians call the "divine procession" in the Trinity. Each important contributor to the play's realization succeeds best by abandoning self and entering into an appropriate role. The result in each case can be an experience of transformative "ecstasy," which opens a new horizon of being. For Balthasar, of course, such self-transcendence recognizes at least implicitly the horizon of the infinite. In answer to critics who see in the term "ecstasy" a Romantic category of emotion—perhaps derived from Balthasar's favorite German authors of the early twentieth century, Balthasar would probably respond:

yes, there is emotion involved, but it is also a phenomenological category with ontological implications.[8]

In rather traditional fashion Balthasar first conceives of the author as a "distinct authority," one who "guarantees the transmission of an inherited myth" (*TD* 1, 261). "The standpoint of the 'author'," he says, "is entirely filled up by the creative activity of a unificatory endeavor that sheds light on existence" (*TD* 1, 262). Later Balthasar quotes Julien Green to the effect that the poet "is God the Father as far as his characters are concerned" (qtd. in *TD* 1, 268). But the author cedes this authority or responsibility. Balthasar quotes with approval Gabriel Marcel: "'There is no dramatic creation without a certain self-alienation on the part of the author for the benefit of the beings to whom he gives life'" (qtd. in *TD* 1, 271). In contrast to critics who proclaim the "death of the author," Balthasar acknowledges the artist's creative uniqueness.[9] He thus stands in the much longer line of critics for whom the author is an important but scarcely divine *terminus a quo* for the work of art. It is also true, however, that Balthasar is aware of the forces that can limit and even distort that creativity.

Perhaps in part because of his having grown up in the twilight of turn-of-the-century German and Austrian culture, Balthasar is fascinated by the actor's role. The following quotation from Georg Simmel reflects Balthasar's sense of the analogy between the actor and the ordinary human being.

> There is a primal histrionic attitude, [namely] playing a part, not hypocritically or to deceive, but by pouring one's own personal life into an [external] form of utterance that is somehow given and pre-existing. This is one of the constitutive functions of our life as it is....Man is meant to live out and represent a reality that is set before [him]; a reality that is different from the self-development he pursues by his own efforts; he does not simply abandon his own

> self, however; he fills this other reality with his own being...(qtd. in *TD* 1, 291).

By pouring "one's own personal life into an [external] form of utterance," the actor or actress is responsible for giving life to the characters created by the author. But "the 'truth' of what is represented," Balthasar says, "can be defined neither as reality (the actor is not really Hamlet) nor as illusion (which presupposes a reality), but a genuine making-present" (*TD* 1, 281).

Quoting Simmel further, Balthasar argues that "the actor's contribution makes the mystery of the theatre a mystery of real presence even before it is a mystery of transformation" (qtd. in *TD* 1, 281). The real presence which the actors bring about is at once a key to the drama's unique effect and an analogy of the eucharistic action. The actor is a mediator (*TD* 1, 285); he "puts himself and all the powers of his soul, including his emotions, at the service of the work of art, at the service of the part he is to play" (*TD* 1, 287). The actor willingly transforms himself, reflecting the fundamental movement that takes place in drama at every level. Balthasar reveals his Jesuit training by employing the Ignatian term *disponibilité* to describe the "total mobilization" of self that is required of the actor (*TD* 1 288). Putting themselves "at the disposal" of the author's work, actors and actresses achieve a self-giving that is simultaneously a fulfillment.

The director, too, mediates the other two creative elements of the drama. "Between the dramatic poet and the actor there yawns a gulf that can be bridged only by a third party who will take responsibility for the play's performance" (*TD* 1, 299). Balthasar acknowledges the potential for the director to usurp the place of actors and author (*TD* 1, 300), but he reaffirms that "the drama is itself a making-present....[I]t speaks (and must speak for today). The producer's or director's concern is to secure this actuality" (*TD* 1, 302). In this fashion Balthasar underlines in a different way the importance of fusing the horizons of past and present.[10] In highlighting the work of Luigi Pirandello and

Thornton Wilder as that work makes explicit the role of the director or stage manager, Balthasar acknowledges the importance of these dramatists' contribution to the growth of drama theory and practice.

In discussing audience, Balthasar manifests yet again the dialectical structure underlying his thinking. Just as author, actor, and director are related by a series of tensions, so actors and audience are similarly related. Referring to the mysterious revelation which the audience comes to the play expecting, Balthasar observes, "For its part the audience also looks for the manifestation of this something else *through* the actor....Audience and actors are not complementary and self-sufficient halves; both of them remain open, expecting some third thing that is to come about in and through both the players and the audience" (*TD* 1, 307). Balthasar then goes on to describe the result of this dialectical relationship as the opening of horizons: "The limitations of both of them [actors and audience] open on to an unlimited horizon. Here, according to Hölderlin, if the poet's word achieves incarnation, the myth can rise again as the word of God, which takes place bodily in the face of the watching crowd" (*TD* 1, 307–8).

Balthasar's analysis has the potential to renew a theater overgrown by problems that Alastair Fowler has rather succinctly described: "The literary development of drama...has been distorted by financial dearth, by lack of adequate theatres, by loss of dependable audiences, by the ephemeral influence of television and by the follies of directors' theatre."[11] From a brief sketch of the author-director-actor-audience-relation in Balthasar, it should be possible to see how his reconceiving these roles restores a balance in the relations between drama and theater and the constituent parts of each. Focusing on the questions that drama raises as well as the cooperative efforts of author, director, and actors to "make present," Balthasar returns theater and the dramatic to its sources in mystery. In modern playwrights like Claudel, Brecht, and Wilder he finds such mystery.

Another insight that derives from a careful reading of *Theo-Drama* concerns the concept of horizon. For Balthasar horizon refers to the limits or dimensions within which we see and understand other human beings, historical events, works of art, and life itself (*TD* 1, 314–23). What he refers to as the "horizontal" coordinate is the finite horizon of human knowing: history and the unfolding of events as if in narrative time. The vertical coordinate is the horizon of transcendence. We might suggest its force by recalling the meaning of the old expression *sub specie aeternitatis*. At the very least the vertical coordinate means referring the particular drama's questions and the whole dramatic event to a horizon of meaning that extends not only back in time but through the present and into an ultimately indeterminable future. The vertical dimension allows us to see drama as asking questions and intimating answers that bear upon the transcendent, the spiritual, the religious.

While for Balthasar the vertical horizon is ultimately theological, he suggests that drama provides an analogous sense of this horizon even when it is not explicitly religious. Whenever a play dramatizes the opposition of competing temporal, moral, or other demands, it opens up an indeterminate space, a horizon which suggests the infinite. In the final analysis, according to Balthasar, these meanings imply and therefore relate the play to the divine. It is by participating in and realizing this horizon that the audience is able "to see and to judge" that aspect of existence illuminated by the play. Such receptivity on the part of the audience is not something that Balthasar is prescribing, but something that is almost self-evident in the very experience of the theater. This disposition is to be distinguished from, even as it comprehends, Brecht's famed "alienation effects." In *The Measures Taken*, even Brecht poses a question that opens a space for the infinite (*TD* 1, 83–84).

Balthasar's analysis of horizon includes a striking revision of Aristotle's concept of catharsis (*TD* 1, 315). He achieves this by taking to task Gotthold Ephraim Lessing, an eighteenth-century German exponent of Aristotle. Rather than relying on the hackneyed terms *pity* and *fear* that Lessing employed (and which subsequent critics have for the most part uncritically adopted), Balthasar refers to catharsis as part of the audience's way of being "struck" by the work. "The spectator, who has a general willingness to be impressed by the fate of the stage characters, is suddenly seized at a deeper level than he expected; he is no longer in charge of his own participation; he himself is called into question by his experience of the play" (*TD* 1, 314–15). It is here, in the lived experience of drama, that the term "ecstasy" applies.

In a brief survey that relates Greek tragedy and Renaissance tragedy derived from Seneca, Balthasar distinguishes the dual horizon of classical drama from the high drama of the baroque. Like the "opaque" borderline between men and gods that exists in classical drama (*TD* 1, 317), the line between fate and providence remains to complicate the horizon of Renaissance Christian drama. "Christian drama," Balthasar observes, "sets forth a horizon that, in virtue of its clarified idea of God, has a more unified effect than that of the ancient world, but at the same time its infinitely deepened dramatic context (embracing man and God) is patient of hidden and diverse interpretation" (*TD* 1, 319). As a result of this change in horizon, Balthasar claims: "All post-Christian drama can be regarded as a fragment of the drama that presses toward the Christian horizon" (*TD* 1, 321). "Everything, in the end, must be regarded as a Christian fragment—perhaps hardly recognizable—that calls for the transformation of the hearts of individuals and of society and its conditions and structures" (*TD* 1, 322). That such transformations are projected into the future (especially by Marxist or other utopian forms of drama) does not invalidate Balthasar's claim for the presence of a "Christian" horizon. Nor does the dramatist's refusal to project such an explicit horizon. Balthasar refers to Brecht's and Beckett's last plays, observing that even "where there is no way out, there is still a horizon, emitting something like a light of meaning" (*TD* 1 322). Insofar as the play leaves open a space of freedom, where an alternative destiny can be imagined, that play, says Balthasar, partakes of a Christian perspective on the future. Throughout *Theo-Drama* Balthasar makes clear that he does not imagine the likelihood of post-Christian drama generally or regularly making explicit reference to a religious horizon. Curiously enough, however, a number of contemporary playwrights—like Peter Shaffer, Brian Friel, and Tony Kushner—do raise this issue explicitly.

Related to Balthasar's discussion of horizon is a consideration of finitude, which for him includes the time of the action, the situation, and the theme of death. With references that range from Ernst Mach to Paul Valéry and Peter Szondi, he reconceives Aristotelian notions of dramatic time in a phenomenological fashion. Balthasar quotes Valéry on the infinite effect of a finite action and how the artist is "double," inasmuch as he works with limited means for a universal impact. The incompleteness of even the most carefully worked out dramatic structure argues, for Balthasar, a sense of infinite wholeness behind or beyond it. "Drama, with its horizontal-temporal restriction that calls for the action to be meaningfully brought to a conclusion within it, provides a metaphor of the dimension of meaning in all human finitude, and hence it also allows us to discern a (vertical) aspect of infinity" (*TD* 1, 345).

Balthasar reconceives dramatic situation in terms of freedom and vocation. Dramatic situation, he maintains, "is essentially determined by antinomies between different persons and their free decisions, made on the basis of how they see their world and their individual vocations" (*TD* 1, 357). While the idea of "antinomies" does not advance much upon existing theories of what constitutes a dramatic situation, Balthasar's stress on the reality of human freedom deepens the significance of situations. Even more importantly, the idea of vocation incorporates a new sense of teleology. Present in most drama through the baroque, such a sense of personal call has been partially or wholly lost in the modern and certainly in the postmodern era. Hitting upon a weakness that others have recognized in postmodern drama.[12] Balthasar recalls us to an issue which, if taken seriously again, could help further rejuvenate contemporary drama.

To understand the power and potential of this dynamic relating of person and vocation, it is necessary to elaborate a bit on Balthasar's understanding of personhood and how it comes about. In his 1971 reflection "Why I am Still a Christian" [which was his half of a book co-authored with Karl Rahner, titled *Two Say Why*], Balthasar returns to the theme of how human love reflects divine love, which we saw earlier in *Love Alone.* He observes that "*genuine love between persons* is probably more rare than one thinks," and then goes on to observe that "the brilliance of the loving choice from the regions of the divine raises the individual, lost in the anonymity of the species, to the uniqueness of a person" (WC 22). Reference to "regions of the divine" is another allusion to how the "vertical dimension" reveals itself in everyday life. The examples which Balthasar cites are significant: Dante and Beatrice, Hölderlin and Diotima, and the chief characters of Paul Claudel's play *The Satin Slipper.* What unites all these instances of "genuine love between persons" is precisely the sense of vocation and mission that results from each person's response to "the brilliance of loving choice." In drama, mission and vocation express themselves concretely in the dramatic situation.

Giving examples of the way in which situations can be developed, Balthasar also intimates the presence of a vertical perspective within which the contradictory structures might be resolved (*TD* 1, 358). Whether being prey to external forces is seen in pagan or Christian terms, Balthasar says, "it [a particular situation] only becomes dramatic when it is dialectically opposed to the possibility of liberation" (*TD* 1, 360). He concludes the discussion of situation by reaffirming the essential tension between external forces and individual freedom, played out in a relation of horizontal and vertical dimensions that does not foreclose the possibility of ultimate mystery.

> While the two aspects of the vertical that codetermine the dramatic situation are most definitely incarnated in the given horizontal conditions (those that prevail between

> human beings and within the individual's soul), they are not completely identical with them. Only thus can human destiny, even the most tragic, avoid seeming completely meaningless and therefore of no interest. Even the *homme revolté* only has meaning if there is a hidden, elusive authority against which he is in revolt. (*TD* 1, 361)

As his numerous examples from such postmodern dramatists as Beckett, Ionesco, Dürrenmatt, and Brecht indicate, Balthasar does not make his claim for a vertical dimension without an awareness of actual postmodern dramatic practice.

A particular case of the horizontal vs. the vertical relation plays itself out to some degree whenever personal desires conflict with some larger good. A person's choices to implement the good take the form of either self-assertion or doing good for "a larger and more significant world" (*TD* 1, 415). Self-assertion remains in tension with self-transcendence; justice with freedom. A survey of examples culminates with Camus' *L' État de siège,* in which one man, Diego, gives his life to overcome tyranny, but whose death, the audience realizes, is ultimately in vain. Balthasar's analysis leads to a realization that "the vault of heaven is present, overarching, in many plays of the modern period, but it is an obscured, distorted, ultimately powerless, annihilated heaven, misinterpreted as man's demonic antagonist" (*TD* 1, 422–23). Meditating on tragedy in the modern period, Balthasar closes with a quote from Jean-Marie Domenach: "Having done so much killing, people wonder what is the point of it....Then tragedy can reemerge. I think we have reached the edge of this new era" (qtd. in *TD* 1, 435).

The final section of the *Prolegomena* returns to the relation between self and role, and by examining models that purport to deal with the question "Who am I?" provides a preliminary resolution to the problem of finite and infinite freedom, mission and role. After examining competing theories of human limitation and alienation, Balthasar explains the dialogic principle and the seminal thinkers on this subject who—it becomes clear—have had a profound and thoroughgoing influence on Balthasar's thought.

Balthasar's reflection on the relation of self and role includes a masterful, brief analysis of psychological theories beginning with Freud's. Balthasar shows that the chief weakness of Freud's deterministic theory is that for the psyche, as Freud conceives of it, there are only objects; there is no Other. The ego is "not a primary phenomenon," and its activity is negligible. Balthasar quotes from Freud's *Collected Works*: "What we call ego is essentially passive in our life; we ourselves are, in fact, 'lived' by powers we do not know and cannot control" (Vol. XIII, 251; qtd. in *TD* 1, 511). Balthasar's analysis presents Freud's theory as a bleak picture of "the suffering human being" (*TD* 1, 512), and in ignoring what some might call its tragic dimension, Balthasar suggests that Freud's theory is in fact a distortion of the Christian mystery: human suffering, but without atonement and redemption. Neither Jung nor Adler fares very well either. Jung's individuation does not make the individual person an autonomous agent but instead, as the etymology of "person" hints, a "mask" for a larger collectivity. Balthasar's slight preference for Adler's thought is based upon the fact that Adler emphasizes action and acceptance of limitation.

In a final sympathetic appropriation, Balthasar examines a typical sociological analysis of role only to find it a place of imprisonment for the person. Balthasar finds confirmation for his view in P. L. Berger's comparison of social roles to puppet theater (*Invitation to Sociology* 140; qtd. in *TD* 1, 543). Concluding that limitation is part of human existence but that acceptance of limitation cannot be the sole end, Balthasar asks whether in the secular world of action, the individual person remains inevitably alienated (*TD* 1, 544).

Balthasar carefully traces alienation from Neoplatonism through Eckhart and Nicholas of Cusa, to Fichte, Schelling, and Hegel. He concludes with the paradox:

> None of the idealists are engaged in a flight from the world: on the contrary, they seek to penetrate and master it (and no more consistent and titanic plans have ever been put forward). The end result is all the more remarkable, namely, the—almost inadvertent—loss of the individual as person. (*TD* 1, 559)

Balthasar's analysis of freedom in Fichte leads back to personal responsibility and the shaping of self through its relationships with others, but despite glimmers of freedom in earlier Romantic thinking, even Hegel's discussion of freedom can only resolve the individual's role into a self-sacrifice of autonomy and freedom (*TD* 1, 588). Rejecting Hegel, then, Balthasar turns from the "aporia of roles" to a creative rethinking of the potential of drama found in the concept of dialogue.[13]

Balthasar's analysis of the alienated self raises a number of issues relevant to understanding drama. First, the tension between self and role is a strong one, involving psychological and sociological levels that theorists have not resolved. One way to conceive of drama's challenge is to say that it poses these tensions in a variety of concrete ways, each time questioning apparently rigid distinctions between self and society, role and inner freedom. Second, his analysis of alienation shows that even Balthasar himself has not escaped the effects of Romantic and later nineteenth-century philosophy.

Balthasar begins the final major subsection of "Transition: From Role to Mission" by pointing out how

> the previous two attempts to answer the question "Who am I?" [by way of Limitation and Alienation] have failed because in each case the personal "I" has had to surrender itself to some all-embracing life or essence, and no necessary connection has been demonstrated between the life/essence and this particular "I." (*TD* 1, 591)

Balthasar then examines four positive attempts to resolve the dichotomy: two pre-Christian and two post-Christian. First, the figure of the king, in primitive culture often believed to be part-god, shares the essence of the god but is a mediator between gods and human beings (*TD* 1, 591). Second, the genius (deriving from the primitive idea of an attendant *daimon*) individualizes self, "placing him above and beyond identifiable categories" (*TD* 1, 604). Neither of these two pre-Christian ideas, Balthasar points out, is sustainable today. He then proposes Simmel's "individual law" as a third, post-Christian response to the problem of self and role.[14] Opposed to the universal humanity of Kant and the Enlightenment, Simmel finds in Schleiermacher an emphasis on the individual's ethical responsibility for shaping common humanity into "an entirely individual form" (*TD* 1, 608). But Balthasar notes that "even great, normative individuality cannot escape the contradiction at the heart of the phenomenon of life" (*TD* 1, 617).

This irreconcilable contradiction leads Simmel to propose that "[f]or men of the more profound sort there is only one way of coping with life, namely, with a certain degree of superficiality" (qtd. in *TD* 1, 617). This position sounds like a version of similar "aesthetic" stances assumed by authors and aesthetes in the late nineteenth century. It also recalls a character in *Der Schwierige,* a comedy by one of Balthasar's favorite dramatists, Hugo von Hofmannsthal. The title character, Hans Karl Bühl, maintains his uniqueness only by acting unconventionally while, simultaneously, assuming the most conventional of roles. The lesson of Hans Karl: in a world where every moment can call forth a different, even contradictory aspect of individuality or uniqueness, it is necessary to live something of a double life. For life to be possible at all, the individual must remain aloof and almost detached from the multiplicity that manifests itself around *and within* himself.

Balthasar's reflection on Simmel and the contradictory multiplicity of selves anticipates recent theorists who celebrate a "loss of the subject." Though Balthasar claims that "Simmel is working toward an affirmation that will embrace the whole of everyday life, with its divine and non-divine aspects, in a single, religious attitude" (*TD* 1, 619), he also admits that Simmel's position is tragic through and through (*TD* 1, 625). The same can be said of those who proclaim the loss of the subject.

Rejecting Simmel's solution, Balthasar turns to the origins of and chief figures in the development of the fourth positive attempt, what he terms "the dialogic principle." Beginning with what Martin Buber meant, Balthasar explains his own use of the concept. He quotes Buber approvingly: "It is the creature who must learn, through the 'I-thou' relationship and 'through the grace of its comings and the pain of its departures', to practice the presence of God" (*TD* 1, 636). From Balthasar's understanding of Buber, too, comes Balthasar's discovering the identity of vocation and mission (*TD* 1, 636). Touching briefly on Franz Rozenzweig's biblical understanding of dialogue, Balthasar examines the thought of Ferdinand Ebner, whose view of the Fall, language, Godforsakenness, and the scandal of the cross (*TD* 1, 642) are fundamental to Balthasar's own conception of theodrama.

For Ebner, Balthasar says, "everything [in the dialogic principle] has its roots in the God-relationship and its solitariness, in a fundamental faith that becomes a full faith only when confronted with Christ's cry of dereliction and that, originating in God and Christ, makes Christian love of neighbor possible" (*TD* 1, 642). Balthasar's assertion in *Science, Religion, and Christianity*, that the modern human being cannot come to God except within community (74–76), achieves its fullness in Balthasar's interpretation of the human need to avoid what Ebner calls "ego loneliness" by seeking "the Kingdom of God among us" (*TD* 1, 643). As Balthasar concludes this final section, it is easy to see how his concern for the particularity of the individual human in relation to God's call can be traced back to the "facticity" of the individual person (*TD* 1, 636) with which all the thinkers involved in the development of the dialogic principle began.

Balthasar's concluding remarks in the *Prolegomena* help turn our attention to what practical critical considerations follow from his theodramatic theory. Reminding readers of how the incarnation and "the processio within the godhead" (*TD* 1, 646) provide a paradigm for the relationship between God's call and the human being's response, Balthasar observes: "It follows quite naturally that if, obedient to his mission, a person goes out into a world that is not only ungodly but hostile to God, he will be led to the experience of Godforsakenness" (*TD* 1, 647). This will also result in passion, in death (*TD* 1, 647). Trying to practice the presence of God, but aware of God's veiled presence in the material world that has resulted from the advance of human consciousness (*SRC* 72–74), we experience in our "departures" into that world the alienation and apparent destruction that are part of our destiny and tragedy.

Implicit in this survey of the *Prolegomena* are a number of potential categories for judging drama. If, with Balthasar, we have reconceived drama as an integrated structure, or texture, of self-giving, of individuals transcending self to inhabit or inform a role given or a mission conferred, it is easier to recognize those qualities in the structures, themes, and characters of specific plays. And what applies to drama may also, with modifications, apply to other forms of narrative as well. Balthasar's theodramatic theory helps identify and judge plays and their effectiveness. Though his theodramatic thinking has almost nothing to say explicitly about comedy, he does offer much for the criticism of serious drama. The stakes, the challenges, the opportunities for sacrifice and for suffering dispossession emerge as ways one better realizes one's role in life, or accomplishes one's mission. Dramatic experiences which make us realize these opportunities or confront us with these challenges are better than those which do not.

Balthasar's *Theo-Drama* belongs to what Paul Ricoeur refers to as a hermeneutics of hope. With its emphasis on receptivity and responsiveness, it yields priority to the work. But such a hermeneutics also requires what George Steiner calls the audience's "answerability" to the claim that originates in the aesthetic experience. Having reconceived the nature of drama in the light of not only its varied history but its relevance to the lived experience of belief, Balthasar is more inclined to emphasize the audience's anticipations of revelation than limitations, frustrations, and irreconcilable contradictions. For this reason critics will have to test the insights of Balthasar's *Theo-Drama*, applying them to a variety of dramatic works. Besides examples from the classical repertoire, Balthasar has illustrated his ideas using the dramas of Brecht, Dürrenmatt, and a number of more recent playwrights. For the beginning of the twenty-first century, however, it will be the job of critics to extend Balthasar's applicability, finding in both classical and more recent—even non-Western—dramas the evidence that Balthasar's thought illumines even these dramatic works.

By way of summary we might say that Balthasar's aesthetic of the drama focuses attention once again on the unique texture of individual dramatic experiences. At the same time, however, his comprehensive view—that all finite experience (including the production, performance, and reception of particular plays) mirrors the drama of God's love—has the potential to provide order and direction to dramatic criticism. It proposes priorities and criteria for classifying and judging not only individual works but the cultures in which artists produce such works, and the historical periods in which they were produced. Not a Hegelian theory of progress, but a dynamic theory that acknowledges differences and distinctions in quality, Balthasar's is a flexible *and* coherent tool of analysis. The baroque world and its theater (including Shakespeare) had a clearer sense than the contemporary world and its theater have of how (via the "world stage" metaphor) human drama reflects the drama of salvation. Romantic and idealist drama was particularly aware of the tension between identity and role and the tension between freedom and necessity. Twentieth-century drama, for its part, has a more explicit sense of limits and horizons, and the "absolute" nature of the oppositions with which human beings are faced. In postmodern drama, particularly, the virtual absence of a transcendent dimension to life challenges authors, actors, directors, and especially audiences to probe the meaning of such experiences, seeking the ways in which divine involvement is nevertheless operative in the unique particularities of everyday life.

Even when undermined by the hegemony of "entertainment," the tyranny of the directors, the desire for profit, or the evils of a "star" system, plays produced and attended continue to pose questions, offer a variety of solutions, and define attitudes with which to face the problems of existence. Drama in the theater continues to engage audiences and provide them with revelations which, to the believer, suggest by analogy the mystery of God's engagement with the world, incarnated in the obedient love and sacrificial death of his Son.

Balthasar's aesthetic is neither apocalyptic nor utopian. Unlike the endlessly recursive exercises of postmodern criticism, it acknowledges a purpose and a goal. We do not repeat with the implicit frustration of the postmodernist who finds only the same—or different—forms of disillusionment, aporia, and betrayal. Rather, enriched by Balthasar's thought, the experience of drama becomes a process of recognition from which we may derive clearer insight and a deeper recognition and acceptance of mystery in the world. Balthasar's aesthetic *is* an aesthetic of hope. It comprehends disillusionment, betrayal, *and* abandonment. To many it may appear to be a hope that is lean and spare, a hope akin to that experienced by the oppressed but faithful poor, but it *is* hope and not despair.

Notes

1. Originally published in German as *Theodramatik*, the five-volume work has now appeared in English under the title *Theo-Drama*. Since part of my purpose in this essay is to demonstrate the richness of Balthasar's work, I shall quote rather extensively. Unless otherwise noted, translations are those by Graham Harrison currently available from Ignatius Press.
2. Chapter 9 of Louis Roberts' *The Theological Aesthetics of Hans Urs von Balthasar* provides a somewhat different kind of summary than the one I present in this essay. For those interested in the *Theodramatik*, I recommend this work. Also relevant is Peter Henrici's "Hans Urs von Balthasar: A Sketch of his Life," in Schindler.

3. Gilbert Keith Chesterton implies the same thing in his discussion of the performance of Shakespearean drama. See his "Realism in Art," in *Chesterton on Shakespeare* (Chester Springs, PA: Dufour Editions, 1971), p. 82.
4. Balthasar's understanding of Heidegger should be clear from a reading of the *Theo-Drama,* but if my oblique references should not satisfy the reader, see *The Glory of God* V.
5. The relevant quotation is: "Both tragedy and the Passion have the same basic nature; they are act. Reality is action, not theory." This recalls the fundamental position of another philosopher-theologian, John Henry Newman, in his "Tamworth Reading Room" letters.
6. Peter Szondi, *Theory of the Modern Drama: A Critical Edition,* ed. and trans. by Michael Hays, Theory and History of Literature Volume 29 (Minneapolis: University of Minnesota Press, 1987), 7, 8.
7. Dr. Joseph Schwartz observes that, according to Chesterton, the biblical book of *Job* was probably performed as a drama before it was written down as a poem.
8. For two other thinkers who similarly reject a dualistic conception of this experience, see John Macmurray, *Religion, Art, and Science,* and Abraham Maslow, *Toward a Psychology of Being.*
9. Patrick Sherry describes the effect of artistic inspiration in a way which, applied to the artist's being inspired, illuminates Balthasar's thinking. See Sherry's *Spirit and Beauty: An Introduction to Theological Aesthetics* (Oxford: Clarendon, 1992, p. 132.
10. This idea of Hans-Georg Gadamer's is given explicit illustration by Balthasar's analysis; see Gadamer's *Truth and Method* (New York: Continuum, 1991) pp. 302–7.
11. Alistair Fowler, *A History of English Literature* (Cambridge, MA: Harvard University Press, 1987), 375.
12. Szondi, *Theory of Modern Drama,* 54.
13. Balthasar finds himself in good company as Szondi and Manfred Pfister both emphasize the creative, almost revolutionary transformation that our understanding of drama undergoes when the concept of dialogue is thus plumbed. See Szondi, *Theory of the Modern Drama,* pp. 6–10; and Pfister, *The Theory and Analysis of Drama.* European Studies in English Literature (Cambridge: Cambridge University Press, 1988), esp. 3.6, 4.5, and 4.6.
14. Simmel is a philosopher whose philosophical mind and roots in the Viennese background of Stefan George make him particularly attractive to Balthasar.

Combined Works Cited

Balthasar, Hans Urs von. *Apokalypse der deutschen Seele.* Salzburg: A. Pustet, 1937–39.

———. *The von Balthasar Reader.* Eds. Medard Kehl, SJ, and Werner Löser, SJ. Trans. Robert J. Daly and Fred Lawrence. New York: Crossroads, 1985.

———. "Current Trends in Catholic Theology and the Responsibility of the Christian." *Communio: International Catholic Review* 5 (1978): 77–85.

———. *Das Ganze im Fragment: Aspekte der Geschichtstheologie.* Einsiedeln: Benziger, 1963. *A Theological Anthropology.* New York: Sheed & Ward, 1967.

———. *Epilog.* Einsiedeln-Trier: Johannes Verlag, 1987.

———. *"Exegese und Dogmatik." Communio: Internationale katholische Zeitschrift* 5 (1976): 385–92.

———. *Explorations in Theology.* Vol. I, *Word Made Flesh.* Trans. A. V. Littledale and Alexander Dru. San Francisco: Ignatius Press, 1989.

———. Explorations in Theology. Vol. III, *Creator Spirit.* Trans. Brian McNeil, CRV. San Francisco: Ignatius Press, 1989, 1993.

———. *Gelebte Kirche: Bernanos.* 3rd ed. Einsiedeln: Johannes Verlag, 1988.

———. *The Glory of the Lord: A Theological Aesthetics.* 7 vols. Edinburgh: T & T Clark; San Francisco: Ignatius Press.

1. *Seeing the Form.* Trans. Erasmo Leiv`a-Merikaki, 1982.
2. *Clerical Styles.* Trans. Andrew Louth, Francis McDonagh, and Brian McNeil, CRV, 1984.

3. *Lay Styles.* Trans. Andrew Louth, John Saward, Martin Simon, and Rowan Williams, 1986.
4. *The Realm of Metaphysics in Antiquity.* Trans. Brian McNeil, CRV, Andrew Louth, John Saward, Rowan Williams, and Oliver Davies, 1989.
5. *The Realm of Metaphysics in the Modern Age.* Trans. Oliver Davies, Andrew Louth, Brian McNeil, CRV, John Saward, and Rowan Williams, 1991.
6. *Theology: The Old Covenant.* Trans. Brian McNeil, CRV, and Erasmo Leiv`a Merikakis, 1991.
7. 7. *Theology: The New Covenant.* Trans. Brian McNeil, CRV, 1989

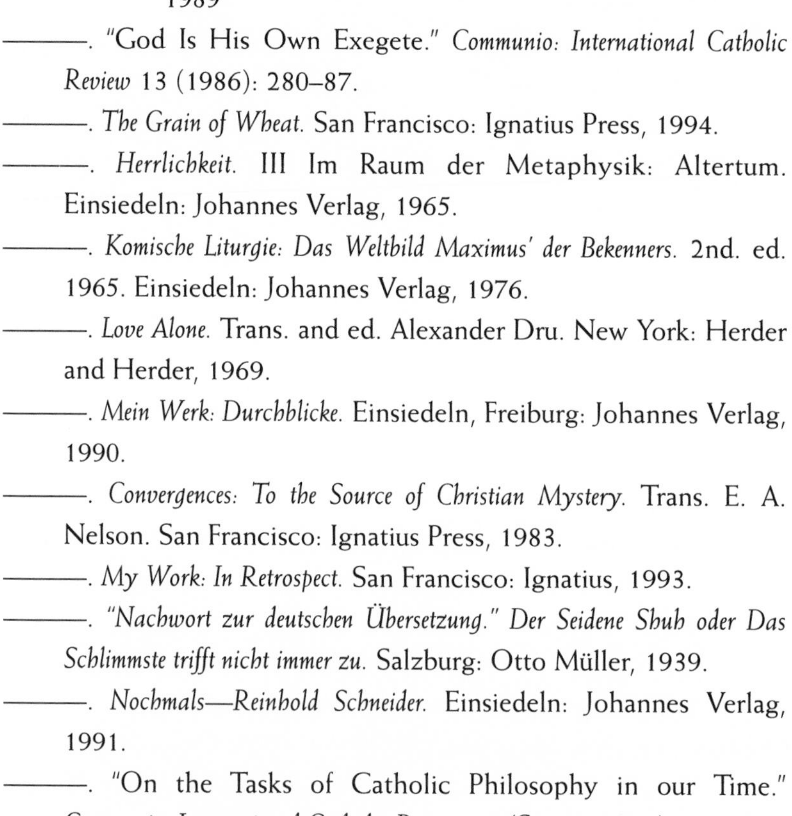

———. "God Is His Own Exegete." *Communio: International Catholic Review* 13 (1986): 280–87.

———. *The Grain of Wheat.* San Francisco: Ignatius Press, 1994.

———. *Herrlichkeit.* III Im Raum der Metaphysik: Altertum. Einsiedeln: Johannes Verlag, 1965.

———. *Komische Liturgie: Das Weltbild Maximus' der Bekenners.* 2nd. ed. 1965. Einsiedeln: Johannes Verlag, 1976.

———. *Love Alone.* Trans. and ed. Alexander Dru. New York: Herder and Herder, 1969.

———. *Mein Werk: Durchblicke.* Einsiedeln, Freiburg: Johannes Verlag, 1990.

———. *Convergences: To the Source of Christian Mystery.* Trans. E. A. Nelson. San Francisco: Ignatius Press, 1983.

———. *My Work: In Retrospect.* San Francisco: Ignatius, 1993.

———. *"Nachwort zur deutschen Übersetzung." Der Seidene Shuh oder Das Schlimmste trifft nicht immer zu.* Salzburg: Otto Müller, 1939.

———. *Nochmals—Reinhold Schneider.* Einsiedeln: Johannes Verlag, 1991.

———. "On the Tasks of Catholic Philosophy in our Time." *Communio: International Catholic Review* 20 (Spring 1993): 147–87.

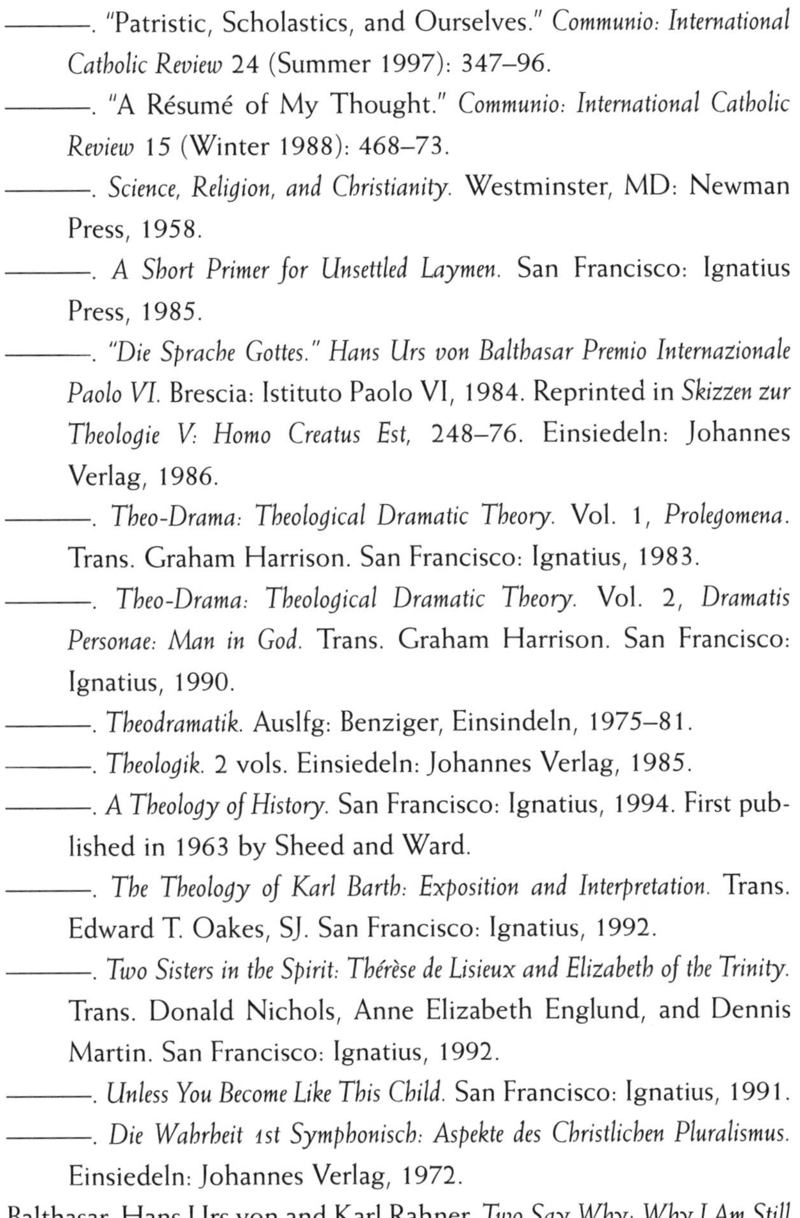

———. "Patristic, Scholastics, and Ourselves." *Communio: International Catholic Review* 24 (Summer 1997): 347–96.

———. "A Résumé of My Thought." *Communio: International Catholic Review* 15 (Winter 1988): 468–73.

———. *Science, Religion, and Christianity*. Westminster, MD: Newman Press, 1958.

———. *A Short Primer for Unsettled Laymen*. San Francisco: Ignatius Press, 1985.

———. *"Die Sprache Gottes." Hans Urs von Balthasar Premio Internazionale Paolo VI*. Brescia: Istituto Paolo VI, 1984. Reprinted in *Skizzen zur Theologie V: Homo Creatus Est*, 248–76. Einsiedeln: Johannes Verlag, 1986.

———. *Theo-Drama: Theological Dramatic Theory*. Vol. 1, *Prolegomena*. Trans. Graham Harrison. San Francisco: Ignatius, 1983.

———. *Theo-Drama: Theological Dramatic Theory*. Vol. 2, *Dramatis Personae: Man in God*. Trans. Graham Harrison. San Francisco: Ignatius, 1990.

———. *Theodramatik*. Auslfg: Benziger, Einsindeln, 1975–81.

———. *Theologik*. 2 vols. Einsiedeln: Johannes Verlag, 1985.

———. *A Theology of History*. San Francisco: Ignatius, 1994. First published in 1963 by Sheed and Ward.

———. *The Theology of Karl Barth: Exposition and Interpretation*. Trans. Edward T. Oakes, SJ. San Francisco: Ignatius, 1992.

———. *Two Sisters in the Spirit: Thérèse de Lisieux and Elizabeth of the Trinity*. Trans. Donald Nichols, Anne Elizabeth Englund, and Dennis Martin. San Francisco: Ignatius, 1992.

———. *Unless You Become Like This Child*. San Francisco: Ignatius, 1991.

———. *Die Wahrheit ist Symphonisch: Aspekte des Christlichen Pluralismus*. Einsiedeln: Johannes Verlag, 1972.

Balthasar, Hans Urs von and Karl Rahner. *Two Say Why: Why I Am Still a Christian*. Trans. John Griffiths. Chicago: Franciscan Herald Press, 1971.

Barr, James. "Exegesis as a Theological Discipline Reconsidered and the Shadow of the Jesus of History." In *The Hermeneutical Quest: Essays in Honor of James Luther Mays on His Sixty-Fifth Birthday*, ed. Donald G. Miller, 11–45 Allison Park, PA: Pickwick Publications, 1986.

Berkowitz, Peter. *Nietzsche: The Ethics of an Immoralist.* Cambridge, MA: Harvard University Press, 1995.

Bieler, Martin. "Meta-anthropology and Christology." *Communio: International Catholic Review* 20 (Spring 1993): 129–46.

Bloom, Harold. *The Western Canon: The Books and School of the Ages.* New York: Riverhead Books, 1994.

Bouyer, Louis. *Erasmus and His Times.* Westminster, MD: Newman, 1959.

Broad, C. D. *Leibniz: An Introduction.* Cambridge: Cambridge University Press, 1975.

Buckley, Michael. *At the Origins of Modern Atheism.* New Haven: Yale University Press, 1987.

Casarella, Peter. "Experience as Theological Category." *Communio: International Catholic Review* 20 (Spring 1993): 118–28.

Catholic Church. *Catechism of the Catholic Church.* Washington, DC: United States Catholic Conference, 1994.

Chantraine, Georges. "Exegesis and Contemplation in the Work of Hans Urs von Balthasar." In *Hans Urs von Balthasar: His Life and Work,* edited by David Schindler, 133–47. San Francisco: Ignatius, 1991.

Chateaubriand, François-René. *Genius of Christianity.* 1802. Repr. Baltimore, MD: J. Murphy Co, no date.

Chesterton, Gilbert Keith. *Chesterton on Shakespeare.* Ed. Dorothy E. Collins. Chester Springs, PA: Dufour Editions, 1971.

Claudel, Paul. *Poetic Art.* New York: Philosophical Library, 1948.

Cousins, Ewert H. "Bonaventure's Mysticism of Language." In *Mysticism and Language,* ed. Steven T. Katz. New York: Oxford University Press, 1992, pp. 236–57.

Cusanus, Nicolaus. *Compendium. Opera Omnia,* vol. XI/3. Eds. K. Bormann and Bruno Decker. Hamburg: Heidelberg Academy of Sciences, 1964.

Dupré, Louis, "Hans Urs von Balthasar's Theology of Aesthetic Form." *Theological Studies* 49 (1988): 299–318.

Edwards, Michael. *Towards a Christian Poetics.* Grand Rapids, MI: Eerdmans, 1984.

Ehrenfels, Christian von. *Gestalthaftes Sehen: Ergebnisse und Aufgaben der Morphologie.* Ed. Ferdinand Weinhandl. Darmstadt: Wissenschaftliche Buchgesellschaft, 1967.

Forster, E. M. *Howard's End.* Ed. O. Stallybrass. London: Edward Arnold, 1973

Fowler, Alistair. *A History of English Literature.* Cambridge, MA: Harvard University Press, 1987.

Frye, Northrop. *Anatomy of Criticism.* Princeton: Princeton University Press, 1957.

Gadamer, Hans-George. *Truth and Method.* New York: Continuum, 1991.

Gilson, E. *Being and Some Philosophers.* 2nd ed. Toronto: PIMS, 1952.

Heidegger, Martin. *Being and Time.* New York: Harper and Row, 1962.

Henrici, Peter. "A Sketch of von Balthasar's Life." In *Hans Urs von Balthasar: His Life and Work,* ed. David Schindler. San Francisco: Ignatius, 1991, 7–43.

Hopkins, G. M. *Journals and Papers of Gerard Manley Hopkins.* Ed. Humphrey House. London: Oxford University Press, 1959.

———. *The Poetical Works of Gerard Manley Hopkins.* Ed. Norman H. Mackenzie. Oxford: Clarendon, 1990.

———. *The Sermons and Devotional Writings of Gerard Manley Hopkins.* Ed. Christopher Devlin. London: Oxford University Press, 1959.

Ivanka, Endre von. *Plato Christianus. Ubernahme und Umgestaltung des Platonismus durch die Vater.* Einsiedeln: Johannes Verlag, 1964.

John Paul II. *Mulieris Dignitatem.* Washington, DC: Office of Pub. and Promotion Services, United States Catholic Conference, 1988.

Kay, Jeffrey. *Theological Aesthetics: The Role of Aesthetics in the Theological Method of Hans Urs von Balthasar.* Berne: Herbert Lang; Frankfurt: Peter Lang, 1975.

Krenski, Thomas Rudolf. *Passio Caritatis: Trinitarische Passiologie im Werk Hans Urs von Balthasar.* Einsiedeln, Freiburg: Johannes Verlag, 1990.

Leibniz, G. W. *La Theodicee.* 1710. Reprint New Haven: Yale University Press, n.d.

Leonard, Andre. *Pensees des jommes et foi en Jesus Christ. Pour un discenement intellectual chretien.* Paris: Namur, 1980.

Lewis, C. S. *Abolition of Man.* New York: Macmillan Co., 1947.

Lichtmann, Maria. *The Contemplative Poetry of Gerard Manley Hopkins.* Princeton: Princeton University Press, 1989.

Lochbrunner, Manfred. *Analogia caritatis. Darstellung und Deutung der Theologie Hans Urs von Balthasar.* Freiburg: Herder, 1981.

Lubac, Henri de. *Augustinianism in Modern Theology.* New York: Herder, 1969.

———. *The Discovery of God.* Grand Rapids, MI: Eerdmans, 1996.

———. *Pico de la Mirandola.* Paris: Aubier Montaigne, 1974.

———. "A Witness of Christ in the Church: Hans Urs von Balthasar." In *Hans Urs Von Balthasar: His Life and Works,* ed. David Schindler, 271–88. San Francisco: Ignatius, 1991.

MacIntyre, Alasdair C. *Against the Self-Images of the Age: Essays on Ideology and Philosophy.* New York: Schocken Books, 1971.

Malebranche, Lochbrunner. "Entretiens sur la metaphysique, sur la religion, et sur la mort." (1696). *Oeuvres.* 2 vols. Paris: Gallimard-Pleiade, 1992.

Marion, Jean-Luc. *God without Being: Hors Texte.* Trans. Thomas A. Carlson. Chicago: University of Chicago Press, 1991.

Maritain, Jacques. *Art and Scholasticism and the Frontiers of Poetry.* Trans. Joseph W. Evans. Notre Dame: University of Notre Dame Press, 1962.

Marshall, Bruce. *Christology in Conflict: The Identity of a Saviour in Rahner and Barth.* Oxford: Blackwell, 1987.

McNeil, Brian. "The Exegete as Iconographer: Balthasar and the Gospels." In *The Analogy of Beauty: The Theology of Hans Urs von Balthasar,* ed. John Riches, 134–46. Edinburgh: T. and T. Clark, 1986.

Millon-Delsol, Chantal. *L'Etat subsidiaire.* Paris: Presses Universitaires do France, 1992.

Moda, Aldo. *Hans Urs von Balthasar, Un' esposizione critica del suo pensiero.* Bari: Ecumenica Editrice, 1976.

Mooney, Hilary A. *The Liberation of Consciousness: Bernard Lonergan's Foundations in Dialogue with the Theological Aesthetics of Hans Urs von Balthasar.* Frankfurt am Main: Verlag Joseph Knecht, 1992.

Morse, Christopher. *The Logic of Promise in Moltmann's Theology.* Philadelphia: Fortress Press, 1979.

Nemoianu, Virgil. "The Beauty of Balthasar." *Crisis* 11 (April 1993): 42–46.

———. "Christian Humanism through the Centuries." *Image* 16 (May 1996): 1–10.

———. "Neoplatonism si cultura romana." *Revista de Istorie si teorie literara* 43 (July–December 1995): 261–71.

———. "Voice of Christian Humanism." *Crisis* 6 (September 1988): 36–40.

Newman, John Henry. "The Tamworth Reading Room." *Essays and Sketches.* Vol. II. Ed. Charles Frederick Harrold. New York: Longmans, Green and Company, 1949.

Nietzche, Friedrich. *The Antichrist + Fragments from a Shattering Mind: Exterminating Texts and Terminal Ecstasies.* Trans. Domino Falls. London: Creation, 2002.

———. *Beyond Good and Evil.* Trans. and commentary by Walter Kaufmann. New York: Vintage Books, 1989.

———. *On the Genealogy of Morals.* Oxford: Oxford University Press, 1999.

———. *The Gay Science with Prelude in Rhymes and an Appendix of Songs.* Trans. and commentary by Walter Kaufmann. New York: Vintage Books, 1994.

———. *Philosophy in the Tragic Age of the Greeks.* Washington, DC: Regenery Gateway, 1962.

———. *Untimely Meditations.* Trans. R. J. Hollingdale. Cambridge: Cambridge University Press, 1983.

———. "Vom Nutzen und Nachteil der Historie für das Leben," *Unzeitgemäss* Betrachtungen, *Nietzsche Werke: Kritische Gesamtausgabe.* III/1. 1873. Reprint Berlin, New York: Walter de Gruyter, 1972.

———. *The Will to Power.* Trans. Walter Kaufmann & R. J. Hollingdale. New York: Random House, 1967.

Oakes, Edward. *Pattern of Redemption: The Theology of Hans Urs von Balthasar.* New York: Continuum, 1994.

O'Donnell, John. SJ. "Alles Sein ist Leibe." In *Hans Urs von Balthasar, Gestalt und Werk.* Eds. K. Lehmann and W. Kasper. Cologne: *Communio,* 1989.

Pascal, Blaise. *Pensées,* Trans. A. J. Krailsheimer. Harmondsworth: Penguin, 1966.

Peelman, Achiel. "Hans Urs von Balthasar: *Un diagnostic théologique de la civilization occidentale.*" *Eglise et théologie* 10 (1979): 257–74.

Pfister, Manfred. *The Theory and Analysis of Drama.* European Studies in English Literature. Cambridge: Cambridge University Press, 1988. (Originally published in German as *Das Drama.* Munich: Wilhelm Fink Verlag, 1977.)

Picard, Max. *Der Mensch und das Wort.* Erlenbach-Zürich: Eugen Rentsch Verlag, 1955.

Potworowski, Christoph. "The Attitude of the Child in the Theology of Hans Urs von Balthasar." *Communio: International Catholic Review* 22 (Spring 1995): 44–55.

———. "Christian Experience in Hans Urs von Balthasar." *Communio: International Catholic Review* 20 (Spring 1993): 107–17.

Propp, Vladimir. *Morphology of the Folktale.* Austin, TX: University of Texas Press, 1968.

Przywara, Erich, "Bild, Gleichnis, Symbol, Mythos, Mysterium, Logos." *Analogia Entis II* (1962): 335–71.

Rad, Gerhard von. *The Message of the Prophets.* Trans. D. M. G. Stalker. New York: Harper & Row, 1972

———. *Old Testament Theology.* Trans. D. M. G. Stalker. New York: Harper & Row, 1965.

Riches, John, ed. *The Analogy of Beauty: The Theology of Hans Urs von Balthasar.* Edinburgh: T. and T. Clark, 1986.

Ricoeur, Paul. *"Contribution d'une réflexion sur le langage à une théologie de la parole." Exégèse et Herméneutique.* Eds. Roland Barthes et al. Paris: Éditions du Seuil, 1971.

Ricoeur, Paul. *Interpretation Theory: Discourse and the Surplus of Meaning.* Fort Worth, TX: Texas Christian University Press, 1976.

Roberts, Louis. *The Theological Aesthetics of Hans Urs von Balthasar.* Washington, DC: Catholic University Press, 1987.

Robinet, Andre, ed. *Malebranche et Leibniz.* Paris: J. Vris, 1953.

Schindler, David, ed. *Hans Urs von Balthasar: His Life and Work.* San Francisco: Ignatius, 1991.

———. *Heart of the World, Center of the Church.* Grand Rapids, MI: Eerdmans, 1996.

Schmitz, Kenneth. "Postmodern or Modern-Plus?" *Communio* 17 (Summer 1990): 152–66.

———. "St. Thomas and the Appeal to Experience." *Catholic Theological Society of America Proceedings* 47 (1992): 1–20.

Sherry, Patrick. *Spirit and Beauty: An Introduction to Theological Aesthetics.* Oxford: Clarendon, 1992.

Siewerth, Gustav. *Philosophie der Sprache.* Einsiedeln: Johannes Verlag, 1962.

Simon, Martin. "Identity and Analogy: Balthasar's Hölderlin and Hamann." In *Hans Urs Von Balthasar: His Life and Works,* ed. David Schindler, 77–104. San Francisco: Ignatius, 1991.

Steinmetz, David C. "The Superiority of Pre-Critical Exegesis." In *The Theological Interpretation of Scripture: Classic and Contemporary Readings*, ed. Stephen E. Fowl. Oxford: Blackwell, 1997, pp. 26–38.

Szondi, Peter. *Theory of the Modern Drama: A Critical Edition*, Ed. and trans. Michael Hays. Theory and History of Literature, Volume 29. Minneapolis: University of Minnesota Press, 1987. (Originally published in Germany as *Theorie des modernen Dramas*, 1965.)

Vatican II Council. *Gaudium et Spes*. Chicago, IL: Catholic Action Federation, 1967.

———. *Lumen Gentium*. Paris: Éditions du Cerf, 1965.

Waldstein, Michael M. "Expression and Form: Principles of a Philosophical Aesthetics According to Hans Urs von Balthasar." PhD diss., University of Dallas, 1981.

———. "Introduction to Balthasar's *The Glory of the Lord*." *Communio: International Catholic Review* 14 (1987): 12–33.

Weinsheimer, Joel. *Philosophical Hermeneutics and Literary Theory*. New Haven: Yale University Press, 1991.

Williams, Rowan. "Balthasar and Rahner." In *The Analogy of Beauty: The Theology of Hans Urs von Balthasar, edited by John Riches*, 11–34. Edinburgh: T. and T. Clark, 1986.

Wippel, John F. *Metaphysical Themes in Aquinas*. Washington, DC: Catholic University of America Press, 1984.

Wojtyla, Karol. "The Radiation of Fatherhood." *Collected Plays and Writings On Theater*. Berkeley, CA: University of California Press, 1987.

Yeago, David S. "The Drama of Nature and Grace: A Study in the Theology of Hans Urs von Balthasar." PhD diss., Yale, 1992.

———. "Jesus of Nazareth and Cosmic Redemption: The Relevance of St. Maximum the Confessor." *Modern Theology* 12.2 (April 1996): 163–94.

Contributors

Ed Block, Jr. is a professor of English at Marquette University. Editor of the scholarly journal *Renascence: Essays on Values in Literature,* Dr. Block has also published *Rituals of Disintegration: Romance and Madness in the Victorian Psychomythic Tale,* edited the book *Critical Essays on John Henry Newman,* and authored numerous essays on Victorian literature. His work on Balthasar includes essays, chapters in books, and a translation of Balthasar's "Foreword" to the German translation of Paul Claudel's *The Satin Slipper* in *Communio.*

Peter J. Casarella is an associate professor of theology at Catholic University of America. He has published on Nicholas of Cusa and Hans Urs von Balthasar in both English and German, including the article "Experience as a Theological Category: Hans Urs von Balthasar on the Encounter with God's Image" in *Communio.*

Virgil Nemoianu is a professor of English and comparative literature at Catholic University of America. He is the author of *Theory of the Secondary: Literature, Progress and Reaction* and of *The Taming of Romanticism: European Literature and the Age of Biedermeier.* He has also written numerous articles on European and English literature in the eighteenth and early nineteenth centuries.

Aidan Nichols, OP, is a lecturer on the Cambridge University Divinity Faculty, prior of Blackfriars Cambridge, and a visiting professor of systematic theology at Oxford University. He is author of over a dozen books on theological subjects, including *Light from the East, Byzantine Gospel,* and *The Shape of Catholic Theology.*

Edward T. Oakes, SJ, is the Chester and Margaret Paluch Professor of Theology at the University of St. Mary of the Lake/Mundelein Seminary in Chicago. He is the author of *Pattern of Redemption: The Theology of Hans Urs von Balthasar,* and the translator of Balthasar's *Spirit and Institution* and *The Theology of Karl Barth.*

Christophe Potworowski is president of Newman Theological College in Canada. For thirteen years before that, he was a professor of theological studies at Concordia University in Montreal. He is the author of *Contemplation and Incarnation: The Theology of Marie-Dominique Chenu* and of several articles on Hans Urs von Balthasar in *Communio.*

David Schindler is editor in chief of the North American edition of *Communio.* He is author of *Heart of the World: Center of the Church* and of over fifty articles translated into eight languages. He is also editor of *Hans Urs von Balthasar: His Life and Work.*

David Yeago is the Michael C. Peeler Professor of Systematic Theology at Lutheran Theological Southern Seminary in Columbia, South Carolina. He has published numerous books, as well as articles in *Pro Ecclesia, Lutheran Forum,* and *Dialog.*

Index of Works by Balthasar

Index of Names

Index of Topics